NOT WITH A BANG
BUT A WHIMPER

NOT WITH A BANG BUT A WHIMPER

The Politics and Culture of Decline

Theodore Dalrymple

Monday Books

© Theodore Dalrymple, 2009

First published in the UK in 2009 by Monday Books
Some elements of this book were originally published in the USA by
Ivan R Dee, Inc

A CIP catalogue record for this title is available from
the British Library

ISBN: 978-1-906308-10-0

Typeset by Andrew Searle

Printed and bound in the UK by CPI Mackays, Chatham ME5 8TD

www.mondaybooks.com
http://mondaybooksblogspot.com/
info@mondaybooks.com

To the memory of my father (1909 - 1983)
and my mother (1920 - 2005).

Contents

Preface

NO AGE is golden to those who live in it, and it is not often that men are more grateful for past progress than worried by current imperfections.

Even so, our current age seems exceptional in the peculiarity of its unease. Never in human history have people lived such long and pain-free lives; never have so many people, and so high a proportion of people, had so much freedom to choose how to live, what goals to pursue and how to divert themselves. On the other hand, never have so many people felt anxious and depressed, and resorted to pills to ease their distress. Mankind has laboured long and hard to produce a cornucopia for itself, only to discover that the cornucopia does not bring the happiness expected, but only a different kind of anxiety.

Of all modern societies, none is more emblematic of this strange disconnection between prosperity and its expected benefits than Britain. Until very recently, the country has experienced continuous economic growth for many years and, however illusory or highly mortgaged that prosperity has been, levels of consumption have risen enormously since the Second World War. And yet it takes very little familiarity with Britain to realise that it suffers from a deep malaise, such that at least half the population would rather live somewhere else. While people pour in from Eastern Europe, Africa, South Asia, the Middle East and (to a lesser extent) South America, in order to earn more money, the population already here seek in large numbers to move to North America, Australasia and the Mediterranean.

Increased levels of consumption have not translated into improvement in subjective quality of life. The country is crime-ridden and the authorities seem impotent, unwilling or unable to do anything about it. Every day come stories of grotesque failure on the part of the criminal justice system. Everyday encounters between citizens ~~talk off~~ ~~on the part~~ ~~from~~ ~~negotiate~~ ~~timber~~

Officialdom interferes in daily lives ever more obtrusively while the public administration seems to be a giant machine efficient only in grinding taxes out of people without returning anything in the way of improved services or infrastructure.

The sturdy, independent, upright citizen has become a neurotic, dependent, frightened wreck. The state is experienced as a juggernaut that cannot be stopped and is no longer under anyone's control. Politicians of all stripes are derided as liars and careerists, *ex officio*, and cynicism about every official's motives is rife. No official explanation of anything is believed, and honesty, straightforwardness and trust have become symptoms of naivety and lack of sophistication. All these traits are mirror images of what, not so very long ago, were the country's virtues.

Perhaps no statistic captures the malaise better than one I saw reported recently in *The Guardian* newspaper, that 79 percent of British children now have a personal television in their bedroom (the 21 percent who don't probably feel resentful and deprived). On the one hand, this appears to be a sign of tremendous prosperity, that so high a proportion of the population can now afford to give its children a piece of apparatus that would once have made kings gasp with amazement; but, on the other, it raises suspicions that children are spending so much time in front of screens that something human, namely ordinary face-to-face contact, is being undermined or lost. Parents feels constrained, apparently, to give each child a television (and a computer) in order to avoid disputes over who watches what, in the process depriving their children of normal play and imbuing them with a bogus sophistication, that is to say, with knowingness rather than knowledge.

On practically all measures of social pathology, Britain leads the Western world, though only half a century ago it was better ordered, as well as freer, than most other societies. There was a subtle, but informal, balance between freedom and social control. The change was wrought not by demand from below, from the majority of the population, but by undermining from above, by intellectuals. Of course, as in all societies, reforms were desirable; but it is doubtful whether, in the headlong rush to create a new and different kind of society, freed from the restraints of the past, anyone spared a thought for what was being lost. If progress has to start from somewhere, so does deterioration; that change can be for ill as well as good is still not a thought that occurs to most projectors and would-be reformers.

Even at the height of its feverish and illusory prosperity, Britain appeared in many ways an unpleasant and charmless society. To the entitlements conferred by the welfare state were now added the entitlements conferred by the consumer society. Mrs Thatcher thought she was introducing free-market reforms into a population which resembled the British population of her youth: self-controlled, dignified, honest, unself-important and with an ironical detachment, and therefore thirsting to be freed from the dead hand of the state. In this she was disastrously mistaken. A cultural *gestalt*-switch had taken place in the meantime: old virtues such as fortitude were now considered vices, or at least self-betrayal, and self-control a form of emotional blockage. The result has been a society in which people demand the right to do anything they choose, but to be protected, as of right, from the consequences of their own choices. The resultant existential supermarket is not pleasant to behold, and it is not a coincidence that more people wish to emigrate from Britain than from any comparable country.

THE REPELLENT MR ROSS

NOWHERE IS THE TACIT ALLIANCE between vulgarity and legalised corruption in Britain better illustrated than in the career of Jonathan Ross, the radio and television presenter to whom the BBC has seen fit to transfer £18 million of tax- and licence-payers' money for three years' activity. The main advantage of such a vast salary, from the BBC's point of view, or at least that of its directors, is to make its yearly payment to the Director-General, Mark Thompson, of £788,000 in 2007, seem comparatively modest.

Let us recall just a couple of highlights of Mr Ross's career so far.

In 2006 he interviewed the leader of the Conservative Party, and possible next Prime Minister of this country, David Cameron (I shall reserve my estimate of Mr Cameron's part in the proceedings for a little later). In the course of this interview, he asked Mr Cameron whether he had masturbated as a 12-year-old boy while thinking of Mrs Thatcher. His precise words were, 'But did you or did you not have a wank thinking of Mrs Thatcher?'

This question came as the culmination of a series of questions as follows:

Ross: Let me ask you a question which you may consider a little risqué. How old were you when Lady Thatcher, back then just plain Margaret Thatcher, was first elected?
Cameron: Twelve, thirteen, something like that.
Ross: That is a time in a boy's life when you begin to look around for women who are attractive.
Cameron: This is when I realise why politicians never come on the show.

Ross: I put it to you, sir, that as a young man, you may have rejected, but I think you probably considered, Margaret Thatcher, in a carnal fashion. As indeed we all did.

Cameron: I wasn't that interested in politics when I was 13.

Ross: We're not talking about that.

Cameron: I wasn't really following it all very closely.

Ross: Did you think of her as a woman? Do you think she might be pin-up material?

Cameron: No.

Ross: You didn't want to see her in stockings?

Cameron: No.

After discussing Mrs Thatcher's political achievements, Ross then asked the question; after which he added, 'I tried but it was a challenge even for me.'

In 2008, in the company of a comedian called Russell Brand, Jonathan Ross telephoned Andrew Sachs, the 78-year-old actor who had played Manuel, the Spanish waiter in the television series *Fawlty Towers*, and made obscene jokes recorded on his answer-phone.

Even without the obscenity that was to come, the manner of both Ross and Brand was extremely vulgar and discourteous. Speaking in a tone of fatuous familiarity, Brand said: 'Hello Andrew Sachs, I am a great appreciator (*sic*) of your work over the decades. You're meant to be on my show now mate, I don't know why you're not answering the phone, it's a bit difficult – I'm here with Jonathan Ross.'

At this point, Ross said, 'Hello Andrew.'

In modern Britain, apparently, this is now deemed a decent and perhaps even admirably informal way in which to address a complete a stranger in public for the first time. Since all men are created equal, no respect is due to age, of course. The ideological imperative to level down trumps by a long way the need to consider the feelings of the person addressed, or what he might expect of others.

Ross and Brand decided to continue talking while the answer-phone recorded. In the course of their inane banter, Ross suddenly blurted out, 'He fucked your grand-daughter.' Then he laughed, and said, 'I'm sorry, I apologise. Andrew, I apologise. I got excited, what can I say, it just came out.'

Brand then said, 'Andrew Sachs, I did not do nothing with Georgina – oh no, I've revealed I know her name! Oh no, it's a disaster.'

They then discussed whether Mr Sachs might hang himself as a result of these revelations.

Ross then made a facetious attempt to exculpate himself. 'How could I carry that round in my head like a big brain blister all day? I had to pop it and let the pressure out.'

A little while later, during a second call to Mr Sachs, Brand recited a kind of poem while Ross hummed in the background:

I'd like to apologise for these terrible attacks – Andrew Sachs.
I'd like to show contrition to the max, Andrew Sachs.
I'd like to create world peace, between the yellow, whites and blacks, Andrew Sachs, Andrew Sachs.
I said some things I didn't of oughta, like I had sex with your grand-daughter.
But it was consensual and she wasn't menstrual, it was consensual, lovely sex.
It's full of respect. I sent her a text. I've asked her to marry me.

At this point, Ross asked Mr Sachs to marry him.

Further on, Brand said, 'And even after the show's finished, Jonathan, we can find out where Andrew Sachs lives, kick his front door in and scream apologies into his bottom. We can just keep on troubling Andrew Sachs, let's do it, OK. You pretend you're Andrew Sachs' answer-phone.'

Ross then said, 'Hello, Manuel is not in right now. Leave your message after the tone.'

This puerile, obscene and mildly menacing drivel continued for nine minutes; it could not therefore be said to be a slip of the tongue or momentary lapse. Moreover, the whole episode was pre-recorded; the BBC saw fit to broadcast it, despite having had ample time and opportunity to suppress it.

It is difficult to conclude anything other than that Jonathan Ross is paid a fortune specifically because of his vulgarity and abusiveness, both fearless and determined.

More important, significant and revealing than the episodes themselves were the responses, public and official, to them.

Protests about the questioning of Mr Cameron were relatively few and muted. Some of the responses were beside the point. Mr Howarth, a Conservative Member of Parliament, said that 'to refer to the most distinguished Prime Minister since Winston Churchill in this way is beneath contempt'. It was not Mrs Thatcher's distinction, however, that made the question objectionable; it would have been no better had it been asked, say, of Mrs Castle, the Labour Minister, or Mrs Williams, the Social Democrat, or indeed of anyone else. It was wrong in itself, pointless in its vulgarity; indeed, its vulgarity was its point, and its whole point. It was vulgarity triumphant, crowing its victory over restraint and refinement.

Jonathan Ross said afterwards, in response to criticism, that he thought his question was 'valid' (not merely valid, in fact, but 'perfectly valid'.) This word in its modern usage is to real thought what viruses are to the operation of computers: it destroys it. What did he mean by saying that his question was valid? That it was correct in grammatical form? That it was susceptible to an answer that might be true or false? That the answer to it was of great political importance? That it was a biographical detail that the British public needed, and had a right, to know? To say of the question that it was 'valid' was an artful way of imputing some value to it without having to go to the trouble of specifying what the value might be.

The response of the Director-General (who at the time was being paid only a paltry £609,000) was absolutely typical of the moral and intellectual pusillanimity of the modern British administrative, bureaucratic and political elite. Before considering it further, let us remind ourselves of a few of the provisions of the BBC Charter, which tells us:

i) that the BBC exists to serve the public interest, and

ii) that its main object is the promotion of its Public Purposes.

The Public Purposes of most relevance here are the following:

a) Sustaining citizenship and civil society.

b) Promoting education and learning.

c) Stimulating creativity and cultural excellence.

In defending Mr Ross, then, and allowing him to be paid £18 million to ask questions such as whether the Leader of the Opposition had masturbated at the age of 12 while thinking of the then Prime Minister, the Director-General considered that he was serving the sustenance of citizenship, the promotion of education and the stimulation of learning and cultural excellence: a misjudgment so bizarre that only utter contempt for the charter itself, corruption, delusion, stupidity or abysmal incompetence could explain it. None of these explanations would suffice to justify his continuance in office.

Mr Thompson, the Director-General, said that Mr Ross was 'outstanding', among 'the very best'. He said he gave enormous enjoyment and represented good financial value. What good financial value is to a public corporation which is not profit-making he did not explain in detail; but there is little doubt one might be able to say the same of public executions, were they broadcast, namely that they gave enormous enjoyment and, being cheap to arrange, represented good financial value.

The Director-General went on to say that, were Ross to leave the BBC, 'you would have headlines about that fact, and I think our licence fee payers would be disappointed'. But popularity, certainly not popularity alone, is not a proper measure of what the BBC was set up to do and what the charter still enjoins it to do.

Thousands of people complained to the BBC about Ross and Brand's broadcast. Ross was suspended for three months and Brand decided that he should refrain from appearing further on the BBC. Before he did so, he issued two 'apologies'. In the first, he spent more time attacking the *Daily Mail*, which had roundly condemned the two men, than in his apology, which was equivocal at best:

I would like to issue a personal Russell Brand apology to Andrew Sachs... for a message Jonathan and I left on his answer-phone, but it was quite funny. But sometimes you mustn't swear on someone's answer-phone...

That he, or anyone else, found his own drivel funny is self-condemnatory; that he thinks being funny is some kind of excuse for pointless cruelty is likewise self-condemnatory; and that he thinks it is often (presumably more often than not) permissible to 'swear', as he calls his obscenity, on people's answer-phones requires no comment either.

He continued:

I would like to remind the *Daily Mail* that while it is a bit bad to leave a swear-word on Andrew Sachs' answer-phone, what's worse – leaving a swear-word on Andrew Sachs' answer-phone or tacitly supporting Adolf Hitler when he took charge of the Third Reich? It's up to you, the listener, to decide which is worse. Offending Manuel, for which I apologise, or is it worse to tacitly support the death of millions?

These are not the words of a man who feels much contrition, indeed any contrition whatsoever; if he did, he would not describe his (and Ross') nine-minute telephone call, grossly discourteous and obscene from beginning to end, as leaving 'a swear-word'. He couldn't really apologise, because he couldn't really see that he had done anything wrong; and as we shall soon see, that is an inability that he shared with many of his countrymen.

Introducing the *Daily Mail*'s inglorious support for Hitler between 1933 and 1939 was the kind of rhetorical smokescreen that is used by many wrongdoers to justify themselves. Here Brand is insinuating a kind of syllogism:

The *Daily Mail* condemns me.

The *Daily Mail* supported Hitler.

People who condemn me are in agreement with the *Daily Mail*.

Therefore, people who condemn me are Nazi sympathisers, and in no moral position to condemn people such as I who leave obscene telephone messages.

Therefore what I did was not very wrong, if it was wrong at all.

It would be tedious to dissect the reasons for the moral irrelevance of this defence, its logical errors and its deeply unpleasant egotism. Suffice it to say that he is not even right historically where the *Daily Mail* is concerned: it changed its tune in 1939, before the Nazis had killed millions (brutal as they already were). As it happens, the *Guardian* also had a few hard words for Brand, but he did not resort to the argument that, in the 1930s, the *Guardian* had suppressed Malcolm Muggeridge's reports of the Ukrainian famine, and which was worse, leaving 'a swear-word' on Andrew Sachs' answer phone, or tacitly supporting the deaths by starvation of millions of Ukrainians?

Brand also failed to mention in his self-exculpation that the very man he selected for his 'prank' was himself a refugee from Nazi Germany, who came to this country to escape Nazi persecution when he was eight years old.

His second apology – made with a portrait of Stalin in the background, not exactly a tactful choice of personage for someone who had recently claimed to be sensitive about the murder of millions – was just as egotistical. In it, he admitted that what he had done was 'really, really stupid', and added that this was especially so since he admired Andrew Sachs so much. Thus it was his admiration for Mr Sachs, which was not so great that it led him to address him with minimal politeness, that made his conduct reprehensible. If he had left obscene messages on the answer-phone of someone he did not know, or worse still had no admiration for, it would not have been nearly so bad.

I was reminded of a recent case in which a woman in a supermarket called her boyfriend to come to her because another customer had accused her of jumping a queue. Upon her pointing out the man, the boyfriend went over and punched him. The man fell and hit his head on the ground, later dying of a head injury. The manager came over to the woman's boyfriend and told him he had got the wrong man – as if there had been a *right* one to punch and kill.

Ross apologised for his behaviour; but he also did not think that leaving obscene phone calls and suggestions that a 78-year-old man might hang himself as a result was not merely a prank, or more than a rush of blood to the head, but a revelation of something much deeper, a coarse, brutal and stupid mentality. Speaking to Brand some time after the 'show', he said that the broadcast had been a mess, and, he added, 'let's face it, an un-entertaining mess'. On this view, entertainment is the highest value; the quality of being entertaining would justify anything, including obscene phone calls.

In the very week after his suspension, which suggested that he had been guilty only of an error of judgment rather than of something far worse, and which left him to scrape by on only £4,500,000 of public money that year, he again made a tasteless sexual joke. Speaking on air to his producer, who had claimed while in Spain to have been accosted sexually by a woman in her eighties who lived near his villa there, Ross said, 'Eighty, oh God! I think you should, just for charity, give her one last night. One last night before the grave. Would it kill you?'

Admittedly in this case Ross did not know that his joke was about a woman who, as it turned out, actually existed and was suffering from Alzheimer's disease (of which sexual disinhibition is sometimes a symptom). But he must have known that either she did not exist, in which case the joke was merely pointless and crude, or that she did, in which case it was likely to be offensive as well as crude.

He had learnt nothing from his suspension, as indeed was no doubt expected and indeed intended by his employers (men of his age do not suddenly learn refinement of feeling), who were simply heading off criticism with as little fuss and inconvenience as possible. It was precisely for being crude and shallow that, *de facto*, agents of the British state were paying him so munificently; they must have thought, or at least have claimed or pretended to think, that the dissemination of such crudity was in the public interest.

The dialectical relationship between a morally and intellectually corrupt elite and a debased population was perfectly illustrated by one part of the public response to the Ross-Brand episode. By the time 10,000 people had complained about the broadcast, 50,000 people had signed up to a petition on Facebook in support of the supposedly-persecuted comedians. Of course, neither figure allows us to say who is in the majority in Britain, and many thousands more did eventually complain, but it seems that, at the very least, a fairly large percentage of the population, especially among the young, is now so morally coarsened that it can no more see what was wrong with the behaviour of the two comedians than can the comedians themselves. A BBC reporter, commenting on the fact that, at the time, the BBC had received six times as many messages of support for the comedians as complaints about them, gave typical examples of the comments received: 'Anybody who thinks it's disgusting should get a grip,' 'Russell is hilarious,' 'Hey, they are comedians – it's their job.'

The flavour of the more extended commentary to be found on the internet in favour of the comedians can be gauged from the following:

> The whole thing is ridiculous, and has brought all kinds of unpleasant people out of the woodwork. Essentially it is a fuss about someone making a joke about fucking someone, you know – that thing lots of adults do for fun – but has played as if Jonathan Ross has somehow tarred Manuel's adult granddaughter by outing the fact that Russell Brand shagged her at one of his hot tub parties. As if sex is somehow dirty and taboo. The headline should be "Man shags woman, tells grumpy elderly relative, incensed newspaper readers foam at the mouth."

The problem here is not lack of intelligence; I should guess that the writer is of above average intelligence, and probably has attended university. The problem is crudity, intellectual, moral, psychological and cultural. What is altogether lacking here, and is culturally disastrous, is an awareness that there is any distinction to be made between the public and the private: that a joke that is permissible, if not particularly funny, in private is not permissible in public. The fact that the writer thinks that the complaint is about 'someone making a joke about fucking someone' demonstrates this.

He continues (*le style est l'homme même*):

> Be sure to check out all of the comments from the new puritans, rabid anti-BBC types, armchair moralists, old people of questionable intelligence, and general fuckwits… It wasn't that funny to begin with but the shitstorm of indignation from the illiterate opinionated twats of Great Britain has made it lolworthy (laughable)… All of those people that are morally outraged have been trolled hard (have been duped into overreaction by a deliberate provocation), and can go fuck themselves. If that's the kind of people Russell Brand and Jonathan Ross have offended – good. Well done BBC – but it's stupid to suspend people for pissing off an elderly guest of the show.

Some supporters of Ross and Brand referred to free speech, and one even mentioned the death of Socrates. Another defence is that he is Jonathan Ross: Jonathan Ross behaves like this, it's what he's known for. I am reminded of a burglar who said, when I suggested that he stopped burgling, 'But I'm a burglar, burglary's what I do.'

When I have mentioned the case of Ross – his persistent and triumphal crudity – to Americans and Frenchmen they have been astonished. Of course, few British people, parochial despite (or perhaps because of) years of lip-service to multiculturalism, are aware of, or care about, the shock that their tastes and behaviour would now evoke in people of other nationalities. Most foreigners have retained some residual, but erroneous, notion of the British as a restrained and self-respecting people. The Americans and Frenchmen to whom I have spoken were even more astonished that the British state has become corrupted enough, morally, intellectually and financially, to subsidise such crudity with such public largesse.

Mr Cameron claimed after he had appeared on the Ross show to have enjoyed it (no doubt an attempt to curry favour with people like the writer of the lovely words I have quoted above). This claim is by itself enough to demonstrate that he is not fit to hold any public office, as indeed is the fact that he agreed to appear on the show in the first place, because the transcript shows that he was fully aware of its nature. Ross, after all, had celebrated his award of the OBE in 2005 by playing a song by the Sex Pistols, whose words went as follows:

God save the Queen, the fascist regime.
They made you a moron, a potential H-bomb.
God save the Queen, she ain't no human being.

Ironically, Ross' conduct with Brand was all the more reprehensible since his insensitivity to the feelings of others was matched by a marked hypersensitivity in regard to his own feelings. He threatened a lawsuit, for beach of privacy, against a man who took and wanted to publish some photographs of him as he played tennis at a private club. It is a sign of the degeneracy of British culture that anyone would be interested in publishing or looking at them.

THE RUSH FROM JUDGMENT

ONE DAY, BEFORE I retired early from medical practice in a slum hospital and the prison next door, I asked a patient of mine how he would describe his own character. He paused for a moment, as if savouring a delicious morsel. 'I take people as they come,' he replied in due course. 'I'm very non-judgmental.'

As his two roommates had recently decamped, stealing his prize possessions and leaving him with ruinous debts to pay, his neutrality towards human character seemed not generous but stupid, a kind of prophylactic against learning from experience. Yet non-judgmentalism has become so universally accepted as the highest, indeed the only, virtue that he spoke of his own character as if pinning a medal for exceptional merit on his own chest.

That same week, I was consulted by another patient who had experienced even worse consequences of non-judgmentalism, though this time not entirely her own. Her life had been that of the modern slum dweller: three children by different fathers, none of whom supported her in any way and the last of whom was a vicious, violent drunk. She had separated from him by fleeing with their two-year-old to a hostel for battered women; soon afterward she found herself an apartment whose whereabouts he did not know.

Unfortunately, sometime later she was admitted to the hospital for an operation. As she had no one to whom she could entrust the child, she turned to Social Services for help. The social workers insisted, against her desperate pleas, that the child should stay with his biological father while she was in the hospital. They were deaf to her argument that he was an unsuitable guardian, even for two weeks: he would regard the child as an encumbrance, an intolerable interference with his daily routine of drinking, whoring and fighting. They said it was wrong to pass judgment on a man like this and threatened her with dire consequences if she did not agree to their plan. So the two year-old was sent to his father as they demanded.

Within the week, he and his new girlfriend had killed the child by swinging him against the wall repeatedly by his ankles and smashing his head. At this somewhat belated juncture, society did, reluctantly, make a judgment: the murderers both received life sentences.

Of course, the rush to non-judgment is in part a reaction against the cruel or unthinking application of moral codes in the past. A friend of mine recently discovered a woman in her nineties who had lived as a 'patient' in a large lunatic asylum for more than 70 years but whose only illness – as far as he was able to discover – had been to give birth to an illegitimate child in the 1920s. No one, surely, would wish to see the return of such monstrous incarceration and cavalier destruction of women's lives: but it does not follow from this that mass illegitimacy (about 50 percent of births in Britain, and far more in the hospital in which I worked) is a good thing, or at least not a bad thing. Judgment is precisely that – judgment. It is not the measure of every action by an infallible and rigid instrument.

Apologists for non-judgmentalism point, above all, to its supposed quality of compassion. A man who judges others will sometimes condemn them and therefore deny them aid and assistance, whereas the man who refuses to judge excludes no one from his all-embracing compassion. He never asks where his fellow man's suffering comes from, whether it be self-inflicted or no: for whatever its source, he sympathises with it and succours the sufferer.

The housing department of my city holds fast to this doctrine. It allocates scarce public housing, it says in its self-congratulatory leaflets, solely on the basis of need (give or take a nepotistic connection or two – after all, even the non-judgmental are human). It never asks how the need arose in the first place: it is there to care, not to condemn.

In practice, things are a little different. It is true that the housing department makes no judgments as to the deserts of the applicants for its largesse, but that is precisely why it cannot express any human compassion whatever. Its estimation of need is mathematical, based on a perverse algebra of sociopathology.

To return to the case of my patient whose child had been murdered: she was afterwards driven from her home by her neighbours, who felt that she was responsible for the death of her child and therefore acted as good, outraged citizens by twice attempting to burn her flat. Thereafter she found cheap lodgings in a house where there also lodged a violent drug addict, who forced his attentions upon her. When she applied to the housing department for help, it refused her on the grounds that she was already adequately housed, in the sense of having four walls around her and a roof over her head (and it would be wholly wrong to stigmatise drug addicts as undesirable neighbours), and also because she had no young dependants – her only young dependent having been murdered and, therefore, not being part of the equation. Stones might have wept at my patient's predicament, but not the housing department: it is far too non-judgmental to do so.

Curiously enough, my patient was perfectly able – with a little encouragement – to accept that her misfortunes did not come entirely out of the blue, that she had contributed to them by her own conduct and was, therefore, not a pure or immaculate victim. Taking the line of least resistance, as she had done throughout her life, she had consented to have a child by a man whom she knew to be thoroughly unsuitable as a parent. Indeed, she had known him to be violent and drunken even before she went to live with him, but she still found him attractive, and she lived in a society that promotes its own version of the Sermon on the Mount – Sufficient unto the day is the attraction thereof. She had learned now from experience (better late than never) which she could never have done had she refrained from making judgments about both herself and others. As a result, she had rejected another violent lover, abjured her own habitual drunkenness and decided to go to college.

In the clinic, of course, a kind of non-judgmentalism does and should hold sway: doctors ought never to refuse treatment on the grounds of moral deficiency. Moses Maimonides, the 12th century rabbi and doctor, wrote: 'May I never see in the patient anything but a fellow creature in pain' – surely a noble aspiration, if somewhat difficult to achieve in practice.

But medicine is not just the passive contemplation of suffering: it is the attempt, by no means always successful, to alleviate it. And it cannot have escaped the attention of doctors that much modern suffering has a distinct flavour of self-infliction. I am not talking now of the physical illnesses that derive from habits such as smoking, but rather of the chronic suffering caused by not knowing how to live, or rather by imagining that life can be lived as an entertainment, as an extended video, as nothing but a series of pleasures of the moment. The whirligig of time brings in its revenges – at least in a cold climate such as ours.

If the doctor has a duty to relieve the suffering of his patients, he must have some idea where that suffering comes from, and this involves the retention of judgment, including moral judgment. And if, as far as he can tell in good faith, the misery of his patients derives from the way they live, he has a duty to tell them so – which often involves a more or less explicit condemnation of their way of life as completely incompatible with a satisfying existence. By avoiding the issue, the doctor is not being kind to his patients; he is being cowardly. Moreover, by refusing to place the onus on the patients to improve their lot, he is likely to mislead them into supposing that he has some purely technical or pharmacological answer to their problems, thus helping to perpetuate them.

For example, I used to be consulted at least once or twice a day – week in, week out; year in, year out – by women who complained of anxiety and depression, and whose biographies contained obvious explanations for these unpleasant feelings. The women had often endured more than one violent sexual relationship, sometimes as many as four in succession, and had more than one young child to bring up. While they feared the loneliness of managing on their own, without help from another adult, they had come to the conclusion that all men were unreliable, even psychopathic. They were in an apparently insoluble dilemma: were they better off beaten, or alone?

Aided by a few simple questions, it didn't take them long to analyse their situation, though at the outset they invariably ascribed their unhappiness to bad luck or to fate. Such is the power of self-deception that even the most obvious considerations escaped them. For instance, a woman came to see me complaining of having been miserable and dissatisfied with her life for 20 years. Her husband treated her like a slave, and when he was not obeyed he became aggressive, either throwing things about the room, smashing windows or beating her.

'Why don't you leave him?' I asked.

'I feel sorry for him.'

'Why?'

'Well, because he's not very bright, doctor, and he doesn't know how to read or write. He couldn't manage on his own; he can't do anything for himself. I even have to dial the telephone for him because he can't read the numbers.'

'Does he work?'

'Yes, he's always worked.'

'What does he do?'

She named a large establishment where he was in charge of security

'How many people work in the security department there?' I asked her.

'Sixteen.

'You mean, every time he has to make a telephone call there, he asks one of his staff to do it for him because he can't read the numbers? Or every time he receives a letter, he has to have someone to read it out to him?'

My patient looked at me, wide-eyed. Obvious as this was, she hadn't thought of it.

'It's not very likely, is it, that such a man would be made the boss?' I added.

She had failed, through cowardice and self-indulgence, to think about the clear discrepancy between her husband's career and his supposed helplessness at home: for had she recognised it, she could no longer think of herself as a victim (with all the psychological comfort that victimhood brings) but rather as the co-author of her own misery. She wanted to avoid a painful dilemma: either to accept the situation as it was or to do something about it.

After two more conversations with me, she did something about it. She delivered an ultimatum to her husband: either he must modify his behaviour or she would leave him. Further, if ever he laid a finger upon her again, she would call the police and press charges against him. After that, he behaved and even did what for 20 years she believed him incapable of doing: he made a cup of tea for himself. Meanwhile she went to art classes instead of imprisoning herself in their flat, awaiting his arbitrary orders.

This patient had only one violent man to contend with; many of my patients had a succession of them. I would ask where they met them, and almost without exception it was in a bar or a night-club when they were both at a loose end, a previous relationship having broken up the week, or even the day, before. I asked what they had in common, apart from loss and loneliness. The invariable answer: sexual attraction and the desire for a good night out.

These are not contemptible in themselves, of course, but as the foundation of long-term relationships and parenthood they are a little thin and soon wear even thinner. I asked what other interests the women and their lovers had in common, and invariably there were none. The day-to-day flux was their whole world: a little shopping, a little cooking, a little tidying up, a lot of television, a visit to the social security office and a few hours in the pub while the money lasts. This aimless routine soon palls but, nevertheless, remains a subject for continual and acrimonious disagreement. Moreover, there is no pressure – either moral pressure from the community or economic pressure from the system of taxation and social security benefits – to keep couples together. Before long, neither necessity nor desire cements relationships – only inertia, punctuated by violence. For the violent man, to have a woman trembling in fear of him is his only guarantee of personal significance.

But how, the women would ask, are they to meet men who are not like this? How is a woman to find someone who will not exploit her alternately as a meal ticket and an object for the relief of sexual tension, who will not spend his own social security money in a single night out and then demand to be given hers as well, despite the fact that this money is needed to feed the children? How is she to find a man who will actually provide something in return, such as companionship and unconditional support?

The answer necessarily involved an examination of how they have lived, from their childhood onward. For if, as I contend and they agreed, it is necessary to have interests in common in order to achieve some depth in a relationship, how are such interests generated in the first place?

The woeful inadequacy of their upbringing, education, and outlook becomes apparent to them, perhaps for the first time.

'What are you interested in?' I would ask.

The question comes like a warning shot.

'Well... nothing, really,' they would reply. They recognised the unsatisfactory nature of their answer – which is all too truthful – at once.

'Did you try hard at school?'

'No.'

'What did you do instead?'

'Messed around, like everyone else.'

Their peers discouraged, sometimes by physical violence, those few who showed some inclination to work. To have resisted the prevailing ethos would have required exceptional courage, as well as parental backing, which was invariably missing. It was better to go along with the crowd and enjoy the illicit pleasures of the moment. It didn't really matter: after all, there would always be enough to eat, a roof over one's head and a television to watch, thanks to subventions from the state. Besides which, it is a truth universally acknowledged in the slums that there is nothing to be gained by individual effort, since the world is so unjustly organised. And in the absence of either fear or hope, only the present moment has any reality: you do what is most amusing, or least boring, at each passing moment.

In the absence of an interest or career, motherhood seems a good choice: only later does it become clear just how entrapping it is, especially when the father – predictably, but not predictedly – takes no share of parental duties.

With no experience or knowledge of the worlds of science, art or literature, and deprived of the sheer necessity to earn their subsistence, my patients were rich in nothing but the time on their hands, and so they embarked upon the *Liaisons dangereuses* of the slums. But the relationships in which they thus embroiled themselves were incapable for long of sustaining the burden placed upon them, and the descent into misery, drudgery, squalor and fear was almost immediate.

In their late twenties, the most intelligent among them would say to me, 'There's something missing in my life, but I don't know what it is.'

They reminded me of the young people I met behind the Iron Curtain, who had never known any other life than that under the Communists, who knew little of the outside world and yet knew that their way of life was both abnormal and intolerable.

My patients medicalised both their own misery and the terrible conduct of their violent lovers, a way of explaining their existential dissatisfaction that absolved them of responsibility. It took little time, however, to disabuse them of their misconceptions, and the fact that I was often able to predict from very near the outset of our consultation how their lovers had behaved towards them astonished them.

Again, I recall a patient who had taken an overdose after her boyfriend beat her up. Our dialogue followed a set pattern.

'And, of course, he sometimes grabs you round the throat and squeezes and tries to strangle you?' I asked.

'How did you know, doctor?'

'Because I've heard it practically every day for many years. And you have marks on your neck.'

'He doesn't do it all the time, doctor.' This is the universal extenuation offered.

'And, of course, he apologises afterward and tells you it won't happen again. And you believe him.'

'Yes. I really think he needs help, doctor.'

'Why do you say that?'

'Well, when he does it, he changes completely; he becomes another person; his eyes stare; it's like he has a fit. I really think he can't help it; he's got no control over it.'

'Would he do it in front of me, here, now, in this room?'

'No, of course not.'

'Then he can help it, can't he?'

The woman's desire to avoid a painful dilemma – love him and be beaten, or leave him and miss him – prevented her from asking herself the very obvious question as to why the 'fits' happened only in the privacy of their flat. Suddenly, inescapably, the responsibility for alleviating her misery became hers: she had to make a choice.

'But I love him, doctor.'

The triumph of the doctrine of the sovereignty of sentiment over sense would have delighted the Romantics, no doubt, but it has promoted an unconscionable amount of misery.

'Your boyfriend is unlikely to change. He strangles you because he enjoys it and gets a feeling of power from doing so. It makes him feel big: "I strangle her, but she still loves me, so I must be really wonderful." If you leave him, he'll find someone else to strangle within the week.'

'But it's difficult, doctor.'

'I didn't say it was easy; I said it was necessary. There's no reason why what is necessary should also be easy. But you can't expect doctors to make you happy while your lover is still strangling you, or to make him stop strangling you. Neither of these things is possible. You must make a choice. There is simply no way round it.'

To tell such a patient that she is responsible, both practically and morally, for her own life is not to deny her help; it is to tell her the truth. To force her to face her complicity in her misery is not to abandon her to her fate. On many occasions I have put such women in touch with lawyers, I have found them safe accommodation, I have found them places in colleges. Nor did I demand an immediate decision; what has taken years to develop is rarely undone in an hour or two. But I stuck to the fundamental truth: that no doctor, no social worker, no policeman can improve the quality of such a woman's life unless she is willing to forgo whatever gratification she derives from her violent boyfriend. There is no painless way of resolving the dilemma.

In almost all cases, the women returned a few weeks later much improved in their mood. The love they thought they felt for their tormentors had evaporated; they found it difficult in retrospect to distinguish it from the fear they felt.

What should we do now? they would ask me.

How was I to answer them? Should I pretend to an agnosticism about what might constitute a better life for them and their children? Should I pretend that a promiscuous granting of their favours to the first man they meet in a pub is as good as taking a little care over such matters? Wouldn't that be the ultimate betrayal?

I advised them that their first responsibility was to do everything in their power to prevent their children from following in their footsteps; they should try to open horizons to them beyond the miserable and sordid ones visible from the slums. This would involve spending time with them, taking an interest in their schoolwork, learning to say no to them when the occasion arises, and, above all, ensuring that they never again witnessed scenes of domestic violence.

As for themselves, they should try to go to college: for even if it failed to render them more employable, they would at least gain a sense of achievement and possibly an enduring interest. And if that meant they had to break the rules governing social security – which decree that they should be theoretically available for work and therefore not engaged in full-time education – well, I was not going to inform the authorities, who (it seems) prefer their dependants utterly passive.

They often took my suggestions. (One of my patients, beaten for 20 years, has since become a nurse, and many others work as assistants in nursing homes, the desire to help others being a corollary of their desire to help themselves.) I was perhaps the only person they had ever met to whom the violence of their lives was not as natural as the air they breathed but the result of human choices; I was the only person who had ever suggested to them that they could behave otherwise than they did behave.

It would be vain to suggest that this approach works in every case. Judgment is necessary, too, in selecting the cases; there are those who are too old, too psychologically fragile, or too young to bear the pain of accepting partial responsibility for their own misery. Alas, there is a period during the downward spiral of self-destruction when little can be done, as if self-destruction has a natural course of its own. Just as alcoholics and drug addicts may take years to accept first, that they are addicted, and second, that addiction is neither an excuse for their conduct nor a fate imposed upon them by circumstances, so the wilful self-destruction that I saw around me often ran a prolonged course, thanks to the powers of human self-deception.

It can rarely be nipped in the bud. For example, in the week in which the woman whose child had been murdered consulted me, two young women came to my notice, neither of whom gave any thought to the future or to the past, and both of whom sleepwalked through the present.

The first was barely 16, a white girl two months pregnant by a Muslim burglar. She was covered in bruises. They had met when he burgled her house, where she had been left alone for the night by her single mother, with whom she fought like a cat and a dog tied up in a sack over the time she should come home at night from clubs and discotheques (her mother suggesting the abominably early hour of midnight). The burglar asked her to come with him, and she did; thenceforth he locked her up, never allowed her out of the flat, forbade all contact with others, beat her black and blue, kicked her regularly in the stomach, demanded her conversion to Islam (he himself was a drunk) and in general expected her to be his slave.

When he went into the hospital for a small operation – the repair of a tendon in his arm, injured in the course of housebreaking – she had an opportunity to escape. I offered her every facility to do so, from a safe house to the services of a lawyer paid for by the public purse.

'I can't leave him,' she said. 'I love him, and he said he'd kill himself if I leave him.'

I know from experience that such a man might take an overdose as a form of emotional blackmail: the vast majority of male overdoses in my ward are of men who have beaten their women – the overdoses serve the dual function of blackmailing the women into remaining with them and of presenting themselves as the victims rather than the perpetrators of their own violence. I also know from experience that the burglar would never actually kill himself. But when a young woman says she fears the suicide of her lover, she is in effect saying that she will not yet leave him, and nothing will induce her to change her mind.

While the Muslim burglar remained in the hospital, she appeared every day, dressed in Punjabi costume, to tend her tormentor-lover, to bring him his Indian delicacies and all the little comforts he lacked.

The second young patient was a black girl, now aged 17, whose parents first knew of her liaison with a white boy a year older than she when her teacher brought her home from school at the age of 14, she having been beaten up by the boy in the schoolyard. A few months later she gave birth to his child, and they went to live together. (No doubt future social historians will find the contradiction between our concern about sexual abuse, on the one hand, and our connivance at and indifference to precocious sexual activity, on the other, as curious as we find the contrast between Victorian sexual prudery and the vast size of the Victorian demimonde.) Fatherhood did not improve the young man's conduct: he broke her jaw, fractured her ribs, partially strangled her, punched her regularly and used her head to break a closed window before pushing her out of it altogether. He did not work, took her money for drink, went to spend nights with other girls, and demanded his meals be ready for him to suit his convenience.

I offered her, too, every opportunity to leave, every legal protection it was possible to provide, but her cup of bitterness, like the first girl's, was not yet full ('It's all right for you, you don't love him') and therefore not yet ready to be drained. All one could do was offer to help whenever she was ready to ask for it.

Neither of these young women was deficient in intelligence, far from it; and I knew that, when they appeared again in my hospital, as inevitably they would, they would be ready to examine the source of their suffering, having wasted so much time. I could but hope that someone would have the courage and compassion to guide them to that source: for only if the veil of self-deception is torn from the eyes can women such as these improve the quality of their lives.

Experience has taught me that it is wrong and cruel to suspend judgment, that non-judgmentalism is, at best, indifference to the suffering of others, and, at worst, a disguised form of sadism. How can one respect people as members of the human race unless one holds them to a standard of conduct and truthfulness? How can people learn from experience unless they are told that they can and should change? One doesn't demand of laboratory mice that they do better: but man is not a mouse, and I can think of no more contemptuous way of treating people than to ascribe to them no more responsibility than such mice.

In any case, non-judgmentalism is not really non-judgmental. It is the judgment that, in the words of a bitter Argentinean tango, '*todo es igual, nada es mejor*': everything is the same, nothing is better.

This is as barbaric and untruthful a doctrine as has yet emerged from the fertile mind of man.

IN THE ASYLUM

THE VICTORIAN LUNATIC ASYLUMS of my city were magnificent, from the purely architectural point of view. Municipal pride, manifested by artistic embellishment without utilitarian purpose, shone out from them. They were built on generous grounds in what were then rural areas, outside the city bounds, on the theory that rustic peace had a healing effect upon fractured minds – and also that remoteness would protect the sane of the city from distressing contact with the insane. The city expanded and soon engulfed the asylums, but the grounds remained, often the only islands of green in a sea of soot and red brick. These grounds, right up until the asylums closed, were tended with a care that spoke of love and devotion.

For all who worked in them, the asylums provided a genuine sense of community. Indeed, by the time of their closure they were the only real communities for miles around, the surrounding society having been smashed into atoms. They held annual cricket matches and other sporting contests on their spacious lawns, and hosted summer and Christmas balls. The staff were often second- or third-generation employees, and the institution was central to their lives.

The patients benefited from the stability; the asylum was a little world in which they could behave as strangely as they pleased without anyone caring too much. They were free of the mockery and disdain with which people elsewhere would greet their strange demeanour, gestures and ideas: for in the asylum, the strange was normal. Within its bounds, there was no stigma.

But of course there was a very dark side as well. Physical conditions, especially for those patients so chronically ill that the wards were in effect their homes, were appalling. There was no privacy, with beds sometimes packed so closely together that no one could walk between them. The smell of urine so deeply impregnated the furnishings and floors of the dayrooms that it seemed ineradicable (not that anyone tried to eradicate it). The stodgy food and physical inactivity meant that chronic constipation was universal; and most patients looked as if they had filtered their food through their shirts, blouses and sweaters. Aimless wandering in the corridors was the principal recreation for many patients, who rarely saw a doctor, therapeutic impotence being more or less taken for granted. Individuals had lived in these conditions for more than half a century; and it was possible until the late 1980s to find women who had been committed to the asylums in the 1920s merely for having borne illegitimate children. As in the Soviet Union (though to a far less sinister degree), deviance was sometimes labelled madness and treated accordingly.

Most of the staff were kindly and well meaning, but, as in any situation in which some human beings have unsupervised care of and power over others, opportunities for sadism abounded. Usually these were minor: I often saw nurses denying cigarettes to patients, telling them to come back in a few minutes, for no other reason than the pleasure of exerting power over a fellow being. But from time to time far worse cruelty would surface, always hushed up in the name of institutional morale. This was easily done, since very few outside the asylum concerned themselves with what went on inside.

For most of their existence, the asylums were custodial rather than therapeutic institutions. Their methods now strike us as laughably crude. One asylum doctor published a memoir just after World War I in which he described how he and his colleagues treated suicidal melancholics and agitated paranoiacs. They sat the melancholics against a wall, placing a bench in front of them to prevent them from moving, while an attendant watched them to ensure that they did not do away with themselves. Croton oil, a very powerful laxative, subdued the agitation of the paranoiacs, who became so preoccupied with the movement of their bowels that they had no time or energy left to act upon the content of their delusions.

Attempts at cures were often more desperate than well advised. One of the asylums of my city had the best-equipped operating theatre of its time, where an enthusiastic psychiatrist partially eviscerated his patients and also removed all their teeth, on the theory that madness was caused by a chronic but undetected and subclinical infection (called 'focal sepsis') in the organs that he removed. Later a visiting neurosurgeon used the theatre to perform lobotomies on patients who were scarcely aware of what was being done to them. Doctors also tried more 'advanced' treatments, such as insulin coma therapy, in which they gave schizophrenic patients insulin to lower their blood sugar to the point at which they became unconscious, sometimes with fatal effect.

It was not difficult, then, to present asylums as chambers of horrors, where bizarre sadistic rituals were carried out for reasons unconnected with beneficent medical endeavour. And it so happened that one of the most powerful critics of both the asylum system and psychiatry as a whole – powerful in the sense of having had the greatest overall effect – published his attack in 1961, not long after the introduction of medications so efficacious in the treatment of psychosis that the asylum populations had already begun to decline, as patients were discharged back into the outside world. The critic was the philosopher Michel Foucault, and within a few years his *Madness and Civilisation* had spawned an entire movement, though of somewhat disparate elements.

Foucault was not so much concerned by the cases of abuse or the poor conditions in asylums, as a mere reformer might have been. In the tortuous prose then typical of French intellectuals, he was concerned to assert that the separation of the mad from the sane, both physically and as a matter of classification, was neither intellectually justified nor motivated by beneficence. Instead, it was an instance of the exertion of power by the rising bourgeoisie, which needed a disciplined and compliant workforce to fuel its economic system and was therefore increasingly intolerant of deviance – not only of conduct but of thought. It therefore locked deviants away in what Foucault called 'the great incarceration' of the 17th and 18th centuries, of which the British asylums of the Victorian Era were a late manifestation.

In Foucault's Nietzschean vision, all human institutions – even, or especially, those of avowedly beneficent intent – are expressions of the will to power, because such a will underlies all human activity. It is not really surprising, then, that asylums had turned into nothing but chambers of horrors: for psychiatry, and indeed the whole of medicine, to the rest of which Foucault soon turned his undermining attention, were not enterprises to liberate mankind from some of its travails – enterprises that inevitably committed errors *en route* to knowledge and enlightenment – but expressions of the will to power of the medical profession. The fact that this will was cloaked under an official ideology of benevolence made it only the more dangerous and sinister. This will needed to be unmasked so that mankind could liberate itself and live in the anarchic Dionysian mode that Foucault favoured. (A sadomasochistic homosexual, he later lived out his fantasies in San Francisco, and died of AIDS as a result.)

Foucault inspired subsequent critics of psychiatry, of varying degrees of scholarliness, rationality and clarity of exposition. Among the best was the influential historian Andrew Scull, whose history of the origins of asylums, *Museums of Madness*, nevertheless implied that the arrogation of insanity to the purview of doctors in the 18th century did not grow out of any natural connection between the phenomena of madness and the endeavour of medicine – still less out of the practical ability of doctors of the time to cure madness (witness their failure in the case of George III) – but on the medical profession's entrepreneurial drive to increase its influence and income. The fact that the mad eventually came under the care of the medical profession was thus a historical accident, the result of the shrewd manoeuvring of the doctors: some other group – the clergymen, for example, or the tailors – might have occupied the same position had they manoeuvred as successfully. Founded on so illegitimate a basis, psychiatry was by implication a totally false undertaking.

This argument overlooks a few obvious facts, however. What could have been said of madness could have been said of dysentery and pneumonia – that the doctors of the time had no power to cure them and that therefore these diseases were not properly the province of physicians and might just as well have been handled by tinkers or topographers. If the Foucauldian style of thought had prevailed at earlier times, with that mindset's failure to understand imaginatively what is required to go from a state of complete ignorance to one of partial knowledge, and how it is often necessary to act in a state of ignorance, no one would ever have discovered anything about the cause or treatment of disease.

Moreover, the connection between madness and medicine is not entirely arbitrary and unfounded, as Scull suggested (though in my opinion the scope of psychiatry has since expanded illegitimately, especially in the grotesque overprescription of psychotropic medication). The 18th century doctors had in this respect a better grasp of reality than Professor Scull, for organic conditions leading to madness and dementia must have been very common at the time. It has been plausibly suggested (though not conclusively proved) that George III was suffering from porphyria, possibly exacerbated by lead poisoning, for instance, and at the end of the 19th century up to a quarter of the population of the asylums was suffering from general paralysis of the insane, the last stage of syphilis. Dare I mention that were it not for modern medicine, I myself would long ago have ended up in an asylum, one of those apathetic creatures that the physiognomists of madness in the 19th century so eloquently portrayed in their drawings, because I suffer from hypothyroidism, which is the most common of all endocrine diseases and which untreated can lead to madness and finally to dementia?

Another rhetorically powerful critic of psychiatry, also influenced by Foucault, was R.D. Laing, himself a psychiatrist. It was he who, in the 1960s and 1970s, gave currency to the idea that madness was an alternative, and in some ways superior, way of being in the world: that madness was in fact true sanity, and sanity true madness, insofar as the world itself was quite mad in its political, social and domestic arrangements. According to Laing, it was the unequal power within families, and the distorted communications to which this inequality gave rise, that caused the condition in young people known as schizophrenia. To hospitalise them and treat them against their will was thus to punish them for the sins of their parents and to maintain an unjust social order at the same time.

This view became extremely popular in an era that uncritically criticised all institutions. The psychotic came to be viewed by right-thinking people as victims of injustice rather than as sufferers from illness (an attitude reinforced when it was discovered that young men of Jamaican origin living in Britain had a rate of schizophrenia six, seven or eight times that of young white men). What was required was not treatment but restitution.

These ideas paved the way for an ill-conceived and hasty deinstitutionalisation of the mentally ill. Thanks to effective treatments, the numbers requiring to be institutionalised were declining anyway; politicians hoped to save money and were all too willing to believe that the mentally ill could be managed almost without any institutions whatever; and finally, criticisms of the Foucauldian mould – that society had no right to impose restraint upon the mad – entered common consciousness. Madmen had a right to wander the streets, and other citizens had the duty to put up with it.

The asylums of my city closed within a few short years. The patients were sent to live in what bureaucrats insisted upon calling 'the community', because of that term's connotations of warmth and welcome. With varying degrees of assistance and supervision, they were expected to live independently; they were given their autonomy, whether they wanted it or not. Many coped adequately with their new-found freedom, but many did not. And meanwhile, hospital provision for the mentally ill declined to such an extent, both for budgetary and ideological reasons (hospital admission was to be avoided at all costs, in a fetishistic kind of way, irrespective of the logic of the individual case), that every time it became imperatively necessary to admit a psychiatric patient, the entire system experienced a crisis. Madmen were left in police cells for days on end while hospital beds were found for them; sometimes, not a single such bed could be found in an area with a population of four or five million.

Every day in my work as a prison doctor I witnessed the effect of this lack of provision. Ironically the splendid new hospital wing of the prison, built with few expenses spared, rose on the grounds of an asylum that had just been closed down; but inside the hospital we were recreating the conditions of 18th century Bedlam. Modern walls do not a modern hospital make. Unearthly screams rent the air; foul smells offended the nostrils. Madmen threw their clothes through the windows, started fires in their cells, tore up their sheets, wrapped towels around their heads, angrily addressed their hallucinatory interlocutors while standing stark naked on their beds, refused all food as poisoned and spat at passersby. All that was lacking were visitors from the outside world who had paid their pennies to laugh at the lunatics; I suggested that we reinstitute this great tradition to improve the prison's finances.

The cases would go like this: a madman would commit an offence – say, a completely unprovoked assault on a person in the street (unprovoked, that is, from the victim's point of view; the perpetrator would believe that the victim had been threatening or insulting him). The police would arrest him and take him to the police station. They would recognise that he was mad – his speech would be rambling and incoherent, he spoke of things that were not, and his behaviour was completely beyond the bounds of reason. They would call a doctor, who would say that yes, the man was mad, but that no, he could not be admitted to a hospital to be treated, because there were no beds available.

The police then faced a dilemma. They could either release the man back into the community, whose sense of social solidarity he had so reinforced by his unprovoked attack on a random stranger, or they could charge him and put him before the courts. Sometimes they would do the one, sometimes the other. I have known lunatics released from police custody who clearly had intended to kill their victims in the street (and were handed back the weapons with which they intended to do it), because a policeman did not want to charge a man who was so obviously not responsible for his actions.

At other times, depending on who knows what factors, the police would bring the man before the courts, where a system of psychiatric screening had been set up. Theoretically the accused found to be psychiatrically unwell by the examining nurse would be diverted from the criminal justice system into the psychiatric system. But the nurse, knowing that no hospital beds would be available were she to declare the accused mentally ill, and not wishing to accept the labour of Hercules involved in trying to find such a bed, declares the madman (so mad that it requires no expertise at all to detect his madness) to be fully sane, or a malingerer, or to be currently under the influence of marijuana, so that his madness will pass within a short time and results from voluntary intoxication which is no excuse under the law for his crime. Thus the madman is remanded into custody; and the nurse calms her conscience with the hope that the prison doctor will recognise the man's madness and will try to find a hospital bed for him.

Unfortunately, things do not go smoothly in the prison. The doctor cannot find a hospital bed for his mad patient; the psychiatrists outside the prison consider that the patient is now in a place of safety – the prison – where he will not be deprived of medical attention, and he is therefore of lower priority for a hospital bed than a lunatic still at large in the community. He is thus kept, often for months, in the prison on remand.

As the law now stands in Britain, prison doctors are not permitted to give treatment against a patient's will, except under the direst emergency, for fear they might abuse such power and forcibly sedate whomever they choose contrary to the patient's human rights. Hence, psychotic patients are now kept in prison hospitals for months without any treatment whatsoever, thus taking part in an interesting if not altogether pleasing experiment in the natural history of psychosis, such as has not been conducted for many years.

For example, I observed a psychotic patient for several weeks who addressed the world night and day through his prison window in words of muddled religious exaltation, who refused all food on the grounds that it was poisoned, his flesh melting away before my eyes, who attacked anyone who came within reach, and who painted religious slogans on the walls of his cell with his own excrement, thus imparting a nauseating faeculent smell to the entire hospital.

It might, of course, be alleged that he behaved in so disturbed a fashion because he was incarcerated, and that his conduct was (in the opinion of R.D. Laing) a meaningful and enlightened response to his terrible social situation, and that he, of all the 1,400 prisoners in the prison, was acting in the most appropriate way under the circumstances. But this would be not only to ignore his medical history but also the fact that he was incarcerated in the first place because he had viciously and without provocation attacked a 79-year-old woman in a church, injuring her badly while reciting verses from the Bible, which suggests that his disturbed mental state preceded his incarceration and was not a consequence of it.

I checked the situation with lawyers. Although he had a fully documented history of psychosis and an entirely favourable response to treatment, attested to by both doctors and relatives (who said that when treated he was a pleasant and intelligent man), I was not entitled, in the name of human rights, to treat him against his will. In the name of human rights, therefore, the prison officers and the other prisoners had to endure weeks of revolting air, as well as disturbed nights in which sleep was all but impossible, while he lived in conditions that Hogarth might well have painted with justified moral fury.

The doctors to whom I proposed to send the patient accepted the conditions in which he lived with Buddha-like calm that would have been admirable had the suffering been theirs. Only the prison officers, among the most despised of all public servants, seemed to be moved by the scandal of the situation. The doctors, by contrast, were now so inured to such situations that they accepted it as normal and nothing to get excited about. The shortage of beds and the administrative difficulties that this shortage caused had steadily eroded their common humanity. It was only when I threatened to expose the scandal publicly and had taken photographs of the man's cell and said I would send them to the government minister responsible for prisons (a proceeding completely against the rules, but supported by the prison governor, who did not want his prison turned into a surrogate lunatic asylum) that the man was finally found a place in a hospital, where he could be treated.

Of course, Foucault might have put a completely different construction on the outrage of the prison officers and the desire of the man's relatives for him to be treated and returned to normality. He might have interpreted all this as an intolerant refusal to accept the man's alternative way of life, a refusal even to try to interpret the meaning of the communications that he coded in his own excrement. For Foucault, their concern, couched in the terms of humanity, concealed a drive for power and domination, used to produce conformity to debilitating and dehumanising bourgeois standards. But such an interpretation would surely mean that common humanity and a feeling for others are qualities whose very possibility he would radically deny: that the only relations that could exist between men are those of power, and that all else is illusion.

I am aware that hard cases make bad law, but I could cite many such cases like the one above; of cases, for example, where doctors have changed their diagnoses in order to avoid the responsibility of finding hospital beds for their patients, and where they have even perjured themselves in court to evade that responsibility, to the great detriment of the patient and the safety of society alike. These are now part of everyday practice.

The shortage of beds, brought about by the desire to make financial savings in the context of an ideological assault on the notion of psychiatric illness, has corrupted doctors and nurses by slow but inexorable steps.

I am also aware that many horror stories could be told of doctors who have been overzealous (to put it mildly) in their attempts to cure their patients or to spread their fields of operations to their own material and social advantage. There is no simple formula for avoiding the Scylla of zealotry on the one hand and the Charybdis of abandonment of responsibility on the other. The art is long, life is short, the occasion fleeting and judgment difficult. But the difficulty must be faced.

One thing is certain: that Foucault and his ilk are no guides to how to treat a man like the one I have described (and such as I came across every day). Should he have been let free to continue his Dionysian assaults on defenceless old ladies, on the grounds that they were life-enhancing? I cannot see that this represents anything but a preference for barbarism.

THE GIFT OF LANGUAGE

NOW THAT I'VE RETIRED, my former colleagues sometimes ask me, not without a trace of anxiety, whether I think I made the right choice or whether I miss my previous life. They are good friends and fine men, but it is only human nature not to wish unalloyed happiness to one who has chosen a path that diverges, even slightly, from one's own.

Fortunately, I do miss some aspects of my work: if I didn't, it would mean that I had not enjoyed what I did for many years and had wasted a large stretch of my life. I miss, for instance, the sudden illumination into the worldview of my patients that their replies to simple questions sometimes gave me. I still do a certain amount of medico-legal work, preparing psychiatric reports on those accused of crimes, and recently a case reminded me of how sharply a few words can bring into relief an entire attitude toward life and shed light on an entire mental hinterland.

A young woman was charged with assault, under the influence of alcohol and marijuana, on a very old lady about five times her age. Describing her childhood, the young accused mentioned that her mother had once been in trouble with the police.

'What for?' I asked.

'She was on the Social and working at the same time.'

'What happened?' I asked.

'She had to give up working.'

The air of self-evidence with which she said this revealed a whole world of presuppositions. For her, and those around her, work was the last resort; economic dependence on state handouts was the natural condition of man.

I delighted in what my patients said. One of them always laced his statements with proverbs, which he invariably mangled. 'Sometimes, doctor,' he said to me one day, 'I feel like the little boy with his finger in the dike, crying wolf.'

And I enjoyed the expressive argot of prison. The prison officers, too, had their own language. They called a loquacious prisoner 'verbal' if they believed him to be mad, and 'mouthy' if they believed him to be merely bad and wilfully misbehaving.

Brief exchanges could so entertain me that on occasion they transformed duty into pleasure. Once I was called to the prison in the early hours to examine a man who had just tried to hang himself. He was sitting in a room with a prison officer. It was about three in the morning, the very worst time to be roused from sleep.

'The things you have to do for Umanity, sir,' said the prison officer to me.

The prisoner, looking bemused, said to him, 'You what?'

'U-manity,' said the prison officer, turning to the prisoner. 'You're Uman, aren't you?'

It was like living in a glorious comic passage in Dickens. For the most part, though, I was struck not by the verbal felicity and invention of my patients and those around them but by their inability to express themselves with anything like facility: and this after 11 years of compulsory education, or (more accurately) supposed attendance at school.

With a very limited vocabulary, it is impossible to make, or at least to express, important distinctions and to examine any question with conceptual care. My patients often had no words to describe what they were feeling, except in the crudest possible way, with expostulations, exclamations and physical displays of emotion. Often, by guesswork and my experience of other patients, I could put things into words for them, words that they grasped at eagerly. Everything was on the tip of their tongue, rarely or never reaching the stage of expression out loud. They struggled even to describe in a consecutive and logical fashion what had happened to them, at least without a great deal of prompting. Complex narrative and most abstractions were closed to them.

In their dealings with authority, they were at a huge disadvantage – a disaster, since so many of them depended upon various public bureaucracies for so many of their needs, from their housing and health care to their income and the education of their children. I would find myself dealing on their behalf with those bureaucracies, which were often simultaneously bullying and incompetent; and what officialdom had claimed for months or even years to be impossible suddenly, on my intervention, became possible within a week. Of course it was not my mastery of language alone that produced this result; rather, my mastery of language signalled my capacity to make serious trouble for the bureaucrats if they did not do as I asked. I do not think it is a coincidence that the offices of all those bureaucracies were increasingly installing security barriers against the physical attacks on the staff by enraged but inarticulate dependants.

All this, it seems to me, directly contradicts our era's ruling orthodoxy about language. According to that orthodoxy, every child, save the severely brain-damaged and those with very rare genetic defects, learns his or her native language with perfect facility, adequate to his needs. He does so because the faculty of language is part of human nature, inscribed in man's physical being, as it were, and almost independent of environment. To be sure, today's language theorists concede that if a child grows up completely isolated from other human beings until the age of about six, he will never learn language adequately; but this very fact, they argue, implies that the capacity for language is 'hard wired' into the human brain, to be activated only at a certain stage in each individual's development, which in turn proves that language is an inherent biological characteristic of mankind rather than a merely cultural artefact. Moreover language itself is always rule-governed, and the rules that govern it are universally the same when stripped of certain minor incidentals and contingencies that superficially appear important but in reality are not.

It follows that no language or dialect is superior to any other and that modes of verbal communication cannot be ranked according to complexity, expressiveness or any other virtue. Thus, attempts to foist alleged grammatical 'correctness' on native speakers of an 'incorrect' dialect are nothing but the unacknowledged and oppressive exercise of social control – the means by which the elites deprive whole social classes and peoples of self-esteem and keep them in permanent subordination. If they are convinced that they can't speak their own language properly, how can they possibly feel other than unworthy, humiliated and disfranchised? Hence, the refusal to teach formal grammar is both in accord with a correct understanding of the nature of language and is politically generous, inasmuch as it confers equal status on all forms of speech and therefore upon all speakers.

The *locus classicus* of this way of thinking, at least for laymen such as myself, is Steven Pinker's book *The Language Instinct*. A best-seller when first published in 1994, it is now in its 25th printing in the British paperback version alone, and its wide circulation suggests a broad influence on the opinions of the intelligent public. Pinker is a professor of psychology at Harvard University, and that institution's great prestige cloaks him, too, in the eyes of many. If Professor Pinker were not right on so important a subject, which is one to which he has devoted much study and brilliant intelligence, would he have tenure at Harvard?

Pinker nails his colours to the mast at once. His book, he says, 'will not chide you about proper usage' because, after all, '[l]anguage is a complex, specialised skill which… is qualitatively the same in every individual… Language is no more a cultural invention than is upright posture,' and men are as naturally equal in their ability to express themselves as in their ability to stand on two legs. 'Once you begin to look at language… as a biological adaptation to communicate information,' Pinker continues, 'it is no longer as tempting to see language as an insidious shaper of thought.' Every individual has an equal linguistic capacity to formulate the most complex and refined thoughts. We all have, so to speak, the same tools for thinking. 'When it comes to linguistic form,' Pinker says, quoting the anthropologist Edward Sapir, 'Plato walks with the Macedonian swineherd, Confucius with the head-hunting savage of Assam.' To put it another way, 'linguistic genius is involved every time a child learns his or her mother tongue'.

The old-fashioned and elitist idea that there is a 'correct' and 'incorrect' form of language no doubt explains the fact that '[l]inguists repeatedly run up against the myth that working-class people… speak a simpler and a coarser language. This is a pernicious illusion… Trifling differences between the dialect of the mainstream and the dialect of other groups… are dignified as badges of "proper grammar".' These are, in fact, the 'hobgoblins of the schoolmarm', and *ipso facto* contemptible. In fact, standard English is one of those languages that 'is a dialect with an army and a navy'. The schoolmarms he so slightingly dismisses are in fact but the linguistic arm of a colonial power – the middle class – oppressing what would otherwise be a much freer and happier populace. 'Since prescriptive rules are so psychologically unnatural that only those with access to the right schooling can abide by them, they serve as shibboleths, differentiating the elite from the rabble.'

Children will learn their native language adequately whatever anyone does, and the attempt to teach them language is fraught with psychological perils. For example, to 'correct' the way a child speaks is potentially to give him what used to be called an inferiority complex. Moreover, when schools undertake such correction they risk dividing the child from his parents and social *milieu*, for he will speak in one way and live in another, creating hostility and possibly rejection all around him. But happily, since every child is a linguistic genius, there is no need to do any such thing. Every child will have the linguistic equipment he needs, merely by virtue of growing older.

I need hardly point out that Pinker doesn't really believe anything of what he writes, at least if example is stronger evidence of belief than precept. Though artfully sown here and there with a demotic expression to prove that he is himself of the people, his own book is written, not surprisingly, in the kind of English that would please schoolmarms. I doubt very much whether it would have reached its 25th printing had he chosen to write it in the dialect of the slums of Newcastle-upon-Tyne, for example, or of rural Louisiana. Even had he chosen to do so, he might have found the writing rather difficult. I should like to see him try to translate a sentence from his book that I have taken at random – 'The point that the argument misses is that, although natural selection involves incremental steps that enhance functioning, the enhancements do not have to be an existing module' – into the language of the back streets of Glasgow or Detroit.

In fact, Pinker has no difficulty in ascribing greater or lesser expressive virtues to languages and dialects. In attacking the idea that there are primitive languages, he quotes the linguist Joan Bresnan, who describes English as 'a West Germanic language spoken in England and its former colonies' (no prizes for guessing the emotional connotations of this way of so describing it). Bresnan wrote an article comparing the use of the dative in English and Kivunjo, a language spoken on the slopes of Mount Kilimanjaro. Its use is much more complex in the latter language than in the former, making far more distinctions. Pinker comments: 'Among the clever gadgets I have glimpsed in the grammars of so-called primitive groups, the complex Cherokee pronoun system seems especially handy. It distinguishes among "you and I", "another person and I", "several other people and I" and "you, one or more other persons, and I", which English crudely collapses into the all-purpose pronoun "we".' In other words, crudity and subtlety are concepts that apply between languages. And if so, there can be no real reason why they cannot apply *within* a language – why one man's usage should not be better, more expressive, subtler, than another's.

Similarly, Pinker attacks the idea that the English of the ghetto, Black English Vernacular, is in any way inferior to standard English. It is rule-governed like all other language. Moreover, 'If the psychologists had listened to spontaneous conversations, they would have rediscovered the commonplace fact that American black culture is highly verbal; the subculture of street youths in particular is famous in the annals of anthropology for the value placed on linguistic virtuosity.' But in appearing to endorse the idea of linguistic virtuosity, he is, whether he likes it or not, endorsing the idea of linguistic *lack* of virtuosity. And it surely requires very little reflection to come to the conclusion that Shakespeare had more linguistic virtuosity than, say, the average contemporary football player. Oddly enough, Pinker ends his encomium on Black English Vernacular with a schoolmarm's pursed lips: 'The highest percentage of ungrammatical sentences [are to be] found in the proceedings of learned academic conferences.'

Over and over again, Pinker stresses that children do not learn language by imitation; rather, they learn it because they are biologically predestined to do so. 'Let us do away,' he writes, with what one imagines to be a rhetorical sweep of his hand, 'with the folklore that parents teach their children language.' It comes as rather a surprise, then, to read the book's dedication: 'For Harry and Roslyn Pinker, who gave me language.'

Surely he cannot mean by this that they gave him language in the same sense as they gave him haemoglobin – that is to say, that they were merely the *sine qua non* of his biological existence as Steven Pinker. If so, why choose language of all the gifts that they gave him? Presumably he means that they gave him the opportunity to learn standard English, even if they did not speak it themselves.

It is utterly implausible to suggest that imitation of parents (or other social contacts) has nothing whatever to do with the acquisition of language. I hesitate to mention so obvious a consideration, but Chinese parents tend to have Chinese-speaking children, and Portuguese parents Portuguese-speaking ones. I find it difficult to believe that this is entirely a coincidence and that imitation has nothing to do with it. Moreover, it is a sociological truism that children tend to speak not merely the language but the dialect of their parents.

Of course, they can escape it if they choose or need to do so: my mother, a native German speaker, arrived in England aged 18 and learned to speak standard English without a trace of a German accent (which linguists say is a rare accomplishment) and without grammatical mistake. She did not imitate her parents, perhaps, but she imitated someone. After her recent death, I found her notebooks from 1939 in which she painstakingly practised English, the errors growing fewer until there were none. I don't think she would have been favourably impressed by Professor Pinker's disdainful grammatical latitudinarianism – the latitudinarianism that, in some British schools and universities, now extends not only to grammar but to spelling, as a friend of mine discovered recently.

A teacher in a state school gave his daughter a list of spellings to learn as homework, and my friend noticed that three out of ten of them were wrong. He went to the principal to complain, but she looked at the list and asked, 'So what? You can tell what the words are supposed to mean.' The test for her was not whether the spellings were correct but whether they were understandable. So much for the hobgoblins of contemporary schoolmarms.

The contrast between a felt and lived reality – in this case, Pinker's need to speak and write standard English because of its superior ability to express complex ideas – and the denial of it, perhaps in order to assert something original and striking, is characteristic of an intellectual climate in which the destruction of moral and social distinctions is proof of the very best intentions.

Pinker's grammatical latitudinarianism, when educationists like the principal of my friend's daughter's school take it seriously, has the practical effect of encouraging those born in the lower reaches of society to remain there, to enclose them in the mental world of their particular *milieu*. This is perfectly all right if you also believe that all stations in life are equally good and desirable and that there is nothing to be said for articulate reflection upon human existence. In other words, grammatical latitudinarianism is the natural ideological ally of moral and cultural relativism.

It so happens that I observed the importance of mastering standard, schoolmarmly, grammatical speech in my own family. My father, born two years after his older brother, had the opportunity, denied his older brother for reasons of poverty, to continue his education. Accordingly, my father learned to speak and write standard English and I never heard him utter a single word that betrayed his origins. He could discourse philosophically without difficulty; I sometimes wished he had been a little less fluent.

My uncle, by contrast, remained trapped in the language of the slums. He was a highly intelligent man and, what is more, a very good one: he was one of those rare men, much less common than their opposite, from whom goodness radiated almost as a physical quality. No one ever met him without sensing his goodness of heart, his generosity of spirit. But he was deeply inarticulate. His thoughts were too complex for the words and the syntax available to him.

All through my childhood and beyond, I saw him struggle, like a man wrestling with an invisible boa constrictor, to express his far from foolish thoughts – thoughts of a complexity that my father expressed effortlessly. The frustration was evident on his face, though he never blamed anyone else for it. When, in Pinker's book, I read the transcript of an interview by the neuropsychologist Howard Gardner with a man who suffered from expressive dysphasia after a stroke – that is to say, an inability to articulate thoughts in language – I was, with great sadness, reminded of my uncle. Gardner asked the man about his job before he had the stroke.

> 'I'm a sig... no... man... uh, well, ... again.' These words were emitted slowly, and with great effort.
> 'Let me help you,' I interjected. 'You were a signal...'
> 'A sig-nal man... right,' [he] completed my phrase triumphantly.
> 'Were you in the Coast Guard?'
> 'No, er, yes, yes... ship... Massachu... chusetts... Coast-guard... years.'

It seemed to me that it was a cruel fate for such a man as my uncle not to have been taught the standard English that came to come so naturally to my father. As Montaigne tells us, there is no torture greater than that of a man who is unable to express what is in his soul.

Beginning in the 1950s, Basil Bernstein, a researcher at London University, demonstrated the difference between the speech of middle- and working-class children, controlling for whatever it is that IQ measures. Working-class speech, tethered closely to the here and now, lacked the very aspects of standard English needed to express abstract or general ideas and to place personal experience in temporal or any other perspective. Thus, unless Pinker's despised schoolmarms were to take the working-class children in hand and deliberately teach them another speech code, they were doomed to remain where they were, at the bottom of a society that was itself much the poorer for not taking full advantage of their abilities, and that indeed would pay a steep penalty for not doing so. An intelligent man who can make no constructive use of his intelligence is likely to make a destructive, and self-destructive, use of it.

If anyone doubts that inarticulacy can be a problem, I recommend reading a report by the Joseph Rowntree Trust about British girls who get themselves pregnant in their teens (and sometimes their early teens) as an answer to their existential problems. The report is not in the least concerned with the linguistic deficiencies of these girls, but they are evident in the transcript in every reply to every question. Without exception, the girls had had a very painful experience of life and therefore much to express from hearts that must have been bursting. I give only one example, but it is representative. A girl, aged 17, explains why it is wonderful to have a baby:

> Maybe it's just – yeah, because maybe just – might be (um) it just feels great when – when like, you've got a child who just you know – following you around, telling you they love you and I think that's – it's quite selfish, but that's one of the reasons why I became a mum because I wanted someone who'll – you know – love 'em to bits 'cos it's not just your child who's the centre of your world, and that feels great as well, so I think – it's brilliant. It is fantastic because – you know – they're – the child's dependent on you and you know that (um) – that you – if you – you know – you've gotta do everything for the child and it just feels great to be depended on.

As I know from the experience of my patients, there is no reason to expect her powers of expression to improve spontaneously with age. Any complex abstractions that enter her mind will remain inchoate, almost a nuisance, like a fly buzzing in a bottle that it cannot escape. Her experience is opaque even to herself, a mere jumble from which it will be difficult or impossible to learn because, for linguistic reasons, she cannot put it into any kind of perspective or coherent order.

I am not of the ungenerous and empirically mistaken party that writes off such people as inherently incapable of anything better or as already having achieved so much that it is unnecessary to demand anything else of them on the grounds that they naturally have more in common with Shakespeare than with speechless animal creation. Nor, of course, would I want everyone to speak all the time in Johnsonian or Gibbonian periods. Not only would it be intolerably tedious, but much linguistic wealth would vanish. But everyone ought to have the opportunity to transcend the limitations of his linguistic environment, if it is a restricted one – which means that he ought to meet a few schoolmarms in his childhood. Everyone, save the handicapped, learns to run without being taught; but no-one runs 100 metres in ten seconds, or even fifteen seconds, without training. It is fatuous to expect that the most complex of human faculties, language, requires no special training to develop it to its highest possible power.

THE ROADS TO SERFDOM

PEOPLE IN BRITAIN who lived through World War II do not remember it with anything like the horror one might have expected. In fact they often remember it as the best time of their lives. Even allowing for the tendency of time to burnish unpleasant memories with a patina of romance, this is extraordinary. The war, after all, was a time of material shortage, terror and loss: what could possibly have been good about it?

The answer, of course, is that it provided a powerful existential meaning and purpose. The population suffered at the hands of an easily identifiable external enemy, whose evil intentions it became the overriding purpose of the whole nation to thwart. A unified and pre-eminent national goal provided respite from the peacetime cacophony of complaint, bickering and social division. And privation for a purpose brings its own content.

The war having instantaneously created a nostalgia for the sense of unity and transcendent purpose that prevailed in those years, the population naturally enough asked why such a mood could not persist into the peace that followed. Why couldn't the dedication of millions, centrally co-ordinated by the government – a co-ordinated dedication that had produced unprecedented quantities of aircraft and munitions – be adapted to defeat what Sir William Beveridge, the head of the London School of Economics, called the 'five giants on the road to reconstruction' in his wartime report on social services that was to usher in the full-scale welfare state in Britain: Want, Disease, Ignorance, Squalor and Idleness?

By the time Beveridge published his report in 1942, most of the intellectuals of the day assumed that the government, and only the government, could accomplish these desirable goals. Indeed, it all seemed so simple a matter that only the cupidity and stupidity of the rich could have prevented these ends from already having been achieved. The Beveridge Report states, for example, that want 'could have been abolished in Britain before the present war' and that 'the income available to the British people was ample for such a purpose'. It was just a matter of dividing the national income cake into more equal slices by means of redistributive taxation. If the political will was there, the way was there; there was no need to worry about effects on wealth creation or any other adverse effects.

For George Orwell, writing a year before the Beveridge Report, matters were equally straightforward. 'Socialism,' he wrote, 'is usually defined as "common ownership of the means of production". Crudely: the State, representing the whole nation, owns everything, and everyone is a state employee... Socialism... can solve the problems of production and consumption... The State simply calculates what goods will be needed and does its best to produce them. Production is only limited by the amount of labour and raw materials.'

A few, equally simple measures would help bring about a better, more just and equitable society. Orwell recommended: 'Nationalisation of land, mines, railways, banks and major industries'; 'Limitation of incomes, on such a scale that the highest does not exceed the lowest by more than ten to one'; and 'Reform of the educational system along democratic lines'. By this last, he meant the total prohibition of private education. He assumed that the culture, which he esteemed but which nevertheless was a product of the very system he so disliked, would take care of itself.

It would scarcely be an exaggeration to say that, by the time Orwell wrote, his collectivist philosophy was an intellectual orthodoxy from which hardly anyone in Britain would dare dissent, at least very strongly. 'We are all socialists now,' declared Bernard Shaw 40 years before Orwell put forward his modest proposals. And before him, Oscar Wilde, in 'The Soul of Man Under Socialism', accepted as incontrovertible – as not even worth supporting with evidence or argument, so obviously true was it – that poverty was the inescapable consequence of private property, and that one man's wealth was another man's destitution. And before Wilde, John Ruskin had argued, in *Unto This Last*, that a market in labour was both unnecessary and productive of misery. After all, he said, many wages were set according to an abstract (which is to say a moral) conception of the value of the job; so why should not all wages be set in the same way? Would this not avoid the unjust, irrational and frequently harsh variations to which a labour market exposed people?

Ruskin was right that there are indeed jobs whose wages are fixed by an approximate notion of moral appropriateness. The salary of the Prime Minister is not set according to the vagaries of the labour market; nor would the number of candidates for the post change much if it were halved or doubled. But if every wage in the United Kingdom were fixed in the same way, wages would soon cease to mean very much. The economy would be demonetised, the impersonal medium of money being replaced in the allocation of goods and services by personal influence and political connection – precisely what happened in the Soviet Union. Every economic transaction would become an expression of political power.

The growing spirit of collectivism in Britain during the war provoked an Austrian economist who had taken refuge there, Friedrich A von Hayek, to write a polemical counterblast to the trend: *The Road to Serfdom*, published in 1944. It went through six printings in its first year, but its effect on majority opinion was, for many years to come, negligible.

Hayek believed that while intellectuals in modern liberal democracies – those to whom he somewhat contemptuously referred as the professional second-hand dealers in ideas – did not usually have direct access to power, the theories they diffused among the population ultimately had a profound, even determining, influence upon their society. Intellectuals are of far greater importance than appears at first sight. He was therefore alarmed at the general acceptance of collectivist arguments – or worse still, assumptions – by British intellectuals of all classes. He had seen the process – or thought he had seen it – before, in the German-speaking world from which he came, and he feared that Britain would likewise slide down the totalitarian path. Moreover, at the time he wrote, the 'success' of the two major totalitarian powers in Europe, Nazi Germany and Soviet Russia, seemed to have justified the belief that a plan was necessary to co-ordinate human activity toward a consciously chosen goal. For George Orwell, the difference between the two tyrannies was one of ends, not of means: he held up Nazi Germany as an exemplar of economic efficiency resulting from central planning, but he deplored the ends that efficiency accomplished. While the idea behind Nazism was 'human inequality, the superiority of Germans to all other races, the right of Germany to rule the world', socialism (of which, of course, the Soviet Union was the only exemplar at the time) 'aims, ultimately, at a world-state of free and equal human beings'. Same means, different ends: but Orwell, at this point in his intellectual development, saw nothing intrinsically objectionable in the means themselves, or that they must inevitably lead to tyranny and oppression, independently of the ends for which they were deployed.

Against the collectivists, Hayek brought powerful – and to my mind obvious – arguments that, however, were scarcely new or original. Nevertheless, it is often, perhaps usually, more important to remind people of old truths than to introduce them to new ones.

Hayek pointed out that the wartime unity of purpose was atypical; in more normal times, people had a far greater, indeed an infinite, variety of ends, and anyone with the power to adjudicate among them in the name of a conscious overall national plan, allowing a few but forbidding most, would exert vastly more power than the most bloated plutocrat of socialist propaganda had ever done in a free-market society.

Orwell's assertion that the state would simply calculate what was needed airily overlooked the difficulties of the matter, as well as his proposal's implications for freedom. The 'directing brains', as Orwell called them, would have to decide how many hairpins, how many shoelaces were 'needed' by the population under their purview. They would have to make untold millions of such decisions, likewise co-ordinating the production of all components of each product, on the basis of their own arbitrary notions of what their fellow citizens needed. Orwell's goal, therefore, was a society in which the authorities strictly rationed everything; for him, and untold intellectuals like him, only rationing was rational. It takes little effort of the imagination to see what this control would mean for the exercise of liberty. Among other things, people would have to be assigned work regardless of their own preferences.

Collectivist thinking arose, according to Hayek, from impatience, a lack of historical perspective, and an arrogant belief that, because we have made so much technological progress, everything must be susceptible to human control. While we take material advance for granted as soon as it occurs, we consider remaining social problems as unprecedented and anomalous, and we propose solutions that actually make more difficult further progress of the very kind that we have forgotten ever happened. While everyone saw the misery the Great Depression caused, for example, few realised that, even so, living standards actually continued to rise for the majority. If we live entirely in the moment, as if the world were created exactly as we now find it, we are almost bound to propose solutions that bring even worse problems in their wake.

In reaction to the unemployment rampant in what W.H. Auden called 'the low dishonest decade' before the war, the Beveridge Report suggested that it was government's function to maintain security of income and employment. This proposition was bound to appeal strongly to people who remembered mass unemployment and collapsing wages; but however high-minded and generous it might have sounded, it was wrong. Hayek pointed out that you cannot give everyone a job irrespective of demand without sparking severe inflation. And you can no more protect one group of workers' wages against market fluctuations without penalising another group than you can discriminate positively in one group's favour without discriminating negatively against another. This is so, and it is beyond any individual human's control that it should be so. Therefore, no amount of planning would ever make Beveridge's goals possible, however desirable they might be in the abstract.

But just because a goal is logically impossible to achieve does not mean that it must be without effect on human affairs. As the history of the 20th century demonstrates perhaps better than any other, impossible goals have had at least as great an effect on human existence as more limited and possible ones.

The most interesting aspect of Hayek's book, however, is not his refutation of collectivist ideas – which, necessary as it might have been at that moment, was not by any means original. Rather, it is his observations of the moral and psychological effects of the collectivist ideal that, 60 years later, capture the imagination – mine, at least.

Hayek thought he had observed an important change in the character of the British people, as a result both of their collectivist aspirations and of such collectivist measures as had already been legislated. He noted, for example, a shift in the locus of people's moral concern. Increasingly it was the state of society or the world as a whole that engaged their moral passion, not their own conduct. 'It is, however, more than doubtful whether a fifty years' approach towards collectivism has raised our moral standards, or whether the change has not rather been in the opposite direction,' he wrote. 'Though we are in the habit of priding ourselves on our more sensitive social conscience, it is by no means clear that this is justified by the practice of our individual conduct.' In fact, 'It may even be... that the passion for collective action is a way in which we now without compunction collectively indulge in that selfishness which as individuals we had learnt a little to restrain.'

Thus, to take a trifling instance, it is the duty of the city council to keep the streets clean; therefore my own conduct in this regard is morally irrelevant – which no doubt explains why so many young Britons now leave a trail of litter behind them wherever they go. If the streets are filthy, it is the council's fault. Indeed, if anything is wrong – for example, my unhealthy diet – it is someone else's fault, and the job of the public power to correct. Hayek – with the perspective of a foreigner who had adopted England as his home – could perceive a further tendency that has become much more pronounced since then: 'There is one aspect of the change in moral values brought about by the advance of collectivism which at the present time provides special food for thought. It is that the virtues which are held less and less in esteem and which consequently become rarer are precisely those on which the British people justly prided themselves and in which they were generally agreed to excel. The virtues possessed by the British people in a higher degree than most other people... were independence and self-reliance, individual initiative and local responsibility... non-interference with one's neighbour and tolerance of the different and queer, respect for custom and tradition and a healthy suspicion of power and authority.'

He might have added the sense of irony, and therefore of the inherent limitations of human existence, that was once so prevalent, and that once protected the British population from infatuation with utopian dreams and unrealistic expectations. And the virtues that Hayek saw in them – the virtues immortalised in the pages of Jane Austen and Charles Dickens – were precisely the virtues that my mother and her cousin also saw when they first arrived in Britain as refugees from Germany in 1938. Orwell saw (and valued) them too, but unlike Hayek he did not ask himself where they came from; he must have supposed that they were an indestructible national essence, distilled not from history but from geography.

The British are sadly changed from Hayek's description of them. A sense of irony is the first victim of utopian dreams. The British tolerance of eccentricity has also evaporated; uniformity is what they want now, and are prepared informally to impose. They tolerate no deviation in taste or appearance from themselves: and certainly in the lower reaches of society, people who are markedly different, either in appearance because of the vagaries of nature, or in behaviour because of an unusual taste they may have, especially for cultivation, meet with merciless ridicule, bullying and even physical attack. It is as if people believe that uniformity of appearance, taste and behaviour are a justification of their own lives, and any deviation an implied reproach or even a declaration of hostility. A young patient of mine, who disliked the noise, the vulgarity and the undertone of violence of the night-clubs where her classmates spent their Friday and Saturday nights, was derided and mocked into conformity: it was too hard to hold out. The pressure to conform to the canons of popular taste – or rather, lack of taste – has never been stronger. Those without interest in football hardly dare mention it in public, for fear of being considered enemies of the people. A dispiriting uniformity of character, deeply shallow, has settled over a land once richer in eccentrics than any other. No more Edward Lears for us: we prefer notoriety to oddity now.

The British are no longer sturdily independent as individuals, either, and now feel no shame or even unease, as not long ago they would have felt, in accepting government handouts. Indeed, 40 percent of them now receive such handouts: for example, the parents of every child are entitled not merely to a tax reduction but to an actual payment in cash, no matter the state of their finances. As for those who, though able-bodied and perfectly capable of work, are completely dependent on the state for their income, they unashamedly call the day when their dole arrives 'pay-day'. Between work and parasitism they see no difference. 'I'm getting paid today,' they say, having not only accepted but thoroughly internalised the doctrine propounded in the Beveridge Report, that it is the duty of the state to assure everyone of a decent minimum standard of life regardless of his conduct. The fact of having drawn 16 breaths a minute, 24 hours a day is sufficient to entitle each of them to his minimum; and, oddly enough, Hayek saw no danger in this and even endorsed the idea. He did not see that to guarantee a decent minimum standard of life would demoralise not only those who accepted it but those who worked in the more menial occupations, and whose wages would almost inevitably give them a standard of living scarcely higher than that of the decent minimum provided merely for drawing breath.

In any case, Hayek did not quite understand the source of the collectivist rot in Britain. It is true, of course, that an individualist society needs a free, or at least a free-ish, market; but a necessary condition is not a sufficient one. It is not surprising, though, that Hayek should have emphasised the danger of a centrally-planned economy when so prominent a figure as Orwell – who was a genuine friend of personal liberty, who valued the peculiarities of English life and who wrote movingly about such national eccentricities as a taste for racy seaside postcards and a love of public school stories – should so little have understood the preconditions of English personal liberty that he wrote, only three years before Hayek's book was published: 'The liberty of the individual is still believed in, almost as in the nineteenth century. But this has nothing to do with economic liberty, the right to exploit others for profit.'

It is depressing to see a man like Orwell equating profit with exploitation. And it is certainly true that Britain after the war took no heed of Hayek and for a time seemed bent on state control of what were then called 'the commanding heights of the economy'. Not only did the Labour government nationalise health care, but also coal mining, electricity and gas supply, the railways and public transportation (including the airlines), telecommunications and even most of the car industry. Yet at no time could it remotely be said that Britain was slipping down the totalitarian path.

The real danger was far more insidious, and Hayek incompletely understood it. The destruction of the British character did not come from Nazi- or Soviet-style nationalisation or centralised planning, as Hayek believed it would. For collectivism proved to be not nearly as incompatible with, or diametrically opposed to, a free, or free-ish, market as he had supposed.

In fact, Hilaire Belloc, in his book *The Servile State*, predicted just such a form of collectivism as early as 1912. Like most intellectuals of the age, Belloc was a critic of capitalism because he held it responsible for the poverty and misery he saw in the London slums. His view was static, not dynamic: he did not see that the striving there could – and would – lift people out of their poverty, and he therefore argued that the liberal, *laissez-faire* state – 'mere capitalist anarchy', he called it – could not, and should not, continue. He foresaw three possible outcomes.

His preferred resolution was more or less the same as Carlyle's half a century earlier: a return to the allegedly stable and happy medieval world of reciprocal rights and duties. There would be guilds of craftsmen and merchants in the towns, supplying mainly handmade goods to one another and to peasant farmers, who in turn would supply them with food. Everyone would own at least some property, thereby having a measure of independence, but no one would be either plutocrat or pauper. However desirable this resolution, though, even Belloc knew it was fantasy.

The second possible resolution was the socialist one: total expropriation of the means of production, followed by state ownership, allegedly administered in the interests of everyone. Belloc had little to say on whether he thought this would work, since in his opinion it was unlikely to happen: the current owners of the means of production were still far too strong.

That left the third, and most likely, resolution. The effect of collectivist thought on a capitalist society would not be socialism but something quite distinct, whose outlines he believed he discerned in the newly established compulsory unemployment insurance. The means of production would remain in private hands, but the state would offer workers certain benefits in return for their quiescence and agreement not to agitate for total expropriation as demanded in socialist propaganda.

Unlike Orwell or Beveridge, however, Belloc realised that such benefits would exact a further price: 'A man has been compelled by law to put aside sums from his wages as insurance against unemployment. But he is no longer the judge of how such sums shall be used. They are not in his possession; they are not even in the hands of some society which he can really control. They are in the hands of a Government official. "Here is work offered to you at twenty-five shillings a week. If you do not take it you shall certainly not have a right to the money you have been compelled to put aside. If you will take it the sum shall stand to your credit, and when next in my judgment your unemployment is not due to your recalcitrance and refusal to labour, I will permit you to have some of your money; not otherwise."'

What applied to unemployment insurance would apply to all other spheres into which government intruded, Belloc intuited; and all of the benefits government conferred, paid for by the compulsory contributions of the taxpayer, in effect would take choice and decision-making out of the hands of the individual, placing them in those of the official. Although the benefits offered by the government were as yet few when Belloc wrote, he foresaw a state in which the 'whole of labour is mapped out and controlled'. In his view, 'The future of industrial society, and in particular of English society... is a future in which subsistence and security shall be guaranteed for the Proletariat, but shall be guaranteed... by the establishment of that Proletariat in a status really, though not nominally, servile'. The people lose 'that tradition of... freedom, and are most powerfully inclined to [the] acceptance of [their servile status] by the positive benefits it confers'.

And this is precisely what has happened to the large proportion of the British population that has been made dependent on the welfare state.

The state action that was supposed to lead to the elimination of Beveridge's five giants of Want, Disease, Ignorance, Squalor and Idleness has left many people in contemporary Britain with very little of importance to decide for themselves, even in their own private spheres. They are educated by the state (at least nominally), as are their children in turn; the state provides for them in old age and has made saving unnecessary or, in some cases, actually uneconomic; they are treated and cured by the state when they are ill; they are housed by the state if they cannot otherwise afford decent housing. Their choices concern only sex and shopping.

No wonder the British have changed in character, their sturdy independence replaced with passivity, querulousness or even, at the lower reaches of society, a sullen resentment that not enough has been or is being done for them. For those at the bottom, such money as they receive is, in effect, pocket money, like the money children get from their parents, reserved for the satisfaction of whims. As a result, they are infantilised. If they behave irresponsibly – for example, by abandoning their own children wherever they father them – it is because both the rewards for behaving responsibly and the penalties for behaving irresponsibly have vanished. Such people come to live in a limbo, in which there is nothing much to hope or strive for and nothing much to fear or lose. Private property and consumerism coexist with collectivism, and freedom for many people now means little more than choice among goods. The free, or at least only partially cartelised, market, as Hayek failed to foresee, has flourished alongside the collectivism that was – and, after years of propaganda, still is – justified by the need to eliminate the five giants. For much of the British population today, the notion that people could solve many of the problems of society without governmental *Gleichschaltung*, the Nazi term for overall co-ordination, is completely alien.

Of course, the current banking and general economic crisis is a boon to those who want increasing administrative control not just of financial markets, but of almost everything else, and who think that the arguments of Hayek have been completely superseded and made irrelevant. But the crisis was brought about as much by the failure of regulators to use the powers they already had as by the ruthless and fundamentally dishonest machinations of the bankers and their subordinates. The nature of Mr Madoff's scheme, for example, was known for years before it collapsed; the Securities Exchange Commission was warned about it years in advance. There is abundant evidence of widespread fraud in sub-prime mortgage lending in the United States, and of a system set up to promote it. But this system can be traced back to the Community Reinvestment Act in the United States that enjoined banks to make loans on racial rather on purely financial grounds, and penalised them if they refused to do so. The banks were forced, by law, to lend in socio-demographic areas where the risks of default were intrinsically very high; and, with the ingenuity for good and evil that characterises capitalism, they soon devised a means of turning a very bad and improvident practice into a goldmine, at least for a few years.

Hayek never intended that there should be no state control over anything: he was not one of those libertarians who think that an acceptable order will arise spontaneously from chaos, nor did he believe in a capitalism red in tooth and claw. He did not advocate a free market in poisons or child pornography. Like Adam Smith, he had a clear view of what kind of morality would make a free society possible and liveable. He clearly saw the state as ring-holder, and would have said of the current conditions that the state had failed in its duty (perhaps because it had taken on so many other responsibilities). He would not have approved of the bonus culture, in which executives appropriate shareholders' funds to themselves the way governments appropriate citizens' funds to increase their own power and importance. But none of this alters the validity of his strictures against centralised economic control and its inevitable effect upon the psychology of populations.

The majority of Britons are still not direct dependants of the state. 'Only' about two fifths of them are: the 25 percent of the working population who are public employees (the government has increased them by nearly one million since 1997, no doubt in order to boost its election chances); and the 15 percent of the adult population either unemployed or registered as medically unfit to work, and thus utterly dependent on government charity. But the state looms large in all our lives, not only in its intrusions but in our thoughts: for so thoroughly have we drunk at the wells of collectivism that we see the state always as the solution to any problem, never as an obstacle to be overcome. One can gauge how completely collectivism has entered our soul – so that we are now a people of the government, for the government, by the government – by a strange but characteristic British locution. When, on the rare occasions that our Chancellor of the Exchequer reduces a tax, he is said to have 'given money away'. In other words, all money is his, and whatever we have in our pockets is what he, by grace and favour, has allowed us.

Our Father, which art in Downing Street…

DELUSIONS OF HONESTY

WHEN MR BLAIR announced his resignation after 10 years as Prime Minister of the United Kingdom, his voice choked with emotion and he nearly shed a tear. He asked his audience to believe that he had always done what he thought was right; it would have been nearer the mark to have said that he thought was right whatever he had done. Throughout his years in office, he kept inviolable his belief in the existence of a purely beneficent essence of himself, a belief so strong that no quantity of untruthfulness, shady dealings, unscrupulousness or constitutional impropriety could undermine or destroy it. Having come into the world marked by Original Virtue, he was a natural-born preacher.

In a confessional mood, he admitted that he had sometimes fallen short of what was expected of him. He did not give specifics, but we were expected to admire his candour and humility in making such an admission. It is no coincidence, however, that Blair reached maturity at the time of the publication of the famous book *Psychobabble*, which dissects the modern tendency to indulge in self-obsession without self-examination. Here was a *mea culpa* without the *culpa*. Bless me, people (Blair appeared to be saying), for I have sinned: but please don't ask me for details.

His support for American policy in Iraq, more from vanity than from calculation of the national interest, won him much sympathy in the United States, of course; there, his eloquence in defence of liberty was taken seriously. And under his leadership, Britain did enjoy 10 years of uninterrupted economic growth, leaving large parts of the country seemingly prosperous as never before. But he had inherited an economy from his predecessor that, for post-war Britain, was unusually healthy. The prosperity of the Blair years, as we now know, was more apparent than real, based as it was upon the expansion of easy credit and borrowing all round; but, unlike previous Labour Prime Ministers, he managed to leave office before the chickens of economic mismanagement came home to roost, at least anywhere near Mr Blair himself. He managed to come out of it all smelling of millions (to change the metaphor).

But how history, rather than his financial adviser, will judge him overall, and whether it will absolve him (to adapt slightly a phrase coined by a famous, though now ailing, Antillean dictator) is another matter. Strictly speaking, history doesn't absolve, or for that matter vindicate, anybody; only people absolve or vindicate, and except in the most obvious cases of villainy or sainthood, they come to different conclusions, using basically the same evidence. There can thus be no definitive judgment of Blair, especially one so soon, relatively-speaking, after his departure. Still, I will try.

Blair's resignation announcement was typical of the man and, one must admit, of the new culture from which he emerged: lachrymose and self-serving. It revealed an unfailing eye and ear for the ersatz and the kitsch, which allowed him so long to play upon the sensibilities of a large section of the population as upon a pipe.

He knew exactly what to say of Princess Diana when she died in a car accident, for example: that she was 'the people's princess'. He sensed acutely that the times were not so much democratic as demotic: that economic egalitarianism having suffered a decisive defeat both in theory and practice, the only mass appeal left to a politician calling himself radical was to cultural egalitarianism. He could gauge the feelings of the people because, in large part, he shared them. A devotee himself of the cult of celebrity, in which the marriage of glamour and banality both reassures egalitarian sentiment and stimulates fantasies of luxury, he sought the company of minor show-business personalities and stayed in their homes during his holidays. The practical demonstration that he worshipped at the same shrines as the people did, that his tastes were the same as theirs, more than compensated for the faint odour of impropriety that this gave off. And differences of taste, after all, unite or divide men more profoundly than anything else.

No Prime Minister had ever been at once so ubiquitous, so informal and so inaccessible. Instinctively understanding the dynamics of the cult of celebrity, Blair was both familiar (he insisted on being known by a diminutive) and distant (he acted more as head of state than as head of government, and spent three times more on his own office than did his predecessor). Having invited 60 ordinary citizens into Downing Street so that they could give him their views, and so that he could say he listened to the people, he proceeded to address them via a huge plasma screen, though he was in the building. So near, and yet so far: this was a grand vizier's durbar for the age of virtual reality. With Blair, communication, like time's arrow, flew in one direction only.

Tony Blair was the perfect politician for an age of short attention spans. What he said on one day had no necessary connection with what he said on the following day: and if someone pointed out the contradiction, he would use his favourite phrase, 'It's time to move on', as if detecting contradictions in what he said were some kind of curious psychological symptom in the person detecting them.

Many have surmised that there was an essential flaw in Blair's makeup that turned him gradually from the most popular to (until the arrival of Mr Brown) the most unpopular Prime Minister of recent history. The problem is to name that essential flaw. As a psychiatrist, I found this problem peculiarly irritating (bearing in mind that it is always highly speculative to make a diagnosis at a distance). But finally a possible solution arrived in a flash of illumination. Blair suffered from a condition previously unknown to me: delusions of honesty.

Blair came to power promising that his government would be 'purer than pure', an expression both self-righteous and somewhat foolish, given the fallen nature of man. The Tories preceding him in government had become notorious for acts of corruption that now appear trifling. Indeed, one objection to those acts – for example, asking questions in the House of Commons in return for payment, handed under the table in used banknotes wrapped in brown paper envelopes – was the derisory sums involved. What kind of person would risk ruin for amounts of money that honest people could make in a week or two?

Soon after Blair took office, however, a billionaire named Bernie Ecclestone offered the Labour party a £1 million donation if the government exempted Formula 1 motor racing, which he controlled, from the ban on cigarette ads at sporting events. The government granted the exemption. After public exposure, Blair declared himself to be such a 'straight kind of guy' that it was inconceivable that he had involved himself in such an unsavoury arrangement – though clearly he had. It was his capacity to believe his own untruths that proved so persuasive to others; it was among his greatest political assets.

Such scandals – involving favours granted to rich men, followed, after exposure, by protestations of injured innocence – punctuated Blair's tenure with monotonous regularity. One of the more notorious was the letter that Blair sent to the Romanian prime minister, Adrian Nastase, encouraging him to sell the state-owned steel producer Sidex to billionaire industrialist Lakshmi Mittal; it would help Romania's application to join the European Union, Blair argued, if a British company bought the steel producer. But Mittal's company was not British; of its 125,000 employees, only 100 worked in Britain; indeed, Mittal himself was not British. He had, however, donated £125,000 to the Labour Party shortly beforehand.

Far from being purer than pure, Blair was infinitely forgiving of impropriety in others, provided they were loyal or politically useful to him. The case of Peter Mandelson is particularly instructive. When first a minister, Mandelson borrowed a large sum of money from another minister, Geoffrey Robinson, a multimillionaire, in order to buy a house. Not only did Mandelson fail to tell the bank that lent him the rest of the money for the purchase that the money he had in hand was not his own (in less well-connected mortals, that would be considered fraud); the government department that Mandelson headed at the time was investigating Robinson's own business affairs for suspected improprieties.

Public exposure forced Blair to accept Mandelson's resignation. But the Prime Minister soon reappointed Mandelson to the cabinet. Blair accepted Mandelson's resignation a second time, however, when it emerged that he had pushed through the passport application of one of the Hinduja brothers, Indian businessmen accused of corruption in India, after a £1 million donation to the Labour Party. Blair then rewarded Mandelson with the lucrative and powerful post of European commissioner. What is one to conclude from this?

Having come into power deeply critical of the previous government's use of private consultants, Blair promptly increased spending on them at least tenfold, ensuring the loyalty of senior civil servants (traditionally a professional cadre, not political appointees) by allowing them to cross back and forth between public and private employment, enriching themselves enormously at public expense in the process. Thus Blair played Mephistopheles to the civil service's Faust, introducing levels of corruption and patronage not seen in Britain since the 18th century. Huge sums of money have disappeared, as if into a black hole, into such organisations as the National Health Service, where bureaucracies have hugely expanded and entwined their interests so closely with those of private suppliers and consultancies that it is difficult to distinguish public from private any longer. Spending on the NHS has increased by two and a half times in the space of ten years; yet it is hard to see any corresponding improvement in the service, other than in the standard of living of those who work in it.

Blair even became the first serving prime minister in history to find himself questioned by the police in Downing Street, under caution of self-incrimination, in the course of a criminal investigation – in this case, into the selling of seats in the House of Lords. Small wonder that for much of the population, truth and Blair now appear to inhabit parallel universes. Reflecting the country's mood is the famous remark that Gordon Brown made to Blair: 'There is nothing that you could say to me now that I could ever believe.'

Blair proved unusually expert in the postmodernist art of spin. A political adviser to the government perfectly captured this approach on September 11, 2001, when she said that it was 'a good day to bury bad news'. In other words, you can get away with anything if the timing is right.

At the outset of his tenure, Blair said that his government would be tough on crime and on the causes of crime. He wanted to appeal – and succeeded in appealing – to two constituencies at once: those who wanted criminals locked up, and those who saw crime as the natural consequence of social injustice, a kind of inchoate protest against the conditions in which they lived.

Blair's resultant task was to obfuscate, so that the electorate and even experts could not find out, without great difficulty, what was going on. For example, Blair's government, aware of public unrest about the number of criminals leaving prison only to commit further serious crimes, introduced indeterminate sentencing – open-ended imprisonment – apparently a tough response to repeat offenders. But the reality was different: the sentencing judges still had the discretion to determine such criminals' parole dates, which in England are *de facto* release dates. The sentences that criminals would serve, in other words, would be no longer than before the new law.

Another way to confuse the public was to corrupt official statistics. In 2006, to take one example, the government dropped three simple but key measures from the compendious statistics that it gathers about people serving community sentences – that is, various kinds of service and supervision outside prison: their criminal histories prior to sentencing, their reconviction rates and the number given prison sentences while serving their community sentences. Instead, it introduced an utterly meaningless measure, at least from a public-safety perspective: the proportion of people with community sentences who abide by such conditions as weekly attendance for an hour at a probation office.

Under Mr Blair's government, the police were encouraged, or at the very least permitted, to treat the recording of crime more as an exercise in spin doctoring or public relations than as an indication of what was happening in society. Trivial offences, that once would not have been deemed crimes at all, were multiplied and recorded as having been solved, while many serious offences went unrecorded, because the police knew that they would not solve them, or were dealt with as though they were as trivial as parking violations: violent thugs and shoplifters, for instance, now often receive on-the-spot fines (which fines they do not always pay, of course). And the long term effect of this lack of intellectual integrity or probity has been what we see now, a demoralised police force that is both bullying and ineffectual, of which only the law-abiding need be afraid. (Many intelligent and insightful police officers understand and regret this bitterly, and some refer to themselves, ruefully, as 'Vichy Cops'.)

The problem of unemployment in Britain illustrates perfectly the methods that Blair's government used to obscure the truth. The world generally believes that, thanks to Labour's prudent policies, Britain now enjoys low unemployment; indeed, Blair often lectured other leaders on the subject. The low rate was not strictly a lie: those counted officially as unemployed were for a long time relatively few, though with the collapse of Britain's virtual economy it has become impossible once again to disguise mass unemployment.

Unfortunately those counted as 'sick' are many; and if you add the numbers of unemployed and sick together, the figure remains remarkably constant in recent years, oscillating around 3.5 million, though the proportion of sick to unemployed has risen rapidly. Approximately 2.7 million people are receiving disability benefits in Britain, 8 or 9 percent of the workforce, highly concentrated in the areas of former unemployment; more people are claiming that psychiatric disorders prevent them from working than are claiming that work is unavailable. In the former coal-mining town of Merthyr Tydfil, about a quarter of the adult population is on disability. Britain is thus the sick man of Europe, though all objective indicators suggest that people are living longer and healthier lives than ever.

Three groups profit from this statistical legerdemain: first, the unemployed themselves, because disability benefits are about 60 percent higher than unemployment benefits, and, once one is receiving them, one does not have to pretend to be looking for work; second, the doctors who make the bogus diagnoses, because by doing so they remove a possible cause of conflict with their patients and, given the assault rate on British doctors, this is important to them; and finally the government, which can claim to have reduced unemployment.

But such obfuscation is destructive of human personality. The unemployed have to pretend something untrue – namely, that they are sick; the medical profession winds up humiliated and dispirited by taking part in fraud; and the government avoids, for a time, real economic problems. Thus the whole of society finds itself corrupted and infantilised by its inability to talk straight; and that Blair could speak with conviction of the low unemployment rate, and believe that he was telling the truth, is to me worse than if he had been a dastardly cynic, more Talleyrand than Walter Mitty.

Tony Blair's most alarming characteristic, however, was his enmity to freedom in his own country, whatever his feelings about it in other countries, and his rhetoric notwithstanding. No British prime minister in 200 years has done more to curtail civil liberties than did Blair.

Starting with an assumption of his infinite beneficence, he assumed infinite responsibility, with the result that Britain has become a country with a degree of official surveillance that would make a Latin American military dictator envious. Sometimes this surveillance is merely ludicrous – parking-enforcement officers wearing miniature closed-circuit security cameras in their caps to capture abusive responses from those ticketed, say, or local councils attaching sensing devices to the dustbins of three million homes to record what people throw away, in order to charge them for the quantity and quality of their rubbish.

But often the government's reach is less innocuous. For example, in the name of national security the government under Blair's leadership sought to make passport applicants provide 200 pieces of information about themselves, including bank account details, and to undergo interrogation for half an hour. If an applicant refused to allow the information to circulate through other government departments, he would not receive a passport, with no appeal. The government also cooked up a plan to require passport holders to inform the police if they changed their address.

A justification presented for these Orwellian arrangements was the revelation that a would-be terrorist, Dhiren Barot, had managed to obtain nine British passports before his arrest because he did not want an accumulation of stamps from suspect countries in any of them. At the same time it came to light that the Passport Office issues 10,000 passports a year to fraudulent applicants – hardly surprising since it employees numbers of illegal immigrants, whose status in the country it is not capable of checking. This would be funny, if it were not typical.

As was often the case with Blair and his government, the solution proposed was not only completely disproportionate to the problem, it was not even a solution. The government has admitted that criminal gangs have already forged the UK's new high-tech passports. The only people, then, whom the process will trouble are the people who need no surveillance. No sensible person denies the danger of Islamic extremism in Britain; but just as the fact that the typical Briton finds himself recorded by security cameras 300 times a day does not secure him in the slightest from crime or anti-social behaviour, which remain prevalent in Britain, so no one feels any safer from the terrorist threat despite the ever-increasing government surveillance.

Blair similarly showed no respect for precedent and gradual reform by Parliament itself, which – in the absence of an American-style written constitution – have been the nation's guiding principles. By decree he made the civil service answerable to unelected political allies for the first time in history; he devoted far less attention to Parliament than did any previous prime minister; the vast majority of legislation under his premiership (amounting to a blizzard so great that lawyers could not keep up with it) passed without effective parliamentary oversight, in effect by decree; one new criminal offence was created every day except Sundays for ten years, 60 percent of them by such decree, ranging from the selling of grey squirrels and Japanese bindweed to failure to nominate someone to turn off your house alarm if it triggers while you are out; he abolished the independence of the House of Lords, the only and very limited restraint on the elected government's power; he eliminated the immemorial jurisprudential rule against double jeopardy; he wanted to introduce preventive detention for people whom the mis deemed dangerous, even though they had as yet committed no crime; he passed a Civil Contingencies Act that permits the British government, if it believes that an emergency anywhere in the world threatens serious damage to human welfare or to the environment in Britain, to confiscate or destroy property without compensation.

That Blair should have turned out to be so authoritarian ought to come as no surprise to those who listened to the timbre of some of his early pronouncements. His early emphasis on youth; his pursuit of what he called, grandiosely, the Third Way (as if no one had thought of it before); his desire to create a 'New Britain'; his assertion that the Labour party was the political arm of the British people (as if people who did not support it were in some way not British) – some have thought all this contained a Mussolinian, or possibly Peronist, ring. It is ridiculous to say that Tony Blair was a fascist; but it would be equally absurd to see him as a defender of liberty, at least in his own country.

Blair found the Muslim threat far easier to tackle abroad than at home, perhaps because it required less courage. Intentionally or not, he pandered to domestic Muslim sentiment. During the 2005 general election, in which the leader and deputy leader of the opposition were Jewish, he allowed Labour to portray them as pigs on election campaign posters. The Jewish vote in Britain is small, and scattered throughout the country; the Muslim vote is large, and concentrated in constituencies upon which the whole election might turn. It is not that Blair is anti-Semitic: no one would accuse him of that. It is simply that he is part of a political culture in which hypothetical ends justify concrete means, and if mild anti-Semitic connotations are necessary to pursue those ends, so be it.

Blair, then, is certainly no hero. Many in Britain believe that he has been the worst prime minister in recent British history, morally and possibly financially corrupt, shallow and egotistical, a man who combined the qualities of Elmer Gantry with those of Juan Domingo Peron. It is intensely frustrating to his countrymen that he should now bestride the world, blithely unaware of the damage he has wrought.

WHAT GOES ON IN
MR BROWN'S MIND?

WHEN Mr Blair resigned, after years of speculation about the timing of this consummation devoutly to be wished, the advent of Mr Brown as his replacement came, at least to me, as something of a relief. Mr Brown did not have Blair's brittle carapace of moral invulnerability; he was not entirely at ease in the limelight, which was all to the good. He was dour rather than glib, and there were even suspicions that he had to be taught how to smile, in which case he did not prove a very apt pupil (the smiles of politicians are more likely to appal than to charm me).

The fact that he had experienced a personal tragedy in his own life raised hopes of depths of character after the fathomless shallows of that of his predecessor. (When a journalist, Jeremy Clarkson, called Mr Brown 'a one-eyed Scottish idiot', I found it distasteful, to say the least. To make mock of an accident that deprived a young man of much of his eyesight is authentically despicable. That Mr Brown overcame his difficulties, and has never used them to attract political sympathy, is much to his credit.)

More intelligent than Mr Blair, above all Mr Brown did not seem to be infatuated with cheap celebrity, either his own or that of others. At least he was not openly a spiv, nor did vulgar ostentation seem part of his character.

But these are all matters of style rather than of substance. When finally he arrived at Number Ten, Mr Brown promised to restore trust in the government, as if he were an opposition leader just elected to office for the first time. At least what he said had the merit of recognition that something had gone wrong during the previous 10 years, in which the promised bright new dawn had turned into a murky twilight; but it was profoundly self-serving and dishonest because Mr Brown himself was not completely unconnected with the events of that decade. During that time he was, after all, the second man in the government, often credited with being more powerful than Mr Blair himself. One was reminded a little of Goering's performance at the Nuremberg trials, when he was asked whether, as the Number Two man in Germany, he had not known of the slaughter of millions. No, he replied, he had not; upon which he was asked whether he thought he ought to have known. How, asked Goering with more dialectical subtlety than frankness, can a man be held responsible for his own ignorance? If he does not know something, he does not know it, and that is all.

Mr Blair was no Hitler, of course, and Mr Brown is no Goering; it is important not to get carried away by dubious analogies. Their authoritarianism notwithstanding, Britain is still not a country in which one fears the midnight knock on the door, however much an undercurrent of fear has crept into daily life, especially among those employed in the public service. Therefore, the two men are still to be judged by the standards of democratic politicians; and, judged by those standards, both men are among the worst of the tribe, though in different ways.

There is no reason to doubt Mr Brown's statement that he went into politics because of his horror at the effects of unemployment. Unfortunately, he forgot one of the few laws of political economy: that the road to unemployment is paved with work creation schemes. He is likely, therefore, to go down in history as something like the patron saint of unemployment. As I write this, the number of unemployed in Britain is above five million, that is to say 14 percent of the population eligible for work (I ignore the patently absurd fiction that all those currently deemed too sick to work are anything other than the unemployed by another name). Indeed, if one includes the hundreds of thousands of paid drones whose employment Mr Brown has assiduously grown apace in the last few years, and no doubt similar numbers of young people who are being encouraged to pay for their own unemployment by pursuing a further education of no conceivable vocational or intellectual value, the number of unemployed is very much higher. And, as if this were not bad enough, the number is destined to go yet higher.

Mr Brown has been a complete, abject and miserable failure with regard to the problem that he says he went into politics to solve. Even before the economic crisis broke (a crisis worsened and in part caused by his own policies), during the halcyon years of Britain's illusory economic prosperity and growth, more than half the new jobs created in the economy were in the public sector, and ninety percent of the increase in the total numbers of people employed was accounted for by foreigners. In other words, Britain was importing labour in order to expand its public service – the make-work nature of the posts in that service is self-evident from the descriptions to be found of situations vacant in, for example, *The Guardian* and the *Health Service Journal* – while keeping millions of native-born unemployed and on the dole. Of course, it is true that one pool of potential labour is not necessarily exchangeable for another; but the vast majority of the people imported were not highly-trained specialists, whom Britain, after years of ever-expanding educational budgets, still lacked, but the unskilled. Moreover, it was certain that, when a downturn occurred, a proportion of the imported labour would not return whence it came, and would thus create social security and other obligations on the part of the British state: in other words, declining revenues and increased expenditures.

Nor was this all, not by a long way. Mr Brown's fiscal policies had long and consistently favoured the destruction of the family, such that by the time the crisis broke, far more children in Britain had a television in their bedroom than a biological father living at home. The telly is father to the child; it and a varying cast of stepfathers in those areas where unemployment was likely to strike the hardest.

So when, as the crisis gathered pace, Mr Brown warned us that we must brace ourselves for a rise in the level of crime, he was probably correct, though for the wrong reasons, genuinely reflective thought not being his strong point. Mr Brown is almost certainly wedded to the old, false but convenient idea that crime is caused by poverty; and therefore he thinks that, since poverty will now increase, so, *pari passu*, will crime.

Now the relation between poverty, even of the relative kind, and crime is far from a straightforward one, and is not directly causative. (If it were, to be poor would be to be criminal: not a very generous or liberal-minded thought, indeed one that is deeply demeaning to millions). The proximal cause of crime is the decision of the criminal to commit it. What goes on in his mind – the ideas he has, his system of morality, his desires, his estimate of his chances of being caught and what will happen to him if he is caught, and so forth – are absolutely crucial. Any theory of crime that does not take into account questions of meaning is inherently absurd; almost certainly, Mr Brown's theory of crime does not do so.

Anyone who has travelled through this country and observed it more closely than through the windows of an official limousine will have noticed that there are large numbers of young people in it who are not well socialised, thanks to the familial chaos in which they were brought up and the vulgar, violent and abusive popular culture which occupies so many of their waking hours, whose strong sense of entitlement is unfortunately accompanied by a weak commitment to the obedience of any rules not of their own making. These are not people who are likely to endure the frustrations of reduced disposable income very philosophically; and unfortunately Mr Brown's social and fiscal policies have done everything possible to maximise the numbers of such young people in the country. (Cultural aspects of the problem were not his remit.) Any rise in crime will not be the consequence of raw poverty, but of supposed but unearned entitlements not met.

All is not modest that is uncomfortable in or declines the limelight. There is a kind of arrogance, or at least self-confidence, too great even to seek the limelight, or to clamour for the gaze of the vulgar, and it is possible that Mr Brown had it while Chancellor. It was this, surely, that accounts for Mr Brown's decision to sell half of Britain's gold reserves at an historically low price, and in such a way as to minimise receipts, against the advice that he received, and indeed against elementary common sense. This episode alone should have ensured that he was never again employed in any paid capacity but the most menial; and the fact that it had so few consequences for him personally is indicative of the degeneracy of our entire political culture, as indeed is the repeated resurrection of figures disgraced not once but several times for dishonesty bordering on the criminal.

One of Mr Brown's first acts was to raise taxes on pension fund dividends, again contrary to strenuous advice. He acted on the assumption that it would make no difference to rates of saving and also that growth in company earnings and the value of their shares would soon make up for the funds' loss of income to taxation. It hardly requires a profound knowledge of financial history to know that profits and share prices can go down as well as up; and it is obvious that these matters are important for people who depend upon a fund of shares for almost their entire income. Deliberately to reduce yields in the hope of eternal ascent is folly of a high (or is it low?) order.

Mr Brown's hubristic failure to understand his own limitations – a failure that, alas, is now a strong cultural trait in our political, bureaucratic and managerial class – no doubt accounts for three boasts that he let fall from his lips in unguarded moments and that revealed to the world what he really thought of himself: boasts that now seem not merely mistaken but ridiculous to the point of fatuity.

When he claimed to have saved the world, one wonders what worse he thinks would have befallen it if he had not intervened and left it to its fate; he claimed to have broken the cycle of 'boom and bust' shortly before presiding over the deepest recession or slump in living memory, worse (not coincidentally) in Britain than in any comparable country; and he claimed for himself a virtue for his economic management which it was perhaps most notable for lacking altogether, namely prudence.

This last claim is the most preposterous of all. In what follows, I admit that I am speculating, but I think my hypothesis a reasonable one. Mr Brown's problem when he arrived as Chancellor of the Exchequer in 1997 was that, by inclination and temperament, he was a socialist, with a belief in the redeeming qualities of state intervention. He saw taxation as an instrument of social justice, and he thought that the state should play a large, even preponderant, part in everyday life. On the other hand, these were not popular views in 1997; no party that espoused them could be elected. General prosperity and a relatively favourable economic conjuncture (always fragile in Britain, at least since the end of the First World War) convinced people that, while a change of government might be necessary, a change of economic direction was not.

For electoral reasons, then, Mr Brown was committed not to raise direct taxes, and also not to increase the public debt beyond 40 percent of the Gross Domestic Product; but a man does not shed his convictions, much less his deepest dyed instincts, as easily as an election promise is made. Thus a form of stealth was required to raise taxes and increase supposedly social-justice-procuring public expenditure, for resort to the crude and obvious measure of expropriating incomes was no longer politically permissible. But how could taxes be increased in pay for expanded public expenditure without the electorate noticing, or at least without complaining, and without increasing the national debt? One method, of course, was the Private Finance Initiative, by means of which the government could borrow money (admittedly at exorbitant rates of interest) without it appearing in the national accounts. Not only was this a means of deferring payment for public expenditure, albeit at a cost double that of borrowing the money directly, but it helped to bind private industry in a pact of mutual self-interest with the government.

The dissolution of the distinction between public service and private enterprise was much advanced by the PFI. Various other taxes gradually increased the proportion of the government expenditure as a proportion of GDP to the highest levels in many years, and higher than (say) Germany's. When the banking crisis broke, Mr Brown naturally (for a politician) tried to pretend that it had nothing to do with him or his policy. Greedy, rogue bankers – many of them without banking qualifications or even (and much more importantly) a lifetime of banking experience – were the villains of the piece. The fact that two of the worst offenders, one of whom brought about by far the biggest corporate loss in British history, had until very recently been among Mr Brown's closest economic advisers was not emphasised in Mr Brown's pronouncements.

The fact is that irresponsible lending and borrowing was not something that, unfortunately, occurred by inadvertence while Mr Brown's otherwise prudent and careful economic policy was carried out; it was Mr Brown's economic policy, or at the very least the *sine qua non* of that policy. Here it is just worth recalling that the first British bank to fail, Northern Rock, and the first to experience a run on its deposits in nearly a century and a half, offered mortgages of up to 125 percent of the value of the value of the mortgaged property. I do not think that you need a banking or accountancy qualification, or a degree in economics, to appreciate the unwisdom, not to say the insane folly, of this.

But why was easy credit so central a part of Mr Brown's strategy? The reason, I think, was this. His real goal was to increase public expenditure, both relatively and absolutely; he believed that the all-powerful and all-benevolent state should weigh heavy in each person's life, and should be a presence in it as God was supposed to be in the Presbyterianism of his upbringing.

For political reasons, however, he had to let the preponderant middle classes, without whose votes he could not be re-elected, imagine that they were doing very well under his dispensation, increased taxes notwithstanding. Obviously, any genuine increase in output was likely to be low by comparison with the increase in the rate of taxation; in any case, it is difficult to increase genuine output in a country like Britain, with a combination of high labour costs, low productivity, shortages of skilled workers, declining research prowess, an inferior infrastructure, poor transport and a generally low cultural level, none of which could be solved either quickly or without very provoking severe political and social conflict.

Easy credit was the answer to the conundrum, the sword that severed the Gordonian knot. Rising asset prices would mean that people would feel rich and spend money accordingly. They would borrow it to do so: for tomorrow their wealth would have increased yet further. Every month for years I would receive offers of loans, up to £25,000, pre-arranged and to be formalised only by a telephone call, so that I might (for example given in some of the brochures) enjoy the holiday of a lifetime. There are two questions to be asked here. The first is what kind of person takes out a £25,000 loan to go on the holiday of a lifetime? The second is, what kind of person offers one? Let us just say that relation between these two types of person is dialectical. No doubt such a loan seemed highly affordable if the value of your house had risen by £100,000 a year for the last three or four years, in fact a mere drop in the bucket of your wealth. The fact that the rise in the value of your house was based upon loans of precisely the same quality probably occurred to very few people. Everyone was getting richer and richer, or so they thought, simply by sitting at home and watching television. Consumption increased dramatically, and everyone lived well for a day: but all forms of indebtedness mounted, national and private.

It requires only minimal common sense, not a degree in economics or anything else, to notice the family resemblance between this situation and the pyramid scheme run by Mr Madoff in the United States: with this difference, that Mr Madoff's scheme, involving only $50 billion, was on a small and amateurish scale by comparison with that run by the British government under the 'prudent' guidance of Mr Brown.

The government, far from reigning in the 'irrational exuberance', to quote Mr Greenspan, depended upon it for its political survival. The surprising thing is not that the pyramid scheme collapsed, but that it took so long to collapse.

It might be objected to my explanation of Mr Brown's policy that it was necessary to expand the role of the supposedly equalising state in national life, that it permitted the emergence of the class of super-rich, so that society would be henceforth divided not into the haves and have-nots, but into the haves and have-yachts. But there is an explanation here, too. The immense concentration of wealth that took place in the Blair-Brown years, far from hindering Mr Brown's aim, was instrumental in achieving it. Any centralising, power-mad government would far rather deal with a relatively small group of plutocrats who are dependent upon or beholden to government favours for their position (like the oligarchs in Russia) than have to deal with a large class of sturdily independent burghers who tend to be prickly and awkward.

We see this effect in many unexpected ways. For example, the government has in effect nationalised charity in Britain; it is now by far the largest single donor to all the most important charities in the country, and he who pays the piper calls the tune. Charities are auxiliaries to government ministries, and those who contribute to them are unwitting and no doubt benevolently-intentioned tax payers, classic useful idiots. Equally, the government has cartelised lawyers who undertake clinical negligence work paid for by public funds. Only designated firms may now undertake it. There is, of course, an argument for specialisation in legal services: clearly lawyers who do a lot of any given work will tend to be better and more expert at it than others who do it only occasionally. But in a free market, such specialisation would tend to occur anyway, albeit more slowly and perhaps less systematically. The great advantage of forced cartelisation, however, is that it means that the selected firms have to dance to the government's tune if they want to keep their contracts, which of course they do.

Many other examples of such centralisation, with its consequent government control of relatively few, but utterly beholden, beneficiaries could be given. The price of Mr Brown's egalitarianism is therefore tolerance of plutocracy.

Where, in all this, is Her Majesty's Loyal Opposition? This is where real depression sets in. Mr Brown is a man who, to achieve his ends, has had to practice deceit, or throw up smokescreens, for years. He is a man bent upon achieving a goal that he thinks good (but I think bad) by unscrupulous means, but he is but a single individual. The utter inability or unwillingness of the opposition to penetrate such smokescreens, an inability or unwillingness caused by its shallow and stupid obsession with opinion polls, which is itself the consequence of its lust for power at any price, is emblematic of the degeneracy of British democracy. Who could be confident that things would be any different under the current opposition's direction?

HOW NOT TO DO IT

NOT LONG AGO, the British government announced – because the normally feeble opposition in Parliament, in a rare display of effectiveness, forced it to announce – that 70 prisoners, including three murderers and an unspecified number of burglars, drug dealers and holders of false passports, had escaped from a single minimum-security prison in one year alone. Twenty-eight of them were still at large.

That so many of them absconded suggested that they were not quite the reformed characters that justified lower levels of security in the first place; but as usual in Britain, temporary embarrassment soon subsides into deep amnesia. The fact is that the whole episode is precisely what we have come to expect of our public administration and was nothing out of the ordinary.

In the same week my former colleagues, senior doctors in the hospital in which I worked until recently, received a leaflet with their monthly pay stubs. It offered them, along with all other employees, literacy training: a little late in their careers as doctors, one might have thought.

The senior doctors could take up to 30 hours of free courses to improve their literacy and numeracy skills, all in working time, of course. In these courses, they could learn to spell at least some words, to punctuate, to add and do fractions, and to read a graph.

'Do you have a SPIKEY [*sic*] profile?' asked the leaflet, and went on to explain: 'A spikey profile is when a person is good at literacy but not at mathematics or visa [*sic*] versa.' The reader could address himself to one of no fewer than four members of the hospital staff who were 'contact persons' for the courses, among them the vocational training coordinator and the nonvocational training coordinator. In case none was available to answer the telephone or reply to emails, the reader could contact one of three central government agencies that deal with the problem of illiterate and innumerate employees.

Here, truly, was a case of the lunatics taking over the asylum; but there is more to the ignorance and incompetence pervading the leaflet than meets the eye. Such ignorance and incompetence are now so systematic and widespread in the British public service that if they are not the result of deliberate policy, they might as well be. In fact, there is now a profoundly catalytic relationship between the intellectual, moral and economic corruption of the British public service and the degeneration of the national character. Which among all the various factors came first and is therefore ultimately causative is not easy to say; as usual, I suspect that intellectual error is at the root of most evil. But why such error should have found so ready an acceptance raises the spectre of an infinite regress of explanation, which perhaps we can avoid only by invoking a dialectical approach.

Three recent books give us an insight into the nature of the corruption that has sprung from the ever-wider extension of self-arrogated government responsibility in Britain, and they shed light as well on the effect that government expansion has upon the population. By the time you have finished reading them, you are unsure as to whether Gogol, Kafka or Orwell offers the best insight into contemporary British reality. Gogol captures the absurdity all right, and Kafka the anxiety caused by an awareness of sinister but unidentifiable forces behind what is happening; but you also need Orwell to appreciate, and sometimes even to admire, the brazenness with which officialdom twists language to mean the opposite of what it would once ordinarily have meant. Two of the books are by men who work in the front line of the public service, one in law enforcement and the other in education. Like me, they write pseudonymously. By describing their day-to-day routine, Police Constable David Copperfield and teacher Frank Chalk show how the British state now works, or rather operates, with devastating effect on the British character.

Copperfield, who describes himself as 'an ordinary constable in an ordinary British town', wrote first a 'blog' and then a book, entitled *Wasting Police Time* (Monday Books). This work so annoyed the then Police Minister, Tony McNulty, that Mr McNulty felt obliged to denigrate it as a work of fiction in Parliament. (He was later forced by the BBC to concede that it was factual in nature.) As Copperfield makes clear in his book, very little of his time at work is spent in activity that could deter crime, discover those who commit it or bring them to justice. His induction into the culture of politically correct bureaucratic incompetence was immediate on joining up: he had naively supposed that the main purpose of his job was the protection of the public by the suppression of malefaction, instead of which he discovered that it was to 'set about changing the racist, homophobic and male-dominated world in which we lived'. The first three days of his training were about prejudice and discrimination – in short, 'diversity training'. There never was to be any training in the mere investigation of crimes, a minor and secondary part of modern police work in Britain.

The mandated, politically-inspired obsession with racism is on view in the crawlingly embarrassing and condescending speech that the deputy chief constable of North Wales, Clive Wolfendale, gave to the inaugural meeting of the North Wales Black Police Association. He decided, Copperfield reports, to speak to the black officers in rap verse, which is about as tactful as addressing Nelson Mandela in pidgin. Here is an extract from Wolfendale's speech:

Put away your cameras and your notepads for a spell.

I got a story that I really need to tell.

Bein' in the dibble [police] is no cakewalk when
you're black. If you don't get fitted, then you'll prob'ly
get the sack. You're better chillin' lie down and just be
passive.

No place for us just yet in the Colwyn Bay Massive
[by 'Colwyn Bay Massive', he was referring to his own
police force].

That must have encouraged the black officers no end: if the (white) deputy chief constable, in his maladroit attempt to demonstrate sympathy with them, had called them a bunch of jungle bunnies he could hardly have made his feelings clearer. His speech reveals what I have long suspected: that anti-racism is the new racism.

It is also, and simultaneously, a job opportunity and work-avoidance scheme. Copperfield recounts how, in 1999, a police officer said to a black motorist who did not answer a question, 'Okay, so you're deaf as well as black.' The report of the official inquiry into the subsequent complaint had 62 pages of attachments, 20 pages of witness statements, and 172 pages of interview transcripts. Legal and disciplinary proceedings took 19 months to complete.

Meanwhile, as the police devote vast energies (and expenditures) to such incidents, crimes such as street robbery and assault continue their inexorable rise and turn much of the country into a no-go area for all but the drunk or the violently inclined.

Copperfield, who joined the police full of idealism, soon notices (as how could he not?) that the completion of bureaucratic procedure is now more important to the police than anything else. All is in order if the forms are filled in correctly. A single arrest takes up to six hours to process, so many and various are the forms. He notices that there are more nonpolice employed in his police station than uniformed officers; and of the latter, the majority are deskbound. The station car park is full nine to five, Monday to Friday, but the whole town has only three or four officers to patrol the streets – in cars, of course, not on foot. The author describes the intellectual and moral corruption that all this bureaucracy brings in its wake. Take, for example, the so-called administrative detection, which allows the police and their political masters to mislead the public about the seriousness and efficiency with which the authorities tackle criminality. It works something like this: someone calls the police about a trifling dispute – one neighbour accuses the other of threatening behaviour, say, and the accused then in turn accuses the accuser. The police record the two complaints as crimes and take statements from every possible witness. This, of course, can take a very long time, because by the time the officers arrive, the witnesses will probably have dispersed. They have to be traced and contacted, and – because the police are now so touchingly-feelingly sensitive to the wishes of the public – mutually convenient times must be arranged for the taking of statements.

When finally the police have gathered all the information, they write it up; but, of course, no prosecution follows, because by then the complainants have withdrawn their complaints, and in any case the prosecuting authorities would regard the whole business as too trivial to be worth a trial. But the two crimes go into the records as having been 'solved'. And since the politicians in charge judge police performance by the proportion of crimes the force solves, there is no incentive for senior officers to focus attention on most real crimes, in which detection is difficult and very uncertain of success. The uselessness of a police force that once excited the admiration of the world is now taken for granted by every Briton who calls the police only to obtain a crime number for insurance purposes, not in the expectation or even hope of any effort at detection. This is not because the individual policeman is lazy, ill-intentioned, corrupt or stupid, though in the present system he might just as well be: for the system in which he works imposes upon him all the effects (or defects) of precisely those qualities. PC Copperfield is clearly a man who wants to do a good job, like most of the policemen I have met, but the system actively and deliberately prevents him from doing so.

I happened, while waiting to interview a man in prison, to be reading Copperfield's book, and two plainclothes policemen in the waiting room saw it. They had read the work, and I asked them whether what Copperfield wrote was true. 'Every word,' they replied.

Frank Chalk's book *It's Your Time You're Wasting* (Monday Books) tells essentially the same story, this time with regard to education. It surely requires some explanation that, in a country that spends many thousands of pounds per year on every child's education, a fifth of children leave school virtually unable to read or write, let alone do simple arithmetic.

It takes considerable organisation to achieve so little, especially when the means by which practically all children can be taught to read to a high standard are perfectly well known. A small local educational authority in Scotland, for example, West Dumbarton, has virtually eliminated illiteracy in children, despite the fact that its population is among the poorest in Scotland, by using simple teaching methods (phonics) at the extremely modest cost of £15 per head.

The intellectual corruption of the English and Welsh education system is near complete (the Scottish system is rather better). For example, OFSTED, the government inspectorate of schools charged with the maintenance of standards, for a long time gave each school it visited several weeks' warning of an impending inspection, ample time for even the dullest-witted school administrators to construct a Potemkin village. And then it criticised all the wrong things: the inspectors criticised Frank Chalk, for example, for having imposed discipline upon his class and thereby having impeded the spontaneity and creativity of the children – which, in the circumstances of the slum school in which he teaches, are principally expressed in vandalism.

The school inspectorate therefore appears to believe in the truth of the anarchist Bakunin's dictum – that the destructive urge is also creative.

The habit of judging educational institutions by non-educational criteria is now quite general. Assessing colleges of Further Education, *The Guardian* said, 'No college or training institution deemed to have a weak approach to equality or diversity will be eligible for a good overall rating, however excellent the quality of its teaching.' Adherence to political correctness is thus more important than the quality of anything imparted to pupils or students.

As an epigraph to his book, Chalk quotes the former British deputy prime minister, John Prescott. In that great man's immortal words, which tell you everything about the calibre of the British government that you really need to know, 'If you set up a school and it becomes a good school, the great danger is that everyone wants to go there.' And that would never do.

In the looking-glass world of modern British public administration, nothing succeeds like failure, because failure provides work for yet more functionaries and confers an ever more providential role upon the government. A child who does not learn to read properly often behaves badly in school and thus becomes the subject (or is it object?) of inquiries by educational psychologists and social workers. As Chalk describes, they always find that the child in question lacks self-esteem and therefore should be allowed to attend only those classes that he feels he can cope with. The so-called senior management team in the school – teachers who have retired into a largely administrative role – deals with all disciplinary problems by means of appeasement, for lack of any other permissible method available to them.

A perverse ideology reigns, in which truth and probity play no part. When grading the children's work, Chalk is expected to make only favourable comparisons, designed to boost egos rather than improve performance. Public examinations are no longer intended to test educational attainment against an invariant standard but to provide the government with statistics that give evidence of ever-better results. In pursuit of such excellence, not only do examinations require ever less of the children, but so-called course work, which may actually be done by the children's parents or even by the teachers themselves, plays an important part in the marks the children receive – and it is marked by the very teachers whose performance is judged by the marks that their pupils achieve. The result, of course, is a swamp of corruption. Wading through it, teachers become utterly cynical, time-serving and without self-respect.

A perfect emblem of the Gogolian, Kafkaesque, and Orwellian nature of the British public administration is the term 'social inclusion' as applied in the educational field. Schools may no longer exclude disruptive children – that would be the very opposite of social inclusion – so a handful of such children may render quite pointless hundreds or even thousands of hours of schooling for scores or even hundreds of their peers who, as a result, are less likely to succeed in life. Teachers such as Chalk are forced to teach mixed-ability classes, which can include the mentally handicapped (their special schools having been closed in the name of social inclusion). The most intelligent children in the class fidget with boredom while the teacher persistently struggles to instil understanding in the minds of the least intelligent children of what the intelligent pupils long ago grasped. The intelligent are not taught what they could learn, while the unintelligent are taught what they cannot learn. The result is chaos, resentment, disaffection and despair all round.

Britain now has more educational bureaucrats than teachers, as well as more health-service administrators than hospital beds. No self-evident or entirely predictable failure, no catastrophe they have brought about at the behest of their political masters, ever affects their careers, in part because they move from post to post so quickly that none of them ever gets held responsible for anything. The public hospital in which my wife worked as a doctor until recently built a £14 million extension, but what had been imperatively necessary for the health of the town's population six years ago became equally superfluous four years later and had to be closed down with great urgency, though with the public assurances of the bureaucrats then in charge that they were 'passionately' committed to the townspeople's welfare. No one, of course, was ever held responsible for this expensive fiasco, which fully partook of the absurdity Gogol portrays, the menace Kafka evokes (employees were, on the whole, too frightened for their careers to speak out) and the mendacity Orwell dramatises.

Insight into why expensive failure is so vitally necessary to the British government – or indeed, to any government once it arrogates responsibility for almost everything, from the national diet to the way people think – glimmers out from management consultant David Craig's recent book, *Plundering the Public Sector*. Craig catalogues what at first sight seems the almost incredible incompetence of the British government in its efforts to 'modernise' the public administration. For example, not a single large-scale information technology project instituted by the government has worked. The National Health Service has so far spent £12 billion on an IT project to unify medical records, without any success. Other projects, costing £200 to £250 million, have similarly failed to work. Modernisation in Britain's public sector means delay and inefficiency procured at colossal expense.

How is this to be explained? I learned a very good lesson when, 20 years ago, I worked in Tanzania. This well-endowed and beautiful country was broken down and economically destitute to a shocking degree. A shard of mirror was a treasured possession; a day's wages bought a small one egg on the open market. It was quicker to go to Europe than to telephone it. Nothing, not even the most basic commodity such as soap or salt, was available to most of the population.

At first, I considered that the president, Julius Nyerere, who was so revered in 'progressive' circles as being halfway between Jesus Christ and Mao Tse-tung, was a total incompetent. How could he reconcile the state of the country with his rhetoric of economic development and prosperity for everyone? Had he no eyes to see, no ears to hear?

But then the thought dawned on me, admittedly with embarrassing slowness, that a man who had been in power virtually unopposed for nearly a quarter of a century could not be called incompetent, once one has abandoned the preposterous premise that he was trying to achieve what he said he was trying to achieve. As a means of remaining in power, what method could be better than to have an all-powerful single political party distribute economic favours in conditions of general shortage? That explained how, and why, in a country of the involuntarily slender, the party officials were fat. This was not incompetence; it was competence of a very high order. Unfortunately it was very bad for the population as a whole.

The scheme in Britain is, of course, rather different. (It is not necessary to believe that such schemes have been consciously elaborated, incidentally; rather, they are inherent in the statism that comes naturally to so many politicians because of their self-importance.) The hoops that bind the government to the consultants who advise it in its perennially failing schemes of modernisation are those of gold. As Craig demonstrates (though without understanding all the implications), the consultants need failure in Britain to perpetuate the contracts that allow them to charge so outrageously and virtually *ad libitum* (Craig suggests that £70 billion has disappeared so far, with no end in sight); and, in turn, the government benefits from having this rich but utterly dependent clientele.

The beauty of the system is that dependence on expensive failure reaches quite low levels of the administration: for example, all those 'civilians' (as non-police workers for the police are called) in PC Copperfield's police station, as well as the educational psychologists whom Frank Chalk derides. The state has become a vast and intricate system of patronage, whose influence very few can entirely escape. It is essentially corporatist: the central government, avid for power, sets itself up as an authority on everything and claims to be omnicompetent both morally and in practice; and by means of taxation, licensing, regulation and bureaucracy, it destroys the independence of all organisations that intervene between it and the individual citizen. If it can draw enough citizens into dependence on it, the central government can remain in power, if not forever, then for a very long time, at least until a crisis or cataclysm forces change.

At the very end of the chain of patronage in the British state is the underclass, who (to change the metaphor slightly) form the scavengers or bottom-feeders of the whole corporatist ecosystem. Impoverished and degraded as they might be, they are nonetheless essential to the whole system, for their existence provides an ideological proof of the necessity of providential government in the first place, as well as justifying many employment opportunities in themselves. Both Copperfield and Chalk describe with great eloquence precisely what I have seen myself in this most wretched stratum of society: large numbers of people corrupted to the very fibre of their being by having been deprived of responsibility, purpose and self-respect, void of hope and fear alike, living in as near to purgatory as anywhere in modern society can come.

Of course, the corporatist system, at least in its British incarnation, is a house of cards, or perhaps a better analogy would be with a pyramid scheme. Hundreds of thousands of people are employed to perform tasks that are not merely useless but actually obstructive of real work and economically counterproductive. The bureaucracy insinuates itself into the smallest cracks of daily life. Renting out a house recently, I learned from an estate agent that the government sends inspectors, in the guise of prospective tenants, to check that the upholstery on chairs is fire-retardant. The inspectors have no other function. The regulations shift like one of those speeded-up meteorological maps on television, creating the need for yet more inspections and inspectors. Recent new regulations for landlords exceed one thousand pages of close print; in the meantime, Britain does not remain short of decaying housing stock while rents are among the highest in the world. The government has to pay for all this activity, supposedly carried out on behalf of the population, somehow. It is simultaneously committed to huge public expenditure and apparent, though not real, control of the public debt. It reconciles the irreconcilable by not including the extravagantly generous pension obligations of the public service in its debt calculations – pension obligations that, properly accounted for, now amount to nearly 56 percent of GDP. Also not included is the government's increasing resort to private finance of government institutions, which involves huge future expenditure obligations without the capital costs having to appear in the national accounts. And all this without consideration of the immense personal debt (£1 *trillion*) that the government has encouraged the population to accumulate, to create the illusion of prosperity.

In other words, the government has turned the words of the confidante of an 18th century absolute monarch, Louis XV, into the guiding principle of its policy: *après nous, le déluge.*

IT'S THIS BAD

RETURNING TO ENGLAND from France for a speaking engagement, I bought three of the major dailies to catch up on the latest developments in my native land. The impression they gave was of a country in the grip of a thorough-going moral frivolity. In a strange inversion of proper priorities, important matters are taken lightly and trivial ones taken seriously.

This is not the charming or uplifting frivolity of Feydeau's farces or Oscar Wilde's comedies; it is the frivolity of real decadence, bespeaking a profound failure of nerve bound to have disastrous consequences for the country's quality of life. The newspapers portrayed frivolity without gaiety and earnestness without seriousness – a most unattractive combination.

Of the two instances of serious matters taken with levity, the first concerned a 42-year-old barrister, Peter Wareing, attacked in the street while walking home from a barbecue with two friends, a man and a woman. They passed a group of seven teenagers who had been drinking heavily, one of whom, a girl, complained that the barrister and his friends were 'staring' at them. Nowadays, English youth of aggressive disposition and porcelain-fragile ego regard such alleged staring as a justified *casus belli*.

The girl attacked the woman in the other party. When Wareing and his male friend tried to separate them, two of the youths, aged 18 and 16, in turn attacked them. They hit the barrister's friend into some bushes, injuring him slightly, and then knocked the barrister to the ground, knocking him down a second time after he had struggled to his feet. This second time, his head hit the ground, injuring his brain severely. He was unconscious and on life support for two months

101

afterward. At first, his face was so disfigured that his three children were not allowed to see him.

The doctors told his wife, a nurse, that he was unlikely to survive, and she prepared the children for their father's death.

She wrote in a journal that she kept as she sat by his bed, 'Very scary feeling that all his natural life is gone.' Nevertheless he made an unexpected, though partial, recovery. His memory remains impaired, as does his speech; he may never be able to resume his legal career fully. It is possible that his income will be much lower for the rest of his life than it would otherwise have been, to the great disadvantage of his wife and children.

One of the two assailants, Daniel Hayward, demonstrated that he had learned nothing – at least, nothing of any comfort to the public – after he had ruined the barrister's life. While awaiting trial on bail, he attacked the landlord of a pub and punched him in the face, for which he received a sentence of 21 days in prison.

Before passing sentence for the attack on Wareing, the judge was eloquent in his condemnation of the two youths. 'You were looking for trouble and prepared to use any excuse to visit violence on anyone you came by. It is the callousness of this that is so chilling... You do not seem to care that others have been blighted by your gratuitous violence.'

You might have thought that this was a prelude to the passing of a very long prison sentence on the two youths. If so, however, you would be entirely mistaken. Both received sentences of 18 months, with an automatic remission of nine months, more or less as of right. In other words, they would serve nine months in prison for having destroyed the health and career of a completely innocent man, caused his wife untold suffering, and deprived three young children of a normal father. One of the perpetrators, too, had shown a complete lack of remorse for what he had done and an inclination to repeat it.

Even at so young an age, nine months is not a very long time. Moreover, when I recall that for youths like these a prison sentence is likely to be a badge of honour rather than a disgrace, I cannot but conclude that the British state is either utterly indifferent to or incapable of the one task that inescapably belongs to it: preserving the peace and ensuring that its citizens may go about their lawful business in safety. It does not know how to deter, prevent or punish. The remarks of the policeman in charge of the case were not encouraging. He said afterward that he hoped 'the sentences... send a clear warning to people who think it is acceptable to consume large quantities of alcohol, then assault members of the public in unprovoked attacks.' If the law supposes that, as Mr Bumble said in *Oliver Twist*, 'the law is a ass – a idiot'.

As for Peter Wareing, even in his brain-damaged state, he had a better appreciation of things. He was evidently a man of some spirit: having been a salesman, he decided to study for the law, supported himself at law school by a variety of manual jobs, and qualified at the bar at the age of 40. The extent of his recovery astounded his neurosurgeon, who attributed it to Wareing's determination and 'bloody-mindedness'. He is avid to get back to work, but the contrast between the nominal 18-month sentence for his attackers and his own 'life sentence', as he called it, of struggle against disability is not lost on him. 'If there were real justice,' he said, 'they would have gone to prison for life.' Could any compassionate person disagree?

Perhaps the final insult is that the state is paying for Wareing to have psychotherapy to suppress his anger. 'I have this rage inside me for the people who did this,' he said. 'I truly hate them.' Having failed in its primary duty, the state then treats the rage naturally consequent upon this failure as pathological, in need of therapy. On reading Peter Wareing's story, ordinary, decent citizens will themselves feel a sense of impotent rage, despair, betrayal and abandonment similar to his. Do we all need psychotherapy?

A second case similarly illustrates the refusal of the British state to take the lives of its citizens seriously. An engineer – Philip Carroll, the father of four – was tinkering with his car outside his home. Four drunken youths sat on a wall on his property, and he asked them to leave. They argued with him, and one of them threw a stone at his car. He chased this youth and caught him, but between 20 and 40 more youths loitering drunkenly nearby rallied round, and one 15-year-old hit the engineer to the ground, where he too banged his head and received severe brain damage. Unconscious for 18 days, he needed three operations to survive; and now he too has an impaired memory and might never work again.

According to his parents, the culprit, Michael Kuba-Kuba, felt deeply ashamed of what he had done, but this did not in the least prevent him during the trial from claiming (unsuccessfully, in the event) that he had been acting in self-defence. This does not sound like genuine shame to me but rather an attempt to get away with it. Before passing sentence, the judge said: 'I have to try to ensure that the courts will treat incidents like this with great severity, to send out a message to other young people that violence is not acceptable.'

Another prelude, you might think, to a stiff sentence – but again you would be wrong. The young man got 12 months, of which he will serve six. Six months for the active life of a man – for having caused 30 or 40 years of disability as well as incalculable suffering to the disabled man's family! It is not difficult to imagine Kuba-Kuba returning from prison to a hero's welcome, because he had simultaneously got away with near-murder and survived the rite of passage that imprisonment now represents. The message the judge sent out to other young people, no doubt unintentionally, was that youths may destroy other people's lives with virtual impunity, for the British state does not care in the least about protecting them or deterring such crimes.

Two aspects of the case went unexamined in the newspapers. The first was that Kuba-Kuba's parents were the owners of a grocery store specialising in African foods, and were deeply religious. The young man doubtless did not grow up in abject poverty, then; nor would he have derived his readiness for violence from anything his parents might have taught him.

The second was that Kuba-Kuba was a talented athlete, apparently of potentially Olympic standard. He was a promising soccer player, so promising that several major teams were seriously interested in recruiting him. If, as seemed likely, he had made the grade, he would have become a multimillionaire by his early 20s, earning more in a year than most people in a lifetime. Lack of economic prospects and the frustration it entails can hardly explain a propensity to violence in his case, therefore.

We must look elsewhere for the source of his violent conduct. Possibly he was born a sport of nature, a creature biologically destined to violence – no doubt there are such cases. But far more likely was that an aggressive popular culture that glorifies egotistical impulsivity and denigrates self-control influenced him. Although his parents presented him, in their statements, as a paragon of virtue, he already had a conviction for theft, and he clearly hung about with teenagers who drank a lot and made a nuisance of themselves. Mr Carroll confronted the youth who threw the stone precisely because he was exasperated by the unruly behaviour that prevailed in his neighbourhood, undeterred and unpunished by the state. A senior policeman said after the attack, 'We have gangs of young people hanging around on street corners being abusive, intimidating and causing trouble... They don't give a damn about the police or the criminal justice system.'

And who can blame them? What deterrent, punishment, vengeance or protection for society is six months in prison for having injured a man so badly that he did not recognise his wife or children for several months afterward, that he now has poor eyesight, has lost his sense of smell and taste, has to wear a brace on one foot and a hard hat to protect his skull, and says of himself, 'I just have no interest in anything or anyone' – having previously been a highly successful man?

(These are but two of countless illustrations of the unholy alliance between politicians and bureaucrats who want to keep prison costs to a minimum, and liberal intellectuals who pretend to see in crime a natural and understandable response to social injustice, which it would be a further injustice to punish. This alliance has engendered an absurd, prolonged and so far unfinished experiment in leniency that has debased the quality of life of millions of people, especially the poor.)

Having seen how the British state takes the serious lightly, let us now see how it takes the trivial seriously.

The newspapers reported the case of an Oxford student who, slightly drunk after celebrating the end of his exams, approached a mounted policeman. 'Excuse me,' said the young man to the policeman, 'do you realise your horse is gay?'

This was not a very witty remark, but it was hardly filled with deep malice either. It was, perhaps, a manifestation of the youthful silliness of which most of us have been guilty in our time. And Oxford was once a city in which drunken students often played, and were even expected to play, pranks on the police, such as knocking off their helmets.

The policeman did not think the student's remark was innocent, however. He called two squad cars to his aid, and, in a city in which it is notoriously difficult to interest the police in so trivial a matter as robbery or burglary, they arrived almost at once. Apparently, the mounted policeman thought – if 'thought' is quite the word I seek –

that the young man's remark was likely to 'cause harassment, alarm or distress'. He was arrested and charged under the Public Order Act for having made a 'homophobic remark'.

The young man spent a night in jail. Brought before the magistrates the following day, he was fined £70, which he refused to pay. The police then sent the case to the Crown Prosecution Service, who brought the student before the courts again but had to admit that there was not enough evidence to prove that his conduct had been disorderly.

The degree to which political correctness has addled British consciousness, like a computer virus, and destroyed all our traditional attachment to liberty, is illustrated by the words of one of the student's friends who witnessed the incident. '[His] comments were... in jest,' he said. 'It was very clear that they were not homophobic.' In other words, the friend accepted the premise that certain remarks, well short of incitement to commit violence or any actual crime – words that merely expressed an unpopular or intolerant point of view – would have constituted reasonable grounds for arrest. One consequence of the liberal intelligentsia's long march through the institutions is the acceptance of the category of Thoughtcrime. On the other hand, political correctness permits genuine incitement to murder – such as the BEHEAD THOSE WHO INSULT ISLAM placards carried by Muslim demonstrators in London four months after the publication of cartoons of Mohammed in a Danish newspaper – to go completely unpunished. Other people, other customs.

Goodness knows how much time of how many people this episode in Oxford had wasted, and at what cost to the taxpayer – all in a country with the highest rate of crime (that is to say, of real crime) in the Western world. I could not help comparing the alacrity with which the police dealt with the 'homophobic' remark with their indifference to an act of arson my wife witnessed.

She noticed some youths setting fire to the contents of a skip just outside our house, a fire that could easily have spread to cars parked nearby. She called the police.

'What do you expect us to do about it?' they asked.

'I expect you to come and arrest them,' she said.

The police regarded this as a bizarre and unreasonable expectation. They refused point-blank to send anyone. Of course, if they had promised to make every effort to come quickly but had arrived too late, my wife would have understood and been satisfied. But she was not satisfied with the idea that youths could set dangerous fires without arousing even the minimal interest of the police. Surely some or all of the youths would conclude that they could do anything they liked, and move on to more serious crimes.

My wife then insisted that the police should at least place the crime on their records. Again they refused. She remonstrated with them at length, and at considerable cost to her equanimity. At last, and with the greatest reluctance, they recorded the crime and gave her a reference number for it.

This was not the end of the matter. About 15 minutes later, a more senior policeman telephoned to upbraid her and tell her she had been wasting police time with her insistence on satisfaction in so trivial a matter. The police, apparently, had more important things to do than suppress arson. Goodness knows what homophobic remarks were being made while the youths were merely setting a fire that could have spread, and in the process learning that they could do so with impunity.

It is not difficult to guess the reason for the senior policeman's anger. My wife had forced his men to record a crime that they had no intention whatever of even trying to solve (though, with due expedition, it was eminently soluble), and this record, in turn, meant the introduction of an unwanted breath of reality into the bogus statistics, the manufacture of which is now every British senior policeman's principal task, with the sole exception of enforcing the dictates of political correctness, thereby to head off the criticism levied at them for many decades by the liberal left – not always without an element of justification. Proving their purity of heart is now more important to them than securing the safety of our streets: and thus Nero fiddled while Rome burned.

Another story in the newspaper then caught my eye: the government wanted to ban smoking in British prisons.

At first sight this might seem like a serious rather than a frivolous idea. More than nine-tenths of prisoners smoke, and if they continue to do so, about half of them will die prematurely as a result. The evidence that smoking is bad for the health has long since been overwhelming and incontrovertible. Therefore the government could reasonably claim that the proposed ban was evidence of its solicitude for the welfare of the most despised of all sections of society, prisoners. And after all, what could be more serious, less frivolous, than saving lives, or trying to do so?

In general I am not sentimental about the rights of prisoners. I do not think the proposed ban infringes any of their rights; but it seems to me that there are plenty of reasons for treating prisoners decently and humanely other than the observance of their supposed rights. Decency and humanity are goods in themselves, after all. The proposed ban was not only hypocritical but gratuitously cruel and inhumane, and likely to prove ineffective into the bargain.

But it would be wrong even if effective.

Smoking is not illegal in Britain, and the government derives large revenues from the consumption of tobacco, indeed far larger than the profits of the tobacco companies. It uses these revenues not to lessen the taxes of nonsmokers but merely as one among many other sources of revenue. Although high taxation on tobacco does discourage smoking, that is not, and never was, its primary aim.

At bottom the proposal looks like the arbitrary bullying of a defenceless population in a fit of Pecksniffian moral enthusiasm. It is to deprive that population of a small privilege long accepted by custom and usage. And, of course, the moral enthusiasts of the government will not bear the practical cost of enforcing the ban; the prison officers will. The proposal is an example of the soft and creeping totalitarianism that comes with unctuous offers of benefits and avowals of purity of intention, rather than the boot-in-the-face variety of Orwell's description. It is the insinuation of the government into the nooks and crannies of everyday life, on the pretext that people are incapable of deciding anything for themselves. Everyone is a child for whom the government is in permanent *loco parentis* (except children, of course, who can consent to sex at age 16 and are to be given the vote at the same age, if Gordon Brown has his way).

The newspapers confirmed what I had long perceived: that the *Zeitgeist* of the country is now one of sentimental moralising combined with the utmost cynicism, where the government's pretended concern for the public welfare co-exists with the most elementary dereliction of duty. There is an absence of any kind of idealism that is a necessary precondition of probity, so that bad faith prevails almost everywhere. The government sees itself as an engineer of souls (to use the phrase so eloquently coined by Stalin with regard to writers who, of course, were expected to mould *Homo sovieticus* by the power of their words). Government thus concerns itself with what people think, feel and say – as well as with trying to change their freely chosen habits – rather than with performing its one inescapable duty: that of preserving the peace. It is more concerned that young men should not smoke cigarettes in prison or make silly jokes to policemen than that they should not attack and permanently maim their elders and betters.

One definition of decadence is the concentration on the gratifyingly imaginary to the disregard of the disconcertingly real. No one who knows Britain could doubt that it has very serious problems – economic, social and cultural. Its public services – which already consume a vast proportion of the national wealth – are not only inefficient but completely beyond amelioration by the expenditure of yet more money. Its population is abysmally educated, to the extent that in a few more years Britain will not even have a well-educated elite. An often cynical and criminally-minded population has been indoctrinated with shallow and gimcrack notions – for example, about social justice – that render it singularly unfit to compete in an increasingly competitive world. Not coincidentally, Britain has serious economic problems, the cracks of which the government managed to paper over for a considerable time, before they were cruelly exposed a few months ago. Unpleasant realities cannot be indefinitely disguised or conjured away: for reality is still reality, no matter how much spin is applied to it.

Therefore I have removed myself: not that I imagine things are much better, only slightly different, in France. But one does not feel the defects of a foreign country in quite the same lacerating way as the defects of one's native land; they are more an object of amused, detached interest than of personal despair.

REAL CRIME, FAKE JUSTICE

IT IS NOT MERELY anecdote which suggests that, for the last 40 years, government policy in Britain, *de facto* if not always *de jure*, has been to render the British population virtually defenceless against criminals and criminality. There is also a wealth of statistical evidence, for those who seek it, which supports the anecdotes and proves their truth (although the sheer weight and volume of anecdotal evidence is significant in itself).

Let us take as an emblematic example the official report into the case of Anthony Rice, who strangled and then stabbed Naomi Bryant to death at her home in Winchester. Rice, a prolific and violent sex offender since 1972, had been convicted for assaulting or raping a total of 15 women, often at knifepoint, before he murdered Miss Bryant. (It is a fair supposition that he had assaulted or raped many more who did not go to the police.)

Having been convicted of rape in 1982 (and released before serving his seven year sentence), he was sentenced to life in prison in 1989 for an attack in which he accosted a woman in the street at night, pushed her into a garden, held a knife to her and attempted to rape her over a 90-minute period. Despite his history, he was transferred to an open prison in 2002 and then released two years later on parole as a 'low-risk' parolee. He received housing in a hostel for ex-prisoners in a village whose inhabitants had been told, to gain their acquiescence, that none of the residents there was violent; five months after his arrival, he murdered Naomi Bryant, stabbing her 15 times. In pronouncing a further life sentence on him, the judge ordered that he should serve at least 25 years: in other words, the law has *still* not quite thrown away the key.

Even *The Observer* (one of the bastions of British liberalism responsible for the present situation) gave prominence to this appalling affair, but there are those who dismiss terrible cases such as this as unrepresentative and of merely 'anecdotal' interest.

Unfortunately, they are not. This year it was revealed that, over the past decade, dozens of killers released on licence from life sentences have gone on to commit serious crimes, including murder, manslaughter, rape, robbery, woundings and offences involving drugs and firearms. One man raped a 10 month-old boy after being paroled; another murdered the wife he had met while serving life for murdering another woman.

Within the same week as the Rice case, the newspapers reported that 1,023 prisoners of foreign origin had been released from British prisons between 1999 and 2006 without having been deported. Among them were five killers, seven kidnappers, nine rapists and 39 other sex offenders, four arsonists, 41 burglars, 52 thieves, 93 robbers and 204 drug offenders. Of the 1,023 prisoners, only 106 had since been traced. The Home Office, responsible for both prisons and immigration, was unable to say how many of the killers, arsonists, rapists and kidnappers were at large; but it admitted that most of them would never be found, at least until they were caught after committing another offence. Although these revelations led to the dismissal of the then home secretary, Charles Clarke, in fact the foreign criminals had been treated only as British criminals are treated: not long afterwards, it was revealed that the government's policy – introduced in 1999 to relieve 'population pressures' on the prisons – of 'tagging' prisoners and releasing them early had allowed more than 1,000 of them to commit further violent offences, including murder, manslaughter and hundreds of assaults, from which the public would have been protected had they served their original sentences in full. At least we can truly say that we do not discriminate in our leniency.

Scandal has followed scandal. A short time later still, we learned that prisoners had been absconding from one open prison, Leyhill, at a rate of two a week for three years – 929 in total since 1999, among them 22 murderers. This outrage came to light only when a senior policeman in the area of Leyhill told a member of Parliament that there had been a crime wave in the vicinity of the prison. The member of Parliament demanded the figures in the House of Commons; otherwise they would have remained secret.

None of these revelations, however, would have surprised a man called David Fraser, author of a book entitled *A Land Fit for Criminals* – the land in question being Great Britain, of course. Far from being mistakes – for mistakes repeated so often cease to be mere mistakes – all these occurrences are in full compliance with general policy in Britain with regard to crime and criminality.

Fraser was a probation officer for more than a quarter of a century. He began to doubt the value of his work in terms of preventing crime and therefore protecting the public, but at first he assumed that, as a comparatively lowly official in the criminal justice system, he was too mired in the grainy everyday detail to see the bigger picture. He assumed also that those in charge not only knew what they were doing but had the public interest at heart.

Eventually, however, the penny dropped. Fraser's lack of success in effecting any change in the criminals under his supervision, and thus in reducing the number of crimes that they subsequently committed, to the great misery of the general public, was not his failure alone but was general throughout the system. Even worse, he discovered that the bureaucrats who ran the system, and their political masters, did not care about this failure, at least from the point of view of its impact on public safety; careerist to the core, they were concerned only that the public should not become aware of the catastrophe. To this end they indulged in obfuscation and outright lies in order to prevent the calamity that public knowledge of the truth would represent for them and their careers.

The collective intellectual dishonesty of those who worked in the system so outraged Fraser – and the Kafkaesque world in which he found himself, where nothing was called by its real name and language tended more to conceal meaning than to convey it, so exasperated him – that, though not a man apt to obtrude upon the public, he determined to write a book. It took him two and a half years to do so, based on 20 years of research, and it is clear from the very first page that he wrote it from a burning need to expose and exorcise the lies and evasions with which he lived for so long, lies and evasions that helped in a few decades transform a law-abiding country with a reputation for civility into the country with the highest crime rate in the Western world, with an ever-present undercurrent of violence in daily life. Like Luther, Fraser could not but speak out. And, as events unfolded, his book has had a publishing history that is additionally revealing of the state of Britain today.

By example after example (repetition being necessary to establish that he has not just alighted on an isolated case of absurdity that might be found in any large-scale enterprise), Fraser demonstrates the unscrupulous lengths to which both bureaucrats and governments have gone to disguise from the public the effect of their policies and decisions, carried out with an almost sadistic indifference to the welfare of common people.

He shows that liberal intellectuals and their bureaucratic allies have left no stone unturned to ensure that the law-abiding should be left as defenceless as possible against the predations of criminals, from the emasculation of the police to the devising of punishments that do not punish and the propagation of sophistry by experts to mislead and confuse the public about what is happening in society, confusion rendering the public helpless in the face of the experimentation perpetrated upon it.

The police, Fraser shows, are like a nearly defeated occupying colonial force that, while mayhem reigns everywhere else, has retreated to their fortress, there to shuffle paper and produce bogus information to propitiate its political masters. Where they agree to investigate crime (and often they do not) they regularly employ a sanction known as the 'caution' – a mere verbal warning – at the behest of their political masters. Indeed, as Fraser points out, the Home Office even reprimanded the West Midlands Police Force for bringing too many apprehended offenders to court, instead of merely giving them a caution. In the official version, only minor crimes are dealt with in this fashion: but as Fraser points out, in the year 2000 alone, 600 cases of robbery, 4,300 cases of car theft, 6,600 offences of burglary, 13,400 offences against public order, 35,400 cases of violence against the person and 67,600 cases of other kinds of theft were dealt with in this fashion – in effect, letting these 127,900 offenders off scot-free. When one considers that the police clear-up rate of all crimes in Britain is scarcely more than one in 20 (and even that figure is based upon official deception), the liberal intellectual claim, repeated *ad nauseam* in the press and on the air, that the British criminal justice system is primitively retributive is absurd.

At every point in the system, Fraser shows, deception reigns. When a judge sentences a criminal to three years' imprisonment, he knows perfectly well (as does the press that reports it) that in the vast majority of cases the criminal in question will serve eighteen months at the very most, because he is entitled automatically, as of right, to a suspension of half his sentence. Moreover, under the scheme of early release, prisoners serve considerably less than half their sentence. They may be tagged electronically under a system of home curfew, intended to give the public an assurance that they are being monitored: but the electronic tag stays on for fewer than 12 hours daily and, as we have seen, this gives criminals plenty of opportunity to follow their careers.

Even when the criminals remove their tags (and it is known that thousands are removed or vandalised every year) or fail to abide by other conditions of their early release, those who are supposedly monitoring them do nothing whatever, for fear of spoiling the statistics of the system's success. When the Home Office tried the tagging system with young criminals, 73 percent of them were reconvicted within three months. The authorities nevertheless decided to extend the scheme. The failure of the British state to take its responsibilities seriously could not be more clearly expressed.

Fraser draws attention to the deeply corrupt system under which a criminal, once caught, may ask for other offences that he has committed to be 'taken into consideration'. (Criminals call these offences TICs) This practice may be in the interests of both the criminal and the police, but not in those of the long-suffering public. The court will sentence the criminal to further prison terms that run concurrently, not consecutively, to that imposed for the index offence: in other words, he will in effect serve the same sentence for fifty burglaries as for one burglary, and he can never again face charges for the 49 burglaries that have been 'taken into consideration'.

Meanwhile the police can preen themselves that they have 'solved' 50 crimes for the price of one.

One Probation Service smokescreen that Fraser knows from personal experience is to measure its own effectiveness by the proportion of criminals who complete their probation in compliance with court orders – a procedural outcome that has no significance whatever for the safety of the public. Such criminals come under the direct observation of probation officers only one hour a week at the very most. What they do the other 167 hours of the week the probation officers cannot possibly know. Unless one takes the preposterous view that such criminals are incapable of telling lies about their activities to their probation officers, mere attendance at the probation office is no guarantee whatever that they are now leading law-abiding lives.

But even if suspension of probation orders were assumed to a surrogate measure of success in preventing re-offending, the Probation Service's figures have long been completely corrupt and for a very obvious reason. Until 1997 the probation officers themselves decided when non-compliance with their directions was so egregious that they 'breached' the criminals under their supervision and returned them to the courts because of such non-compliance. Since their own effectiveness was measured by the proportion of probation orders 'successfully' completed, they had a very powerful motive for disregarding the non-compliance of criminals. In such circumstances all activity became strictly *pro forma*, with no purpose external to itself.

While the government put an end to this particular statistical legerdemain, probation orders still go into the statistics as 'successfully completed' if they reach their official termination date – even in many cases if the offender gets arrested for committing further offences before that date. Only in this way can the Home Office claim that between 70 and 80 percent of probation orders are 'successfully completed'.

In their effort to prove the liberal orthodoxy that prison does not work, criminologists, government officials and journalists have routinely used the lower reconviction rates of those sentenced to probation and other forms of non-custodial punishment (the word 'punishment' in these circumstances being used very loosely) than those imprisoned. But if the aim is to protect the law-abiding, a comparison of reconviction rates of those imprisoned and those put on probation is irrelevant. What counts is the re-offending rate – a point so obvious that it is shameful that Fraser should not only have to make it but to hammer it home repeatedly, for the politicians, academics and journalistic hangers-on have completely obscured it.

By definition, a man in prison can commit no crimes (except against fellow prisoners and prison staff). But what of those out in the world on probation? Of 1,000 male criminals on probation, Fraser makes clear, about 600 will be re-convicted at least once within the two years that the Home Office follows them up for statistical purposes. The rate of detection in Britain of all crimes being about 5 percent, those 1,000 criminals will actually have committed not 600, but at least 12,000 crimes (assuming them to have been averagely competent criminals chased by averagely incompetent police). Even this is not quite all. Since there are, in fact, about 150,000 people on probation in Britain, it means that at least 1.8 million crimes – more than an eighth of the nation's total – must be committed annually by people on probation, within the very purview of the criminal justice system, or very shortly after they have been on probation. While some of these crimes might be 'victimless', or at least impersonal, research has shown that these criminals inflict untold misery upon the British population: misery that they would not have been able to inflict had they been in prison for a year instead of on probation.

To compare the reconviction rates of ex-prisoners and people on probation as an argument against prison is not only irrelevant from the point of view of public safety but is also logically absurd. Of course the imprisoned will have higher reconviction rates once they get out of jail – not because prison failed to reform them but because it is the most hardened, incorrigible and recidivist criminals who go to prison. Again, this point is so obvious that it is shameful that anyone should have to point it out; yet politicians and others continue to use the reconviction rates as if they were a proper basis for deciding policy.

Relentless for hundreds of pages, Fraser provides examples of how the British government and its bloated and totally ineffectual bureaucratic apparatus, through moral and intellectual frivolity as well as plain incompetence, has failed in its elementary duty: to protect the lives and property of the citizenry. He exposes the absurd prejudice that has become a virtually unassailable orthodoxy among the intellectual and political elite, that we have too many prisoners in Britain, as if there were an ideal number of prisoners, derived from a purely abstract principle, at which, independent of the number of crimes committed, we should aim. He describes in full detail the moral and intellectual corruption of the British criminal justice system, from decisions by the authorities not to record crimes or to charge wrongdoers, to the absurdly light sentences given after conviction and the administrative means by which prisoners end up serving less than half their time, irrespective of their dangerousness or the likelihood that they will re-offend.

According to Fraser, at the heart of the British idiocy is the condescending and totally unrealistic idea – which, however, provides employment opportunities for armies of apparatchiks as well as being psychologically gratifying – that burglars, thieves and robbers are not conscious malefactors who calculate their chances of getting away with it, but people in the grip of something rather like a mental disease, whose thoughts, feelings and decision-making processes need to be restructured. The whole criminal justice system ought therefore to act in a therapeutic or medical, rather than a punitive and deterrent, fashion. Burglars do not know, poor things, that householders are upset by housebreaking, and so we must educate and inform them on this point; and we must also seek to persuade them of something that all their experience so far has taught them to be false, namely that crime does not pay.

All in all, Fraser's book is a searing and unanswerable (or at least so far unanswered) indictment of the British criminal justice system, and therefore of the British state. As Fraser pointed out to me, the failure of the state to protect the lives and property of its citizens, and to take seriously its duty in this regard, creates a politically dangerous situation, for it puts the very legitimacy of the state itself at risk. The potential consequences are incalculable, for the failure might bring the rule of law itself into disrepute and give an opportunity to the brutal and the authoritarian.

You might have thought that any publisher would gratefully accept a book so urgent in its message, so transparently the product of a burning need to communicate obvious but uncomfortable truths of such public interest, conveyed in a way that anyone of reasonable intelligence might understand them. Any publisher, you would think, would feel fortunate to have such a manuscript land on his desk. But you would be wrong, at least as far as Britain is concerned.

So uncongenial was Fraser's message to all right-thinking Britons that 60 publishers to whom he sent the book turned it down. In a country that publishes more than 10,000 books monthly, not many of which are imperishable masterpieces, there was no room for it or for what it said, though it would take no great acumen to see its commercial possibilities in a country crowded with crime victims. So great was the pressure of the orthodoxy now weighing on the minds of the British intelligentsia that Fraser might as well have gone to Mecca and said that there is no God and that Mohammed was not His prophet. Of course, no publisher actually told him that what he said was unacceptable or unsayable in public: his book merely did not 'fit the list' of any publisher. He was the victim of British publishing's equivalent of Mafia *omerta*.

Fortunately he did not give up, as he sometimes thought of doing. The 61ˢᵗ publisher to whom he sent the book accepted it. I mean no disrespect to her judgment when I say that it was her personal situation that distinguished her from her fellow publishers: for her husband's son by a previous marriage had not long before been murdered in the street, stabbed by a drug-dealing Jamaican immigrant, aged 20, who had not been deported despite his criminal record but instead allowed to stay in the country as if he were a national treasure to be at all costs cherished and nurtured. Indeed, in court his lawyer presented him as an unemployed painter and decorator, the victim of racial prejudice (a mitigating circumstance, of course), a view that the prosecution did not challenge, even though the killer had somehow managed alchemically to transmute his unemployment benefits into a new convertible costing £34,000.

The maternal grandmother of the murdered boy, who had never been ill in her life, died of a heart attack a week after his death, and so the funeral was a double one. It is difficult to resist the conclusion that the killer killed not one but two people. He received a sentence of eight years – which, in effect, will be four or five years.

I asked the publisher the impossible question of whether she would have published the book if someone close to her had not had such firsthand experience of the frivolous leniency of the British criminal justice system. She said she thought so: but what is beyond dispute is that the murder made her publication of the book a certainty.

A Land Fit for Criminals has sold well and has been very widely discussed, though not by the most important liberal newspapers, which would find the whole subject in bad taste. But the book's publishing history demonstrates how close we have come to an almost totalitarian uniformity of the sayable, imposed informally by rightthinking people in the name of humanity, but in utter disregard for the truth and the reality of their fellow citizens' lives. Better that they, the right-thinking, should feel pleased with their own rectitude and broadmindedness, than that millions should be freed of their fear of robbery and violence. It is sad that Fraser's voice could be heard only over someone's dead body.

HOW CRIMINOLOGISTS
FOSTER CRIME

CRIME HAS NOW COME to seem normal to many Britons, not least to its perpetrators.

Once, in the prison, I asked a young man why he was there.

'Just normal burglaries,' he replied.

'Normal for whom?' I asked.

'You know, just normal.'

He meant, I think, that burglaries were like grey skies in an English winter: unavoidable and to be expected. In an actuarial sense, he was right: Britain is now the burglary capital of the world, as almost every householder here will attest. But there was also a deeper sense to his words, for statistical normality slides rapidly in our minds into moral normality. The wives of burglars often talk to me of their husband's 'work', as if breaking into other people's homes were merely a late shift in a factory. Nor is only burglary 'normal' in the estimation of its perpetrators. 'Just a normal assault' was another frequent answer prisoners gave to my question, the little word 'just' emphasising the innocuousness of the crime.

But how has this sense of normality come about? Is it merely a recognition of the brute fact of a vastly increased crime rate? Or could it be, on the contrary, one of the very causes of that increase, inasmuch as it represents a weakening of the inhibition against criminality?

As usual, one must look first to the academy when tracing the origins of a change in the *Zeitgeist*. What starts out as a career-promoting academic hypothesis ends up as an idea so widely accepted that it becomes not only an unchallengeable orthodoxy but a cliché even among the untutored. Academics have used two closely linked arguments to establish the statistical and moral normality of crime and the consequent illegitimacy of the criminal justice system's sanctions.

First, they claim, we are all criminal anyway; and when everyone is guilty, everyone is innocent.

Their second argument, Marxist in inspiration, is that the law has no moral content, being merely the expression of the power of certain interest groups – of the rich against the poor, for example, or the capitalist against the worker. Since the law is an expression of raw power, there is no essential moral distinction between criminal and non-criminal behaviour. It is simply a question of whose foot the boot is on.

Criminologists are the mirror image of Hamlet, who exclaimed that if each man received his deserts, none should escape whipping. On the contrary, say the criminologists, more liberal than the prince (no doubt because of their humbler social origins): none should be punished. These ideas resonate in the criminal's mind. If his illegal conduct is so very normal, he thinks, what's all the fuss about in his case, or why should he be where he is – in prison? It is patently unjust for him to be incarcerated for what everyone still at liberty does. He is the victim of illegitimate and unfair discrimination, rather like an African under apartheid, and it is only reasonable that, on his release, he should take his revenge upon so unjust a society by continuing, or expanding, his criminal activity.

It is impossible to state precisely when the *Zeitgeist* changed and the criminal became a victim in the minds of intellectuals: not only history, but also the history of an idea, is a seamless robe. Let me quote one example, though, now almost half a century old. In 1966 (at about the time when Norman Mailer in America, and Jean-Paul Sartre in Europe, portrayed criminals as existential heroes in revolt against a heartless, inauthentic world), the psychiatrist Karl Menninger published a book with the revealing title *The Crime of Punishment*. It was based upon the Isaac Ray lectures he had given three years earlier – Isaac Ray having been the first American psychiatrist who concerned himself with the problems of crime. Menninger wrote: 'Crime is everybody's temptation. It is easy to look with proud disdain upon those people who get caught – the stupid ones, the unlucky ones, the blatant ones. But who does not get nervous when a police car follows closely? We squirm over our income tax statements and make some adjustments. We tell the customs official we have nothing to declare – well, practically nothing. Some of us who have never been convicted of crime picked up over two billion dollars' worth of merchandise last year from the stores we patronise. Over a billion dollars was embezzled by employees last year.'

The moral of the story is that those who go to court and to prison are victims of chance at best and of prejudice at worst: prejudice against the lowly, the unwashed, the uneducated, the poor – those whom literary critics portentously call the Other. This is precisely what many of my patients in the prison tell me. Even when they have been caught *in flagrante*, loot in hand or blood on fist, they believe the police are unfairly picking on them. Such an attitude, of course, prevents them from reflecting upon their own contribution to their predicament: for chance and prejudice are not forces over which an individual has much personal control. When I ask prisoners whether they'll be coming back after their release, a few say no with an entirely credible vehemence; they are the ones who make the mental connection between their conduct and their fate. But most say they don't know, that no one can foresee the future, that it's up to the courts, that it all depends – on others, never on themselves.

It didn't take long for Menninger's attitude to permeate official thinking. A 1968 British government document on juvenile delinquency, *Children in Trouble*, declared: 'It is probably a minority of children who grow up without ever misbehaving in ways which may be contrary to the law. Frequently, such behaviour is no more than an ⁣⁣⁣

In a sense this is perfectly true, for in the absence of proper guidance and control, the default setting of human beings is surely to crime and anti-social conduct, and everyone breaks the rules at some time. But in a period of increasing permissiveness, many draw precisely the wrong conclusion from human nature's universal potential for delinquency: indeed, the only reason commentators mention that potential at all is to draw a predetermined liberal conclusion from it – that acts of delinquency, being normal, should not give rise to sanctions.

In this spirit, *Children in Trouble* treats the delinquency of normal children as if its transience were the result of a purely biological or natural process rather than of a social one. Delinquency is like baby teeth: predetermined to come and go at a certain stage of a child's development.

Not so very long ago, such an attitude would have struck almost everyone as absurd. Everyone knew, as if by instinct, that human behaviour is a product of consciousness, and the consciousness of a child must be moulded. I can best illustrate what I mean by my own experience. At the age of eight, I stole a penny bar of chocolate from the corner shop. It gave me a thrill to do so, and I enjoyed the chocolate all the more for the fact that it had not made an inroad into my weekly pocket money (sixpence). Unwisely, however, I confided my exploit to my elder brother, in an attempt to win his respect for my bravery, which was much in question at the time. Even more unwisely, I forgot that he knew this incriminating story when, furious at him because of his habitual teasing, I told my mother that he had uttered a word that at that time was never heard in respectable households. In retaliation, he told my mother that I had stolen the chocolate.

My mother did not take the view that this was a transient episode of delinquency that would pass of its own accord. She knew instinctively (for, at that time, no one had yet befuddled minds by suggesting otherwise) that all that was necessary for delinquency to triumph was for her to do nothing. She did not think that my theft was a natural act of self-expression, or a revolt against the inequality between the power and wealth of children and that of adults, or indeed of anything other than my desire to have the chocolate without paying for it. She was right, of course. What I had done was morally wrong, and to impress the fact upon me she marched me round to Mrs Marks, the owner of the store, where I confessed my sin and paid her tuppence by way of restitution. It was the end of my shoplifting career.

Since then, of course, our understanding of theft and other criminal activity has grown more complex, if not necessarily more accurate or realistic. It has been the effect, and quite possibly the intention, of criminologists to shed new obscurity on the matter of crime: the opacity of their writing sometimes leads one to wonder whether they have actually ever met a criminal or a crime victim. Certainly it is in their professional interest that the wellsprings of crime should remain an unfathomed mystery, for how else is one to convince governments that what a crime-ridden country (such as Britain) needs is further research done by ever more criminologists?

It is probably no coincidence that the profession of criminology underwent a vast expansion at about the same time that criminal activity began the steepest part of its exponential rise. Criminologists in Britain once numbered in the low dozens, and criminology, considered unfit for undergraduates, was taught only in one or two institutes. Today hardly a city or town in the country is without its academic criminology department. Half of the 800 or so criminologists now working in Britain had their training (mostly in sociology) in the late

127

sixties and early seventies, during the heyday of radical activism, and they trained the other half.

Of course, it might have been that the problem of crime called forth its students. But since social problems are often of a dialectical nature, could it not also have been that the students called forth their problem? (British economist John Vaizey once wrote that any problem that became the subject of an 'ology' was destined to grow serious.) Since the cause of crime is the decision of criminals to commit it, what goes on in their minds is not irrelevant. Ideas filter down selectively from the academy into the population at large, through discussions (and often bowdlerisations) in the papers and on TV, and become intellectual currency. In this way, the ideas of criminologists could actually become a cause of crime. In addition, these ideas deleteriously affect the thinking of the police. In the hospital in which I worked, for example, the police posted notices everywhere warning staff, patients, and visitors about car theft. *Motorists!* proclaimed one such. *Your car is at risk!* This is a very criminological locution, implying as it does a mysterious force – like, say, gravity – against which mere human will, such as that exercised by thieves and policemen, can be expected to avail nothing.

In the process of transmission from academy to populace, ideas may change in subtle ways. When the well-known criminologist Jock Young wrote that 'the normalisation of drug use is paralleled by the normalisation of crime', and, because of this normalisation, criminal behaviour in individuals no longer required special explanation, he surely didn't mean that he wouldn't mind if his own children started to shoot up heroin or rob old ladies in the street. Nor would he be indifferent to the intrusion of burglars into his own house, ascribing it merely to the temper of the times and regarding it as a morally neutral event. But that, of course, is precisely how 'just' shoplifters, 'just' burglars, 'just' assaulters, 'just' attempted murderers, taking their cue from him and others like him, would view (or at least say they viewed) their own actions: they have simply moved with the times, and therefore done no wrong. And, not surprisingly, the crimes that now attract the deprecatory qualification 'just' have escalated in seriousness even in the fifteen years I attended the prison as a doctor before my comparatively early retirement, so that I have even heard a prisoner wave away 'just a poxy little murder charge'.

The same is true of the drugs that prisoners use: where once they replied that they smoked 'just' cannabis, they now say that they take 'just' crack cocaine, as if by confining themselves thus they were paragons of self-denial and self-discipline.

Of course, the tendency of liberal intellectuals such as Jock Young not to mean quite what they say, and to express themselves more to flaunt the magnanimity of their intentions than to propagate truth, is a general one. I was once involved in a radio discussion with a distinguished film critic about the alleged social (or anti-social) effects of the constant exposure of children to depictions of violence. He strenuously denied that any ill effects occurred or were likely to occur, but admitted *en passant* that he would not permit a diet of violence for his own children. He perhaps did not notice that, underscoring his contradictory attitude, was an unutterable contempt for at least half of mankind. In effect, he was saying that the proles were so beyond redemption, so immoral by nature, that nothing could make them either better or worse. They did not make choices; they did not respond to moral or immoral influences; they were violent and criminal by essence. His own children, by contrast, would respond appropriately to his careful guidance.

Criminologists, needless to say, are not monolithic in their explanations of criminality: an academic discipline needs theoretical disputes as armed forces need potential enemies. But above the cacophony of explanations offered, one idea makes itself heard loud and clear, at least to criminals: to explain all is to excuse all. Criminological writing generally conceives of criminals as objects, more nearly than responding mechanically to other billiard balls that impinge upon them. But even when they are conceived of as subjects, whose actions are the result of their ideas, criminals remain innocent: for their ideas, criminologists contend, are reasonable and natural in the circumstances in which they find themselves. What more natural than that a poor man should want material goods, especially in so materialistic a society as ours?

Recently, in the last ten or fifteen years, biological theories of crime have come back into fashion. Such theories go a long way back: 19th century Italian and French criminologists and forensic psychiatrists elaborated a theory of hereditary degeneration to account for the criminal's inability to conform to the law. But until recently, biological theories of crime – usually spiced with a strong dose of bogus genetics – were the province of the illiberal right, leading directly to forced sterilisation and other eugenic measures.

The latest biological theories of crime, however, stress that criminals cannot help what they do: it is all in their genes, their neurochemistry or their temporal lobes. Such factors provide no answer to why the mere increase in recorded crime in Britain between 1990 and 1991 was greater than the total of *all* recorded crime in 1950 (to say nothing of the accelerating increases since 1991), but that failure does not deter researchers in the least. Scholarly books with titles such as *Genetics of Criminal and Antisocial Behaviour* proliferate and do not evoke the outrage among intellectuals that greeted the 1964 publication of H.J. Eysenck's *Crime and Personality*, a book suggesting that criminality is an hereditary trait. For many years, liberals viewed Eysenck, professor of psychology at London University, as virtually a fascist for suggesting the heritability of almost every human characteristic, but they have since realised that genetic explanations of crime can just as readily be grist for their exculpatory and all-forgiving mills as they can be for the mills of conservatives.

In the 1990s, an entire television series in Britain focused on the idea that crime is the result of brain dysfunction. The book that accompanied the series states that the two authors 'believe that – because we accept the findings of clinicians with no penal axe to grind – many criminals act as they do because of the way their brains are made. The past two decades have vastly extended the horizons of knowledge, and we believe it is time to benefit from that knowledge – the result of the work of endocrinologists, bio-physiologists, neurophysiologists, biostatisticians, geneticists and many others.'

But despite the alleged lack of penal axe to grind, the ultimate message is all too familiar: 'What stands out from literally hundreds of papers and studies of the various types of criminal is widespread and cogent evidence of disordered minds resulting from dysfunctional brains... But we do not recognise; we merely condemn. Incarceration is an expensive and wasteful reaction.'

Both parts of this message were welcome to my patients in the prison: that they are ill and in need of treatment, and that imprisonment is not only pointless but cruel and morally unjustified – less justified, indeed, than their crimes. After all, the judges who sentence them to imprisonment cannot exculpate themselves by virtue of their dysfunctional brains.

No wonder that each week prisoners told me, 'Prison's no good to me, doctor; prison's not what I need.'

I asked them what they did need, then.

Help, treatment, therapy.

The idea that prison is principally a therapeutic institution is now virtually ineradicable. The emphasis on recidivism rates as a measure of its success or failure in the press coverage of prison ('Research by criminologists shows...' etc.) reinforces this view, as does the

131

theory put forward by criminologists that crime is a mental disorder. *The Psychopathology of Crime* by Adrian Raine of the University of Southern California claims that recidivism is a mental disorder like any other, often accompanied by cerebral dysfunction. *Addicted to Crime?*, a volume edited by psychologists working in one of Britain's few institutions for the criminally insane, contains the work of eight academics. The answer to the question of their title is, of course, Yes; addiction being – falsely – conceived as a compulsion that it is futile to expect anyone to resist. (If there is a second edition of the book, the question mark will no doubt disappear from its title, just as it vanished from the second edition of Beatrice and Sidney Webb's book about the Soviet Union, *The Soviet Union: A New Civilisation?* – which included everything about Russia except the truth.)

Is it surprising that recidivist burglars and car thieves now ask for therapy for their addiction, secure in the knowledge that no such therapy can or will be forthcoming, thereby justifying the continuation of their habit?

'I asked for help,' they often complained to me, 'but didn't get none.'

One young man aged 21, serving a sentence of six months (three months, with time off for good behaviour) for having stolen 60 cars, told me that in reality he had stolen more than 500 and had made some £100,000 doing so. It is surely an unnecessary mystification to construct an elaborate neuropsychological explanation of his conduct.

Burglars who told me that they were addicted to their craft, thereby implying that the fault would be mine for not having treated them successfully if they continued to burgle after their release, always reacted in the same way when I asked them how many burglaries they had committed for which they were not caught: with a contented but not (from the householder's point of view) an altogether reassuring smile, as if they were recalling the happiest times of their life – soon to return.

Criminals call for therapy for all anti-social behaviour – curiously, though, only *after* it has led to imprisonment, not before. For example, a young man finally imprisoned for repeated assaults on his girlfriend and his mother, among others, told me that prison was not doing him any good, that what he needed was anger management therapy. I remarked that his behaviour in prison had been exemplary: he was always polite and did as he was told.

'I don't want to be taken down the block [the punishment floor], do I?' he replied, rather giving the game away. He had been violent to his girlfriend and his mother because hitherto there were advantages, but no disadvantages, to his violence. Now that the equation was different, he had no problem 'managing' his anger.

The great majority of the theories criminologists propound lead to the exculpation of criminals, and criminals eagerly take up these theories in their desire to present themselves as victims rather than as victimisers. For example, not long ago 'labelling theory' took criminology by storm. According to these theorists, the quantity of crime, the type of person and offence selected to be criminalised and the categories used to describe and explain the deviant are social constructions. Crime, or deviance, is not an objective 'thing' out there. I did not try this theory out on my non-criminal patients whose houses were burgled three times in a year – or who had been attacked in the street more than once, as is common among these patients – but I think I can imagine their response.

For criminals, of course, a theory that suggests that crime is an entirely arbitrary social category without justifiable moral content is highly gratifying – except when they themselves have been the victim of a crime, when they react like everyone else.

Since criminologists and sociologists can no longer plausibly attribute crime to raw poverty, they now look to 'relative deprivation' to explain its rise in times of prosperity. In this light they see crime as a quasi-political protest against an unjust distribution of the goods of the world. Several criminological commentators have lamented the apparently contradictory fact that it is the poor who suffer most, including loss of property, from criminals, implying that it would be more acceptable if the criminals robbed the rich.

In discussing the policy of zero tolerance, criminologist Jock Young avers that it could be used selectively for 'progressive' ends: 'One can,' he says, 'be zero-tolerant of violence against women and tolerant about the activities of the dispossessed.' One might suppose from this that among those tolerable activities of the dispossessed there was never any violence against women.

Moreover, the very term 'dispossessed' carries its own emotional and ideological connotations. The poor have not failed to earn, the term implies, but instead have been robbed of what is rightfully theirs. Crime is thus the expropriation of the expropriators – and so not crime at all in the moral sense. And this is an attitude I have encountered many times among burglars and car thieves. They believe that anyone who possesses something can, *ipso facto*, afford to lose it, while someone who does not possess it is, *ipso facto*, justified in taking it. Crime is but a form of redistributive taxation from below.

Or – when committed by women – crime could be seen 'as a way, perhaps, of celebrating women as independent of men', to quote Elizabeth Stanko, an American feminist criminologist teaching in a British university. Here we are paddling in the murky waters of Frantz Fanon, the West Indian psychiatrist who believed that a little murder did wonders for the psyche of the downtrodden, and who achieved iconic status precisely at the time of criminology's great expansion as a university discipline.

'Justice' in the writings of many criminologists does not refer to the means by which an individual is either rewarded or punished for his conduct in life. It refers to social justice. Most criminologists cannot distinguish between unfairness and injustice, and they conclude that any society in which unfairness continues to exist (as it must) is therefore unjust. And the question of social justice usually boils down to the question of equality. As Jock Young puts it starkly: 'Zero tolerance of crime must mean zero tolerance of inequality if it is to mean anything.' Since one of the inhibitions against crime (as crime is commonly understood, by people who have suffered it or are likely to suffer it) is the perceived legitimacy of the legal system under which the potential criminal lives, those who propagate the idea that we live in a fundamentally unjust society also propagate crime. The poor reap what the intellectual sows.

No one gains kudos in the criminological fraternity by suggesting that police and punishment are necessary in a civilised society. To do so would be to appear illiberal and lacking faith in man's primordial goodness. It is much better for one's reputation, for example, to refer to the large number of American prisoners as 'the American gulag', as if there were no relevant differences between the former Soviet Union and the United States.

In fact, criminals know all about the power of punishment: both its deterrent and rehabilitative effect. For prison is a society divided clearly in two, between officers and prisoners. Prisoners maintain the rigid division by their own extremely severe code of punishment. Should an individual prisoner try to break down this division, other prisoners will inflict immediate, severe and public punishment. The division therefore holds, even though many prisoners would prefer to side with the officers than with their peers.

Criminology is not monolithic, and there are more dissenters now than there once were, as Jock Young recognises. 'This recent pattern [of criminologists who believe in detection and punishment] is in contrast to a generation of liberal opinion and scholarship whose aim was to minimise police intervention and lower police numbers. One might even say that this has been the hidden agenda of academic criminology since the Nineteenth Century.'

From the criminal's point of view, criminology has served him proud.

OPIATE LIES

NOT LONG AGO, the British government ran an advertising campaign to warn young people against taking up smoking. It showed dramatic pictures of established smokers with large and nasty fishing hooks piercing their cheeks. Tension on the attached line fishing line pulled their cheeks in the direction of whoever was doing the pulling. The implication was clear: once you started smoking you were 'hooked', that is to say you lost all control over yourself, and had no choice but to go wherever your addiction took you.

The advertising campaign fitted in very well with prevailing ideas about addiction, particularly addiction to opiate drugs such as heroin. On this view of the matter, the addict is in the grip of a compulsion over which he has no control, so strong, in fact, that he cannot really be blamed for what he does in order to 'feed his habit', as the cant phrase puts it. For example, Polly Toynbee, the influential columnist for *The Guardian*, suggested that addicts should be given their drugs free so that they did not 'have to' steal and burgle to obtain them. In other words, drug addicts are not like you and me: they do not choose what they do. Having no choice, they are, in effect, automata; and we must forgive them, for they choose not what they do.

Of course, this view has potentially very illiberal consequences that are usually quite unnoticed by its proponents. If it were true that addicts could do no other than to steal, rob and burgle because of their addiction, and if, as a matter of fact, there were no way of treating them that would eliminate their addiction, then society would be justified, in order to protect itself, in imprisoning them indefinitely, for life, or at least until such an age that the addiction disappeared of its own accord. Fortunately, the prevailing view of addiction being completely and obviously wrong, no such illiberal consequences do actually follow from the facts of addiction.

Most people imagine that addicts are unwitting, unwilling and unlucky victims of heroin. Describing the life of five prostitutes murdered by a psychopath in Ipswich, for example, a headline in *The Guardian* said, 'Girls put in harm's way by drugs'. In other words, the girls didn't seek the drugs, the drugs sought them. The girls were more or less at the intellectual level of fish, who are, of course, quite rightly not blamed for their own misfortunes when caught by anglers and unable to escape.

On the prevailing view, young people quietly go about their business when they are suddenly attacked by drugs, which capture and enslave them by binding them in chains (the same metaphor has been used ever since De Quincey and Coleridge wrote their dishonest and self-serving accounts of their addiction to laudanum, tincture of opium in alcohol, in the 1820s). The active participant in the transaction between man and drug is not man, but drug: man is but drug's helpless victim.

This is preposterous. It is true that man, being a creature in a permanent and unavoidable state of dissatisfaction, is perennially tempted to alter his state of mind by extraneous substances (even change for the worse is often welcomed in preference to the boredom of stasis). But it is most definitely not true that the proportion of people addicting themselves to drugs is the same at all times and in all places.

Moreover, it still takes considerable effort and determination to become a heroin addict in our society. It is not the case that people take one or two doses of heroin, more or less by accident, and then find themselves unable to stop taking it. Most addicts have long periods of apprenticeship, during which they take the drug intermittently, before they take it regularly and develop physiological dependence on it. Learning about the equipment, apparatus and ceremonial of addiction – citric acid, needles, syringes etc – requires more concentration and attention than many addicts have been prepared to devote to schoolwork.

Nor is it true that those who become addicts first try heroin, and then take it regularly, through ignorance or naivety. This might just have been true once, I suppose; but in the areas where there are most addicts (in the mid 1950s, there were about 60 addicts registered by the Home Office in the whole of Great Britain, while now it is estimated that there are up to 300,000 addicts, that is to say a 5,000-fold increase), the young people may not know very much about history or geography, or be able to spell, but they do know about heroin addiction, addicts and the addicted way of life. They become heroin addicts because they choose to become heroin addicts; for, terrible commentary on our society as it may be, the addicted life seems better to them, more interesting and full of incident, more romantic, than any alternative way of life easily available to them.

But, you say, once they have become addicts, surely they have to fear the most terrible of consequences of addiction, namely withdrawal or (as it is popularly known) 'cold turkey'? The idea that most people have of withdrawal from morphine and heroin is entirely derived from books or films, in which it is portrayed as being so terrible that no person could be blamed for going to almost any length to avoid it. This was reflected in an out-of-court settlement recently when the Home Office gave three heroin-addicted prisoners at Winchester prison £11,000 each of taxpayers' money in compensation for having undergone such withdrawal in the prison without benefit of reducing doses of their drug or a substitute to alleviate their symptoms. According to reports, this terrible experience was accepted by the Home Office to be contrary to their human rights, and therefore indefensible in court.

But the idea that withdrawal from heroin is either dangerous or results in intolerable suffering is pharmacological nonsense. There are drugs from which withdrawal can be dangerous, but heroin is not one of them. Withdrawal from alcohol, for example, can kill; so can withdrawal from barbiturates. But withdrawal from heroin, as portrayed in thoroughly misleading films such as *Trainspotting*, is a benign, self-limiting condition lasting two or three days at most, and at worst like a dose of a mild viral illness. No one dies of it, and the textbooks of medicine are quite clear about its trivial nature. (Niesink, Jaspers, Komet and van Ree say in *Drugs of Abuse and Addiction*: 'Withdrawal is time-limited and not life-threatening, and thus can be easily controlled by reassurance, personal attention and general nursing care without the need for any pharmacotherapy.' Lowinson, Ring, Millman and Langrod say in *Substance Abuse: A Comprehensive Textbook*: 'The acute withdrawal syndrome is a time-limited phenomenon, generally of brief duration. Following the abrupt withdrawal from heroin, withdrawal signs and symptoms usually subside on the second or third heroin-free day. Although uncomfortable for the addict, the withdrawal syndrome, in contrast to the syndrome associated with the withdrawal of other drugs such as benzodiazepines and alcohol, does not pose a medical risk to the patient.')

There is good evidence that, in so far as the suffering of withdrawal from heroin is real and not exaggerated in order to obtain drugs from gullible doctors, it is largely caused by anticipatory anxiety. Many (though not all) addicts accept the mythology peddled by films like *Trainspotting*, and therefore do genuinely fear withdrawal. An Austrian experiment demonstrated not only that self-reported suffering of heroin addicts bore no relation to the physical symptoms that they suffered, but that their self-reported suffering reached almost to its maximum before they had missed even their first dose, which is to say that the suffering of withdrawal is overwhelmingly caused by what they expect to happen, not by what actually does happen. Moreover, experiments conducted in the 1930s (and therefore conveniently forgotten) demonstrated that withdrawing addicts could not reliably tell the difference between injections of morphine and water if they were misinformed in advance as to which was which. It follows from this that those people – writers, film directors, those involved in the so-called treatment of drug addicts, many of them no doubt acting from the best motives – who persist in peddling the myth of the seriousness of suffering from withdrawal are actually responsible for most of the suffering from withdrawal, and not the withdrawal itself.

Nor is this all. While no one dies of withdrawal from opiates, plenty of people die from the drugs which the Home Office thought it was the human right of the compensated prisoners to receive. Hundreds of people die each year of the effects of both heroin and the most commonly used substitute; and so, by a piece of intellectual alchemy that is truly astonishing, it becomes a human right for a non-serious condition to be treated by life-threatening methods. There could be no clearer illustration of Bentham's famous dictum, that talk of rights is not only nonsense, but nonsense on stilts.

Be that as it may, addicts do feel impelled to avoid abstinence from their drug; and – so the popular conception has it – since the drug is expensive, and its effects preclude regular work, addicts are driven to crime as sheep to market, addiction being merely an extenuation of crime rather than (as Aristotle would have had it) as an aggravation. Like all of the popular conceptions of heroin addiction and its relation to crime, this is a mistaken view. Addiction to opiates is certainly not necessarily incompatible with normal work. During the 1920s and 1930s, the majority of morphine addicts in the United States went to work normally, and it would be perfectly possible, from the economic point of view, for addicts in Britain to earn enough money by normal work to pay for their drug, if only they were self-disciplined enough to do so. Unfortunately, they are often drawn from chaotic, disintegrated and criminal backgrounds where work, even for non-addicts, is a rarity, and they choose instead to pursue criminal means to achieve their ends. (Indeed, most of them have to 'work' quite hard at their crime in order to raise enough for their drug; many have described to me how they go out early to burgle or steal, and in not a few statements made to the police that I have read in the course of my medico-legal work, I have found such locutions from heroin addicts as 'On Tuesday, I went out to work as usual.' For them, crime is the continuation of work by other means.)

Furthermore, the great majority of addicts who end up in British prisons have served prison sentences before they ever addicted themselves (a better and more accurate way of putting it than 'became addicted to') to heroin. Let us just reflect for a moment upon what this means. The majority of people who go to prison have been convicted of criminal offences about ten times before they receive their first prison sentence (unless – as is unusual – their first conviction is for a very serious offence). The clear-up rate for reported crimes in Britain, a considerable underestimate of all the crimes that are committed, is about one in 20. Thus, if (and admittedly this is a fair-sized, though not completely unreasonable, if) heroin-addicted criminals are like other criminals, they have committed up to two hundred crimes before they ever addicted themselves to heroin.

In other words, in so far as there is a relationship between heroin addiction and criminality, it is that a liability to addict oneself to heroin is a consequence of a tendency to criminality rather than the other way round. It is more true that crime causes addiction than that addiction causes crime. And indeed a certain number of addicts claim to have addicted themselves while in prison.

The reverse relationship between crime and addiction to the one that has gained currency is borne out in the biography of William S. Burroughs, the psychopathic literary hero of the counter-culture. Born into the wealthy Burroughs family, he was for much of his life in receipt of an allowance from that very family that he affected to despise. He went to Harvard, but found nothing there worthy of his sustained attention; what really interested him was the life of criminals whom he so admired that he wished to join them. This fascination preceded by many years his addiction to heroin; he was much influenced at the age of 12 by reading the memoirs of a criminal, for which he wrote an introduction to a much later edition, that described in graphic detail a brutal murder that Burroughs later extolled in his introduction as an instance of human authenticity. This was tactless of him, since he had murdered his own wife in Mexico, using the money of his despised family to escape the consequences of his crime, and suggests less than obsessive repentance for it.

Before he was ever addicted to heroin, Burroughs would go on to the New York subway and 'roll' (that is to say, steal from the pockets of) down-and-out drunks on the benches and platforms of the subway. At the time he was in receipt of an allowance adequate for his living expenses, so he could certainly not plead necessity in extenuation. What kind of mind would entertain, even for a moment, stealing from tramps? There could be no clearer illustration of the precedence of criminality to addiction.

This nevertheless leaves the question of 'treatment'. I use quotation marks because the very word implies that addicts are suffering from a *bona fide* illness that it is the duty and within the capacity of doctors to treat.

No one can doubt that heroin addiction has a physiological aspect, but the part that the physiological aspect plays overall is a small one. No one can doubt, either, that addicts often do themselves serious physical harm. Many of those whom I examined as they came into the prison in which I worked were clearly not a picture of health. Quite often I would tell them that if a film director were looking for extras to play the part of concentration camp inmates, they would be ideal (they understood at once the point I was making). They were thin and grossly malnourished, often to the point of near starvation; their skins were often covered in sores; they had fresh abscesses and sinuses from old unhealed ones. They had suffered from thrombosis of their veins, and occasionally life-threatening emboli in their lungs.

But the complications caused by behaviour do not make the behaviour itself an illness. Indeed, almost all behaviour has conceivable medical complications: certainly sport does, for example. Once when I explained my opinion to an addict he asked me whether I did not consider his addiction to be an illness because he had contracted hepatitis and other diseases as a result of it; to which I replied that I considered it no more an illness than I considered playing a football an illness when I saw a footballer with a broken leg.

Still the question of treatment, so-called, arises. The main form of such treatment in the recent past has been the substitution of heroin for methadone, usually in the form of a syrup taken once a day. The idea, in Britain at least, is that addicts should take this drug, as addictive as heroin, for at least 18 months. (Indeed, the government judges the success of drug clinics by the number of people whom they can persuade to take methadone for this prolonged period at least.) Does it work? The question is a vexed one.

In the first place, the treatment is itself dangerous. In some places, such as Dublin, more people die of the methadone poisoning than of heroin poisoning. In England and Wales there were 7,072 deaths caused by heroin between 1993 and 2004 and 3,298 caused by methadone. Since far fewer than a third of heroin addicts are treated with methadone, this suggests that methadone increased the total number of deaths rather than reduced them. It is a strange form of treatment that adds to mortality.

However, when addicts are given methadone in controlled trials, they tend to do better by comparison with those who are given placebo. Their level of criminality is reduced (but far from eliminated, the reduction in their criminality quite possibly being caused by the continual sedation that results from taking methadone), they use less heroin and indulge in fewer risk-taking activities such as sharing needles.

But this does not address the question as to whether such treatment answers the social problem of heroin addiction.

In the first place, it is in the very nature of the trials that the treated addicts are selected by their willingness to participate: they are not representative of addicts as a whole. This is particularly important where the disease, so-called, is a form of behaviour rather than a form of pathology.

Second, it is completely unjustified to conclude from the fact that a group decreases its use of heroin in a course of such a trial that giving methadone decreases the use of heroin in society as a whole. If you treat a person with open tuberculosis with anti-tubercular drugs, you not only treat the individual but interrupt the spread of the disease; but this is not the case with methadone treatment of heroin addiction for a very obvious reason. A little thought experiment will clarify this. Suppose you are the drug addict and I am your dealer. One day you come to me and say, 'Thank you very much, but I no longer need heroin because I am now getting methadone.' What do I do with the heroin I had earmarked for you? Do I simply flush it away down the lavatory as surplus to requirements, or do I find someone else to take it? Thus your supposed treatment has this result: a methadone *and* a heroin addict, whereas before there was only a heroin addict. And this fits far better what has happened in Britain than the idea that methadone is to heroin addiction what antituberculous treatment is to tuberculosis.

Nevertheless, the fact that there is a favourable response to methadone treatment according to some measures, and furthermore that large doses seem to be more effective than small ones, suggests to some people that addiction is an authentic disease. Why else would it respond to medicine?

Let us now consider the terrible disease of burglary. Is it not clear that the sufferers from this dread disease, burglars, could be successfully treated with donations of money? And is it not true that the larger the donations, the more successful the treatment would be? The supposition that addicts 'need' treatment, and cannot be expected to desist without it, overlooks the fact that many, indeed millions, of people have given up without it. The textbooks note that such experiences as religious conversion often 'cure' addiction; and although there are many undoubtedly pathophysiological diseases whose outcome is influenced by the sufferer's mental state, we should nevertheless be surprised if we found that a textbook of oncology stated that many cases of, say, cancer of the colon or the liver had been cured by religious conversion.

Moreover, two historical experiences suggest that addiction is more a question of meaning than of raw physiology. When Mao Tse-tung came to power in 1949, he took a pretty hard line with the millions of Chinese opium addicts. His ultimate method of persuasion was to have them shot if they did not give up: and they gave up, by the million. Let me be clear about the point I am trying to make, because I was once wilfully misunderstood by a well-known advocate of the medical treatment response to addiction. I am not saying, let us follow Mao; I am saying that, if Mao had told people with, say, rheumatoid or osteo-arthritis, for example, that they must have normal joints by next Friday or be shot, this would not have made sense; but it *did* make sense (though it was not very humane) to threaten addicts with being shot. Therefore, there is an important conceptual difference between most medical conditions and addiction.

Another important historical example is that of American conscripts during the Vietnam War. Scores of thousands of them addicted themselves to heroin while there; within two years of returning home, their rate of heroin addiction was no higher than that of conscripts who were drafted to go to Vietnam but never made it because the war ended (ie the 'normal' rate of the population from which they were drawn). The great majority of them received no medical assistance whatsoever.

Thus, heroin addiction is fundamentally a problem of the soul, if I may so put it: it is a problem of the meaning of life and of meaning *in* life. The vast majority of young addicts in Britain come from disastrous home backgrounds that our social and fiscal policies have so assiduously fostered and encouraged; they are without religious or political belief, they have no culture other than the most debased popular culture of which they are largely passive consumers, their economic prospects are poor, they live surrounded by the most hideous physical ugliness, their social world is Hobbesian, the households in which they live are unstable and of kaleidoscopically-changing membership, their level of education is a tribute to the wilful and sadistic incompetence of educationists of the past half century. Yet even they have a choice, and they know it full well, for when I ask them why they tried heroin, they often reply, 'I fell in with the wrong crowd'; they understand immediately and without difficulty the import of my reply, when I say to them, 'Is it not strange that while I meet many people who fell in with the wrong crowd, I never seem to meet any members of the wrong crowd itself?' Their laughter proves that they are by no means as stupid or incapable of reflection as the condescending professional saviours of the socially excluded, so-called, would have us believe.

All the information I have used is well-known and easily available in textbooks, yet no official notice whatever is taken of it, quite the reverse. Why? The reasons are no doubt numerous. It is flattering to the philanthropic vanity of some that there should be many helpless victims in our society. (There are such helpless victims, but comparatively few, and heroin addicts are not among them. One of the consequence of treating large numbers of people as helpless is that the genuine cases are often abominably neglected.) The supposedly helpless are, of course, an employment and career opportunity: large organisations depend upon the helplessness of one sector or another of the population. The poor, said a German bishop of the 16th century, are a goldmine; and so it has proved to be for our bureaucracies of welfare.

Finally, one must not forget the sheer moral cowardice that is so marked a feature of the intellectual life of our society: the fact that no one dares to say that heroin addicts have chosen not merely a foolish, but a bad, path. Victims must be immaculate and without sin; therefore heroin addicts are immaculate and without sin, above all not responsible for their own condition.

Here we see not only how sophisticated but how much more realistic and genuinely compassionate is the traditional religious world outlook than that of the sociological secularist, who sees in his fellow-beings only human billiard balls, acted upon by forces that they cannot resist. And I say this as one without religious belief.

DON'T LEGALISE DRUGS

THERE IS A PROGRESSION in the minds of men: first the unthinkable becomes thinkable, and then it becomes an orthodoxy whose truth seems so obvious that no one remembers that anyone ever thought differently. This is just what is happening with the idea of legalising drugs: it has reached the stage when millions of thinking people are agreed that allowing others to take whatever they like is the obvious, indeed only, solution to the social problems that arise from the consumption of drugs.

Man's desire to take mind-altering substances is as old as society itself – as are attempts to regulate their consumption. If intoxication in one form or another is inevitable, then so is customary or legal restraint upon that intoxication. But no society until our own has had to contend with the ready availability of so many different mind-altering drugs, combined with a citizenry jealous of its right to pursue its own pleasures in its own way.

The arguments in favour of legalising the use of all narcotic and stimulant drugs are twofold: philosophical and pragmatic. Neither argument is negligible, but both are mistaken, I believe, and both miss the point.

The philosophic argument is that, in a free society, adults should be permitted to do whatever they please, always provided that they are prepared to take the consequences of their own choices and that they cause no direct harm to others. The *locus classicus* for this point of view is John Stuart Mill's famous essay *On Liberty*: 'The only purpose for which power can be rightfully exercised over any member of the community, against his will, is to prevent harm to others,' Mill wrote. 'His own good, either physical or moral, is not a sufficient warrant.'

149

This radical individualism allows society no part whatever in shaping, determining or enforcing a moral code: in short, we have nothing in common but our continual agreement not to interfere with one another as we go about seeking our private pleasures.

In practice, of course, it is exceedingly difficult to make people take all the consequences of their own actions – as they must, if Mill's great principle is to serve as a philosophical guide to policy. Addiction to, or regular use of, most currently prohibited drugs cannot affect only the person who takes them – and not his spouse, children, neighbours or employers. No man, except possibly a hermit, is an island; and so it is virtually impossible for Mill's principle to apply to any human action whatever, let alone shooting up heroin or smoking crack. Such a principle is virtually useless in determining what should or should not be permitted.

Perhaps we ought not be too harsh on Mill's principle: it is not at all clear that anyone has ever thought of a better one. But that is precisely the point. Human affairs cannot be decided by an appeal to an infallible rule, expressible in a few words, whose simple application can decide all cases, including whether drugs should be freely available to the entire adult population. Philosophical fundamentalism is not preferable to the religious variety, and because the *desiderata* of human life are many, and often in conflict with one another, mere philosophical inconsistency in policy – such as permitting the consumption of alcohol while outlawing cocaine – is not a sufficient argument against that policy. We all value freedom, and we all value order; sometimes we sacrifice freedom for order, and sometimes order for freedom. But once a prohibition has been removed, it is hard to restore, even when the newfound freedom proves to have been ill-conceived and socially disastrous.

Even Mill came to see the limitations of his own principle as a guide for policy and to deny that all pleasures were of equal significance for human existence. It was better, he said, to be Socrates discontented than a fool satisfied. Mill acknowledged that some goals were intrinsically worthier of pursuit than others.

This being the case, not all freedoms are equal, and neither are all limitations of freedom: some are serious and some trivial. The freedom we cherish – or should cherish – is not merely that of satisfying our appetites, whatever they happen to be. We are not Dickensian Harold Skimpoles, exclaiming in protest that 'Even the butterflies are free!' We are not children who chafe at restrictions because they are restrictions. And we even recognise the apparent paradox that some limitations to our freedoms have the consequence of making us freer overall. The freest man is not the one who slavishly follows his appetites and desires throughout his life – as all too many of my patients have discovered to their cost.

We are prepared to accept limitations to our freedoms for many reasons, not just that of public order. Take an extreme hypothetical case: public exhibitions of necrophilia are quite rightly not permitted, though on Mill's principle they should be. A corpse has no interests and cannot be harmed, because it is no longer a person; and no member of the public is harmed if he has agreed to attend such an exhibition.

Our resolve to prohibit such exhibitions would not be altered if we discovered that millions of people wished to attend them or even if we discovered that millions already were attending them illicitly. Our objection is not based upon pragmatic considerations or upon a head count: it is based upon the wrongness of the would-be exhibitions themselves. The fact that the prohibition represents a genuine restriction of our freedom is of no account.

It might be argued that the freedom to choose among a variety of intoxicating substances is a much more important freedom and that millions of people have derived innocent fun from taking stimulants and narcotics. But the consumption of drugs has the effect of reducing men's freedom by circumscribing the range of their interests. It impairs their ability to pursue more important human aims, such as raising a family and fulfilling civic obligations. Very often, particularly in the case of drugs such as cannabis and crack cocaine, it impairs their ability or desire to pursue, and suitability for, gainful employment and promotes parasitism. Moreover, far from being expanders of consciousness, most drugs severely limit it. One of the most striking characteristics of drug-takers is their intense and tedious self-absorption; and their journeys into inner space are generally forays into inner vacuums. Drug-taking is a lazy man's way of pursuing happiness and wisdom, and the shortcut turns out to be the deadest of dead ends. We lose remarkably little by not being permitted to take drugs.

The idea that freedom is merely the ability to act upon one's whims is surely very thin and hardly begins to capture the complexities of human existence; a man whose appetite is his law strikes us not as liberated but enslaved. And when such a narrowly conceived freedom is made the touchstone of public policy, a dissolution of society is bound to follow. No culture that makes publicly sanctioned self-indulgence its highest good can long survive: a radical egotism is bound to ensue, in which any limitations upon personal behaviour are experienced as infringements of basic rights.

Distinctions between the important and the trivial, between the freedom to criticise received ideas and the freedom to take LSD, are precisely the standards that keep societies from barbarism.

So the legalisation of drugs cannot be supported by philosophical principle. But if the pragmatic argument in favour of legalisation were strong enough, it might overwhelm other objections. It is upon this argument that proponents of legalisation rest the larger part of their case.

The argument is that the overwhelming majority of the harm done to society by the consumption of currently illicit drugs is caused not by their pharmacological properties but by their prohibition and the resultant criminal activity that prohibition always calls into being. Simple reflection tells us that a supply invariably grows up to meet a demand; and when the demand is widespread suppression is useless. Indeed, it is harmful, since – by raising the price of the commodity in question – it raises the profits of middlemen, which gives them an even more powerful incentive to stimulate demand further. The vast profits to be made from cocaine and heroin – which, were it not for their illegality, would be cheap and easily affordable even by the poorest in affluent societies – exert a deeply corrupting effect on producers, distributors, consumers and law enforcers alike. Besides, it is well known that illegality in itself has attractions for youth already inclined to disaffection. Even many of the harmful physical effects of illicit drugs stem from their illegal status: for example, fluctuations in the purity of heroin bought on the street are responsible for many of the deaths by overdose. If the sale and consumption of such drugs were legalised, consumers would know how much they were taking and thus avoid overdoses.

Moreover, since society already permits the use of some mind-altering substances known to be both addictive and harmful, such as alcohol and nicotine, in prohibiting others it appears hypocritical, arbitrary and dictatorial. Its hypocrisy, as well as its patent failure to enforce its prohibitions successfully, leads inevitably to a decline in respect for the law as a whole. Thus, things fall apart and the centre cannot hold.

It stands to reason, therefore, that all these problems would be resolved at a stroke if everyone were permitted to smoke, swallow, or inject anything he chose. The corruption of the police, the luring of children of 11 and 12 into illegal activities, the making of such vast sums of money by drug dealing that legitimate work seems pointless and silly by comparison, and the turf wars that make poor neighbourhoods so exceedingly violent and dangerous, would all cease at once were drug taking to be decriminalised and the supply regulated in the same way as is that of alcohol.

But a certain modesty in the face of an inherently unknowable future is surely advisable. That is why prudence is a political virtue: what stands to reason should happen does not necessarily happen in practice. As Goethe said, all theory (even of the monetarist or free-market variety) is grey, but green springs the golden tree of life. If drugs were legalised, I suspect that the golden tree of life might spring some unpleasant surprises.

It is of course true, but only trivially so, that the present illegality of drugs is the cause of the criminality surrounding their distribution. Likewise, it is the desirability of cars, their restricted supply and the lack of serious sanction for their misappropriation which creates car thieves; as far as I am aware, no one has ever suggested that the law which proscribes the taking of other peoples' cars, however weakly enforced, should therefore be abandoned. Similarly, the impossibility of winning the 'war' against burglary, robbery or fraud has never been used as an argument that these categories of crime should be abandoned.

And so long as the demand for material goods outstrips supply, people will be tempted to commit criminal acts against the owners of property. This is not an argument, in my view, against private property or in favour of the common ownership of all goods. It does suggest, however, that we shall need a police force for a long time to come.

In any case, there are reasons to doubt whether the crime rate would fall quite as dramatically as advocates of legalisation have suggested. Amsterdam, where access to drugs has been relatively unproblematic, is among the most violent and squalid cities in Europe. The idea behind crime – of getting rich, or at least richer, quickly and without much effort – is unlikely to disappear once drugs are freely available to all who want them. And it may be that officially sanctioned anti-social behaviour – the official lifting of taboos – breeds yet more anti-social behaviour, as the 'broken windows' theory would suggest.

Having met large numbers of drug dealers in prison, I doubt that they would return to respectable life if the principal article of their commerce were to be legalised. Far from evincing a desire to be reincorporated into the world of regular work, they express a deep contempt for it and regard those who accept the bargain of a fair day's work for a fair day's pay as cowards and fools. A life of crime has its attractions for many who would otherwise lead a mundane existence. So long as there is the possibility of a lucrative racket or illegal traffic, such people will find it and extend its scope. Therefore, since even legalisers would hesitate to allow children to take drugs, decriminalisation might easily result in dealers turning their attentions to younger and younger children, who – in the permissive atmosphere that even now prevails – have already been inducted into the drug subculture in alarmingly high numbers. They would also find something else to deal in.

Those who do not deal in drugs but commit crimes to fund their consumption of them are, of course, more numerous than large-scale dealers. And it is true that once opiate addicts, for example, enter a treatment programme, which often includes maintenance doses of methadone, the rate at which they commit crimes sometimes falls markedly. The drug clinic in my hospital claimed an 80 percent reduction in criminal convictions among heroin addicts once they had been stabilised on methadone.

This is impressive, but it is not certain that the results should be generalised. First, as we have already seen, the patients are self-selected: they have some motivation to change, otherwise they would not have attended the clinic in the first place. Only a minority of addicts attend, and therefore it is not safe to conclude that, if other addicts were to receive methadone, their criminal activity would similarly diminish.

Second, a decline in convictions is not necessarily the same as a decline in criminal acts. If methadone stabilises an addict's life, he may become a more competent criminal, one who is harder to catch. Moreover, when the police in our city do catch an addict, they are less likely to prosecute him if he can prove that he is undergoing anything remotely resembling psychiatric treatment. They return him directly to his doctor. Having once had a psychiatric consultation is an all-purpose alibi for a robber or a burglar; many police officers, who do not want to fill in the 20-odd forms it now takes to charge anyone with anything in England, appear to consider a single contact with a psychiatrist sufficient to deprive anyone of legal responsibility for crime forever.

Third, the rate of criminal activity among those drug addicts who receive methadone from the clinic, though reduced, remains very high. The deputy director of the clinic estimates that the number of criminal acts committed by his average patient (as judged by self-report) was 250 per year before entering treatment and 50 afterward. It may well be that the real difference is considerably less than this, because the patients have an incentive to exaggerate it to secure the continuation of their methadone. But clearly, many opiate addicts who receive their drugs legally and free of charge continue to commit large numbers of crimes. In my clinics in prison, I see numerous prisoners who were on methadone when they committed the crime for which they are incarcerated.

Why do addicts given their drug free of charge continue to commit crimes? Some addicts, of course, continue to take drugs other than those prescribed and claim to have to fund their consumption of them. So long as any restriction whatever regulates the consumption of drugs, many addicts will seek them illicitly, regardless of what they receive legally. In addition, drugs such as cannabis and crack cocaine may themselves exert a long-term effect on a person's ability to earn a living and severely limit rather than expand his horizons and mental repertoire. They sap the will or the ability of an addict to make long-term plans. While drugs are the focus of an addict's life, they are not all he needs to live, and many addicts thus continue to procure the rest of what they need by criminal means.

For the proposed legalisation of drugs to have its much-vaunted beneficial effect on the rate of criminality, such drugs would have to be both cheap and readily available. The legalisers assume that there is a natural limit to the demand for these drugs, and that if their consumption were legalised, the demand would not increase substantially. Those psychologically unstable persons currently taking drugs would continue to do so, with the necessity to commit crimes removed, while psychologically stabler people (such as you and I and our children) would not be enticed to take drugs by their new legal status and cheapness. But price and availability, I need hardly say, exert a profound effect on consumption: the cheaper alcohol becomes, for example, the more of it is consumed, at least within quite wide limits.

I have personal experience of this effect. I once worked as a doctor on a British government aid project to Africa. We were building a road through remote African bush. The contract stipulated that the construction company could import, free of all taxes, alcoholic drinks from the United Kingdom. These drinks the company then sold to its British workers at cost, in the local currency at the official exchange rate, which was approximately one-sixth the black-market rate. A litre bottle of gin thus cost less than 50 pence and could be sold on the open market for almost five pounds, those five pounds being then available to recycle into more bottles of gin, and so on, quite literally *ad nauseam*. So it was theoretically possible to remain dead drunk for several years for an initial outlay of less than a pound.

Of course, the necessity to go to work somewhat limited the workers' consumption of alcohol. Nevertheless, drunkenness among them far outstripped anything I have ever seen, before or since. I discovered that, when alcohol is effectively free of charge, a fifth of British construction workers will regularly go to bed so drunk that they are incontinent both of urine and faeces. I remember one man who very rarely got as far as his bed at night: he fell asleep in the lavatory, where he was usually found the next morning. Half the men shook in the mornings and resorted to the hair of the dog to steady their hands before they drove their bulldozers and other heavy machines (which they frequently wrecked, at enormous expense to the British taxpayer). The men were either drunk or hung over for months on end.

True, construction workers are notoriously liable to drink heavily, but in these circumstances even formerly moderate drinkers turned alcoholic and eventually suffered from *delirium tremens*. The heavy drinking occurred not because of the isolation of the African bush: not only did the company provide sports facilities for its workers, but there were many other ways to occupy oneself there. Other groups of workers in the bush whom I visited, who did not have the same rights of importation of alcoholic drink but had to purchase it at normal prices, were not nearly as drunk. And when the company asked its workers what it could do to improve their conditions, they unanimously asked for a further reduction in the price of alcohol, because they could think of nothing else to ask for.

The conclusion was inescapable: that a susceptible population had responded to the low price of alcohol, and the lack of other effective restraints upon its consumption, by drinking destructively large quantities of it. The health of many men suffered as a consequence, as did their capacity for work, and they gained a well-deserved local reputation for reprehensible, violent, antisocial behaviour.

It is therefore perfectly possible that the demand for drugs, including opiates, would rise dramatically were their price to fall and their availability to increase. And if it is true that the consumption of those drugs such as cannabis and cocaine in itself predisposes to criminal behaviour (as data from our clinic suggested), it is also possible that the effect on the rate of criminality of this rise in consumption would swamp the decrease that resulted from decriminalisation. We would have just as much crime in aggregate as before, but many more addicts.

The intermediate position on drug legalisation, such as that espoused by Ethan Nadelmann, director of the Lindesmith Center, a drug policy research institute sponsored by financier George Soros, is emphatically not the answer to drug-related crime. This view holds that it should be easy for addicts to receive opiate drugs from doctors, either free or at cost, and that they should receive them in municipal injecting rooms, such as now exist in Zurich. But in Liverpool, 2,000 people of a population of 600,000 receive official prescriptions for methadone: and this once proud and prosperous city was for long the world capital of drug-motivated burglary, according to the police and independent researchers.

Of course, many addicts in Liverpool are not yet on methadone, because the clinics are insufficient in number to deal with the demand. If the city expended more money on clinics, perhaps the number of addicts in treatment could be increased five- or tenfold. But would that solve the problem of burglary in Liverpool? No, because the hypothesis on which the increased prescription is based (which I believe to be mistaken in any case) means that new addicts, as yet not prescribed heroin, would commit the same crimes as those who were now prescribed heroin would once have committed. Yet more clinics dispensing yet more methadone would then be needed, and so on, if not *ad infinitum*, at least until there were very many of them.

In fact Britain, which has had a relatively liberal approach to the prescribing of opiate drugs to addicts since 1928 (I myself have prescribed heroin to addicts), has seen an explosive increase in addiction to opiates and all the evils associated with it since the 1960s, despite that liberal policy. A few hundred have become more than a hundred thousand. At the heart of Nadelmann's position, then, is an evasion. The legal and liberal provision of drugs for people who are already addicted to them will not reduce the economic benefits to dealers of pushing these drugs, at least until the entire susceptible population is addicted and in a treatment programme. On the argument of the legalisers, so long as there are addicts who have to resort to the black market for their drugs, there will be drug-associated crime. Nadelmann assumes that the number of potential addicts would not soar under considerably more liberal drug laws. I cannot muster such Panglossian optimism.

The problem of reducing the amount of crime committed by individual addicts is emphatically not the same as the problem of reducing the amount of crime committed by addicts as a whole. I can illustrate what I mean by an analogy: it is often claimed that prison does not work because many prisoners are recidivists who, by definition, failed to be deterred from further wrongdoing by their last prison sentence. But does any sensible person believe that the abolition of prisons in their entirety would not reduce the numbers of the law-abiding? The murder rate in New York and the rate of drunken driving in Britain have not been reduced by a sudden upsurge in the love of humanity, but by the effective threat of punishment. An institution such as prison can work for society even if it does not work for an individual.

Don't Legalise Drugs

The situation could be very much worse than I have suggested hitherto, however, if we legalised the consumption of drugs other than opiates. So far I have considered mainly opiates, which exert a generally tranquillising effect. If opiate addicts commit crimes even when they receive their drugs free of charge, it is because they are unwilling to meet their other needs any other way; but there are, unfortunately, drugs whose consumption directly leads to violence because of their psychopharmacological properties and not merely because of the criminality associated with their distribution. Stimulant drugs such as crack cocaine provoke paranoia, increase aggression and promote violence. Much of this violence takes place in the home, as the relatives of crack-takers will testify. It is something I know from personal acquaintance by working in casualty and in the wards of our hospital. Only someone who has not been assaulted by drug-takers rendered psychotic by their drug could view with equanimity the prospect of the further spread of the abuse of stimulants.

And no one should underestimate the possibility that the use of stimulant drugs could spread very much wider, and become far more general, than it is now, if restraints on their use were relaxed. The importation of the mildly stimulant khat is legal in Britain, and a proportion of our community of Somali refugees devotes its entire life to chewing the leaves that contain the stimulant, miring these refugees in far worse poverty than they would otherwise experience. The reason that the khat habit has not spread to the rest of the population is that it takes an entire day's chewing of disgustingly bitter leaves to gain the comparatively mild pharmacological effect. The point is, however, that once the use of a stimulant becomes culturally acceptable and normal, it can easily become so general as to exert devastating social effects. And the kinds of stimulants on offer in Western cities – cocaine, crack, amphetamines – are vastly more attractive than khat.

In claiming that prohibition, not the drugs themselves, is the problem, Nadelmann and many others – even policemen – have said that 'the war on drugs is lost'. But to demand a yes or no answer to the question 'Is the war against drugs being won?' is like demanding a yes or no answer to the question 'Have you stopped beating your wife yet?' Never can an unimaginative and fundamentally stupid metaphor have exerted a more baleful effect upon proper thought.

Let us ask whether medicine is winning the war against death.

The answer is obviously no, it isn't winning: the one fundamental rule of human existence remains, unfortunately, one man one death. And this is despite the fact that upwards of 8 percent of our gross domestic product (to say nothing of the efforts of other countries) goes into the fight against death. Was ever a war more expensively lost?

And if the war against drugs is lost, then so are the wars against theft, speeding, incest, fraud, rape, murder, arson and illegal parking. Few, if any, such wars are winnable. So let us all do anything we choose.

Even the legalisers' argument that permitting the purchase and use of drugs as freely as Milton Friedman suggests will necessarily result in less governmental and other official interference in our lives is not plausible. To the contrary, if the use of narcotics and stimulants were to become virtually universal, as is by no means impossible, the number of situations in which compulsory checks upon people would have to be carried out, for reasons of public safety, would increase enormously. Pharmacies, banks, schools, hospitals – indeed, all organisations dealing with the public – might feel obliged to check regularly and randomly on the drug consumption of their employees. The general use of such drugs would increase the *locus standi* of innumerable agencies, public and private, to interfere in our lives; and freedom from interference, far from having increased, would have drastically shrunk.

Don't Legalise Drugs

The present situation is bad, undoubtedly; but few are the situations so bad that they cannot be made worse by a wrong policy decision.

The extreme intellectual elegance of the proposal to legalise the distribution and consumption of drugs, touted as the solution to so many problems at once (AIDS, crime, overcrowding in the prisons and even the attractiveness of drugs to foolish young people) should give rise to scepticism. Social problems are not usually like that. Analogies with the Prohibition era, often drawn by those who would legalise drugs, are false and inexact: it is one thing to attempt to ban a substance that has been in customary use for centuries by at least nine-tenths of the adult population, and quite another to retain a ban on substances that are still not in customary use, in an attempt to ensure that they never do become customary.

Surely we have already slid down enough slippery slopes in the last 40 years without looking for more such slopes to slide down.

MULTICULTURALISM STARTS LOSING ITS LUSTRE

MULTICULTURALISM RESTS ON the supposition – or better, the dishonest pretence – that all cultures are equal in all respects and that no fundamental conflict can arise between the customs, mores and philosophical outlooks of two different cultures. The multiculturalist preaches that, in an age of mass migration, society can (and should) be a kind of salad bowl, a receptacle for wonderful exotic ingredients from around the world, the more the better, each bringing its special flavour to the cultural admixture. For the salad to be delicious, no ingredient should predominate and impose its flavour on the others.

Even as a culinary metaphor, this view is wrong: every cook knows that not every ingredient blends with every other. But the spread and influence of an idea is by no means necessarily proportional to its intrinsic worth, including (perhaps especially) among those who gain their living by playing with ideas, the intelligentsia.

Reality, though, has a way of revenging itself upon the frivolous, and September 11 has seemingly concentrated minds a little. Some signs indicate that in Britain the pieties of multiculturalism, for years an official orthodoxy, are beginning to face a challenge.

The then Home Secretary, David Blunkett, for example, suddenly announced that immigrants to Britain should learn English. Blunkett made this heterodox suggestion in response to riotous clashes in northern England between white youths and Muslim youths of Pakistani descent. Liberals predictably decried his comments as tactless at best and proto-fascist at worst. Didn't they give succour to the vicious xenophobic elements in British society, perhaps even portending a new dark age of intolerance?

In fact Blunkett's remarks were both on and off the mark. Doubtless all of the rioting Muslim youths spoke English. Hardly any British-born young men and women of South Asian descent do not speak it – though some, given the undemanding British school system, speak it poorly. So it is not true, as Blunkett implied, that a failure to learn English was to blame for the rioters' aggrieved sense of being unequal citizens in British society.

Yet Blunkett was right in other respects. Though the rioting youths could speak English, the brides they would bring back from Pakistan would not – and, furthermore, never would. Many women I have encountered as patients who came to Britain from Pakistan 30 years ago, at age 16 or 18, still know little English – but not necessarily from any unwillingness to learn. Their husbands actively prevented them from learning the language, to make sure that they would stay enclosed in a ghetto and not get any ideas above their station. The same rioting youths who protested at British society's failure to accept them as equal citizens have themselves sought to reproduce the unequal social patterns of rural Pakistan, half a world away, because it suited them to do so.

Multiculturalism encourages this stance. If all cultures are equal, and none has the right to impose its standards on any other, what is wrong with the immigrant ghettos that have emerged, where the population (that is to say, the male population) enjoys, *de facto*, extraterritorial rights? If it is the custom of their ancestral culture to keep girls out of school and force them into marriages that they do not want and to confiscate the passports that the British government issues them for their personal use, what can a multiculturalist object to without asserting the superiority of his own values?

Giving further weight to Blunkett's remarks is the silliness of the government language practices that multiculturalism has spawned. For example, one can take the driver's licence test in Britain in a startling variety of languages. Spoken instructions come even in the various dialects of Albanian, Kurdish and Lingala. For the written part, test takers need not know how to read the Latin alphabet (that would be discriminatory): officials provide the questions in the script of your choice. Never mind that traffic signs are still in English.

Nor is the driver's test anomalous. Government pamphlets, including those concerning health and social security benefits, now routinely appear in myriad languages – at public expense. When I went to vote in the local elections not long ago, I saw notices in various Indian languages and in Vietnamese explaining how to cast a vote. And at my local airport, the sign directing travellers to the line for returning British passport holders is written not only in English, but in Bengali, Hindi, Punjabi and Urdu (each with its own script): proof that the granting of citizenship requires no proficiency in the national language.

These practices send the message that newcomers to Britain have no obligation to learn English – indeed, that the obligation is the other way around: that the British state must make itself clear in Arabic, Farsi, Russian, Somali, Swahili and many other languages. British officialdom doubtless does not know that the confusion of languages after the Tower of Babel fell was meant as a punishment, not a reward.

In today's multicultural climate the general population, it seems, has the duty to be familiar with the immigrant tongues too. My local state schools now teach Bengali and Urdu, so that the 'local' (ie, white) population may learn to mix better with the immigrant population. While I have no objection to the children of immigrants speaking their parents' native tongue at home, or to the private decision of anyone to master any language he chooses, a private choice is very different from the government's ideological decision to offer such languages (of minor global importance) in the state schools. How is it possible not to see such a decision as deliberately subversive of belief in the primacy (in Britain) of European culture – with which, after all, the immigrants have chosen to throw in their lot?

Clumsy and maladroit as Blunkett may have been, then, he drew attention to an important issue – one that makes clear what an absurd and at heart insincere doctrine multiculturalism is. Yet it is also a dangerous doctrine, inspiring policies certain to maintain minorities in their impoverishment, stoke their resentment and exacerbate racial tensions – while providing employment for a growing number of bureaucrats.

Another Blairite who once uncritically espoused multicultural pieties has recently undergone a conversion: Trevor Phillips, the then chairman of the Commission for Racial Equality and now head of the Commission for Equalities and Human Rights. In an interview with *The Times*, Phillips, a black man born in Guyana, argued that England should abandon the whole concept of multiculturalism since it was doing more harm than good. Officials should even stop using the word itself, he added.

Phillips noted that Britain has a long and mostly distinguished history of accepting people to its shores and integrating them into its national life, while at the same time deriving benefits from whatever skills they may have brought with them. Britishness has been a cultural, not a racial or biological, concept with a tradition of tolerance, compromise, civility, gentlemanly reserve, respect for privacy, individuality (evident as far back as Chaucer's time), a ready acceptance of and even affection for eccentricity, a belief in the rule of law, a profound sense of irony and a desire for fair play: in short, the common decency that Orwell wrote of so eloquently.

Utopian intellectuals, including the theorists of multiculturalism, deride many of these now-weakened British characteristics, on the grounds that they were never universal among the population (but what characteristics are?) and had more drawbacks than advantages. But Britain's common decency proved self-evident to generations of immigrants and refugees, among them my mother, who, arriving in Britain from Germany in 1938, noticed them instantly, to her relief and great admiration.

My family history attests further to British society's generous capacity to absorb. My father, whose immigrant parents never learned to speak English well, attended a slum school during and just after World War I, with classmates so poor that they went hungry and barefoot. Despite his background, my father found himself inducted into British culture by teachers who did not believe that the ability to understand and appreciate Milton or Shakespeare, or to make a contribution to national life, depended on social class or required roots in the soil going back before the Norman conquest. His teachers had the same faith in the liberating power of high culture, in its universal value and appeal, that many British workers then shared. As the historian Jonathan Rose has beautifully demonstrated in *The Intellectual Life of the British Working Classes*, many ordinary English working-men, who led lives of sometimes numbing toil and financial hardship, nevertheless devoted much of their little spare time and tiny wages to improving their lives by strenuous reading of good literature, of whose transcendent value they had no doubt – a faith borne out by the success many of them attained in later years.

My father's teachers were the only people I ever heard him mention with unqualified admiration and gratitude. And he was right to do so: their philosophy was infinitely more generous than that of the multiculturalists who succeeded them. They had no desire to enclose my father in the world that his parents had fled. And they understood that, for society to avoid bitter internal conflicts, everyone had to share important elements of culture and historical knowledge that would result in a shared identity. Not by chance did Trevor Phillips regret 80 years later that teachers were instructing children less and less in the great works of English literature, especially Shakespeare – a deprivation wrought not because teachers were complying with any spontaneous demand from below but because they were implementing the theories of elite educationists, especially the multiculturalists.

Phillips rightly pointed out that English literature is the perfect vehicle for promoting a shared identity. Not to teach Shakespeare or other giants of British culture is to provide no worthwhile tradition with which the increasingly diverse population can identify. Without such a tradition, nothing deeper than the ephemeral products of popular culture will be on hand to unite that population, even as profound cultural differences divide it. A shared culture consisting of nothing but pop ephemera will likely arouse the justified contempt of immigrants and their children, driving them into ethnic, cultural or ideological enclaves in search of something more mentally and spiritually nourishing – thereby increasing social tensions, sometimes disastrously.

The shared identity that my father's teachers believed in was not an imposed uniformity, as present-day critics allege; they did not seek to turn out mental clones. Far from it. Part of that shared identity – a source of pride – was inventiveness and freedom of thought, the permission for the mind to voyage forever on strange seas of thought alone (as Wordsworth described Newton). And this shared identity relieved those who participated in it of the need to cling too strongly to other, potentially conflicting, identities. The national identity was strong but loose, permitting a great deal of personal freedom and give-and-take – much more so, usually, than the ethnic identities that immigrants bring with them. Freedom of religious belief was complete, as was practice, provided that it complied with the law and claimed no special privileges for itself. Induction into British culture did not fetter or circumscribe the immigrant, therefore, any more than speaking English determines what anyone has to say.

Britain's openness is precisely what made it so attractive to immigrants. While by no means without blemish, Britain's history of openness (compared with most societies) goes back a long way, and it has allowed many groups of newcomers to become national assets. The Huguenots, for example, immensely enriched British cultural and economic life. Before their arrival, all silk in Britain came from France; after their arrival, most French silk came from Britain. In time the Huguenots became intensely British – is any writer more British than De Quincey? – but for many years they had their own churches, and some spoke French at home until well into the 19th century.

It was this tradition of integration that Phillips eloquently invoked in his interview. Since the chairmen of quasi-governmental bodies such as his are not known for speaking courageously out of turn, his words most likely reflected the thinking of the government, alarmed at the extent of sympathy in the Muslim population for the September 11 terrorists.

Phillips failed to mention one vital difference between previous and contemporary influxes into Britain, however. The relative tolerance and flexibility that he praises were spontaneous, informal, and undirected, without official interference. It never occurred to anyone in my father's day that the children of immigrants should or would have a fundamentally different culture from that of the larger population, or that they would have any cultural peculiarities or sensibilities that needed catering to. They would be British without qualification. These immigrants, of course, arrived during a prolonged era of national self-confidence, when Britain was either a rising or a risen power. The generosity of my father's teachers grew out of pride in their culture and country.

Since then, much has changed. We live in a time of deep mistrust of spontaneous, undirected social processes – a mistrust of which Phillips's former organisation was one symptom. The Commission for Racial Equality that he chaired believed that racial prejudice and unfairness could only be eradicated if the government ceaselessly monitored racial statistics for inequalities (several professional organisations that I belong to repeatedly try to extract from me my 'ethnic' group, though I refuse to answer). Paradoxically, the commission simultaneously denied, at least in theory, any underlying reality to the racial and ethnic categories into which it divided people for monitoring purposes, since it took for granted that any low levels in achievement among the monitored racial groups must result from prejudice alone, not from any differences in the attitude or behaviour of those groups. Without official bureaucratic interference, in this view, society will remain mired in racial prejudice. Minorities will stagnate or even retrogress.

In addition, confidence in Britain's historical and cultural record, as embodying anything worthwhile, let alone uniquely valuable, has all but vanished. Those things that the nation once glorified, it now derides and satirises. Not so long ago the then prime minister attacked the very notion that the British past held anything worth preserving, the 'forces of conservatism' being for him a synonym for evil. Reality, belatedly, taught him otherwise.

No doubt the shift in attitude partly results from the collapse of British power and the nation's long retreat from world importance. But it also results from the growth of the intellectual class, whose livelihood depends on ceaseless carping.

Thanks to the intellectuals, for instance, the teaching of history has become an ideological minefield, with grievance groups demanding that their ancestors' suffering enjoy special status in the narrative. And if British history and culture are nothing but the story of internal and external oppression, of injustice and exploitation, why should those who come to these shores learn our national traditions and culture? Much better for them just to keep their own. One professor of race relations, Bikhu Parekh, has even suggested that Britain should change its name, which has so many negative historical connotations for millions around the world. Now that Britain has become so ineradicably multicultural, he says, there is no justification for it to be 'British' any more.

Such fatuities are likely, and perhaps are intended, to produce an extreme reaction from the native-born population, demonstrating that the original contention was correct: that the British tradition is simply one of violent intolerance and oppression – from which we need such luminaries as the professor, wielding coercive administrative powers, to deliver us.

A new mass immigration to Britain from every region of the globe, in which the differences between the immigrants and the host population are profound, has occurred precisely at the moment when the multiculturalists have helped undermine the capacity of British culture to absorb them, in the hope that 'a community of communities' (to use Parekh's phrase) would emerge: in short, that the lion of the Somali tribal ethic would somehow lie down with the lamb of the British law.

To be sure, many people flee their homelands to live under our rule of law. Among my patients were some refugees, most of them people of intelligence, drive and clear-sightedness. They had no doubts about the benefits of the rule of law, having experienced the opposite in their own flesh and blood. They knew the relief of not fearing the nocturnal knock at the door and of passing a man in uniform without trembling with anxiety.

They knew also that the rule of law is an historical achievement, not the natural state of man. It was a pleasure to hear my refugee patients descant on that great historical achievement. Because of their own experience, they did not take it for granted. They knew that it arose from a long philosophical and political development, one unique in world history. They knew that it is a fragile achievement and easily destroyed.

I recall a highly intelligent Iranian refugee who consulted me. The medical part of the consultation over, we began to chat about Iranian affairs. He was a political philosopher not by training or inclination but by experience and necessity. He felt that, in the end, the clerical regime had done an immense service to the cause of political secularism in Iran, because even previously religious people now deeply opposed clerical rule. The clerics had done more damage to the cause of Islam among the Iranian population by their brutality and corruption than the infidels could ever inflict. His problem, of course, was that he lived in the personal short term, not the historical long run.

He appreciated deeply the British institutions that now protected him. He had experienced occasional hostility from individual Britons, but he realised that it was the product of ineradicable human nature, not of official malice. Above all, he said, Britain had a different history from Iran's – of struggle no doubt, but also of compromise – which allowed us to take our liberty for granted (a dangerous thing to do). It was, he said, a very valuable and inspiring history. What impressed him first when he arrived was how everyone just assumed that he could say what he liked, without fear of retribution – a freedom above price. But he recognised that he could only be part of that worthy society if he chose to fit in, abandoning any aspects of his Iranian culture incompatible with it, which he was only too happy to do. The fundamental demands and responsibilities, he felt, were upon the immigrant, not upon the host country.

It would be vain to suggest that all immigrants are as conscious of these demands and responsibilities as he. And if we are to avoid violently disaffected and resentful ethnic enclaves in our midst, we need to teach immigrants that the freedom, prosperity and tolerance they enjoy result from a long spiritual and cultural development, not to be taken for granted, and that they have a magnificence and grandeur.

In the modern multicultural climate, though, there is no quick way of doing this. Because of the ideological cacophony that drowns out this cardinal, though obvious message, it is impossible to relay it unself-consciously, as my father's teachers had done. Nor would one wish the message to harden into an official dogma: the answer to a false orthodoxy is not another orthodoxy that denies contrary evidence. We must persuade, not coerce or indoctrinate, and to do so we must first disabuse our intellectuals of the notion – frivolous but damaging – that society should be a cultural salad.

THE MARRIAGE OF REASON
AND NIGHTMARE

DESPITE THE UNPRECEDENTED prosperity that reigned until recently, we British were not as happy as we should have been, at least if the causes of human happiness were mainly economic. It turned out, however, that ever-rising consumption was not the same thing as ever-greater contentment. Yet no one was quite sure what else was necessary. Anti-depressants in the water supply, perhaps? Urban life — and in the modern world, most life is urban — has an unpleasant edge in Britain, even in the midst of plenty. You hardly dare look a stranger in the eye, lest he take violent offence; the young, poor and prosperous alike, have imposed a curfew on the old after dark, and on everyone on Friday and Saturday nights; the age at which fellow citizens provoke fear declines constantly, so that one avoids even aggregations of eight-year-olds, as though they were piranhas in a jungle river.

The British state, for its part, is able to bully and regulate at will, thanks to technology — yet it seems to carry out these actions for their own sake, not for any higher purpose. The privatisation of morality is so complete that no code of conduct is generally accepted, save that you should do what you can get away with; sufficient unto the day is the pleasure thereof. Nowhere in the developed world has civilisation gone so fast and so far into reverse as here, at least to the extent to which civilisation is made up of the small change and amenities of life.

No contemporary British writer captures our malaise better than did J.G. Ballard. In a writing career of half a century, he explored with acuity, from the eyrie of his respectable suburban home outside London, the anxieties of modern existence — of what he called the marriage of reason and nightmare. The reason is our technological advance, the nightmare the uses to which we have put it.

Much in Ballard's biography explains his sensitivity to aspects of modern decomposition that escape more superficial observers. But a biography cannot explain everything: as Pasteur once said, chance favours only a mind prepared. It is not only experience, therefore, but reflection upon it that makes the writer. A rich seam of ore is worthless without the will and ability to mine it.

Ballard's ore was his childhood. Born in Shanghai in 1930, the son of well-to-do British parents, he did not come to Britain until he was 16. The defining experience of his life, colouring all of his writing, was his internment by the Japanese, at 13, in a civilian camp during World War II. But it was not the internment alone that marked him; rather, it was the contrast with his earlier life. 'Anyone who has experienced a war at first hand knows that it completely overturns every conventional idea of what makes up day-to-day reality,' Ballard observed. 'You never feel quite the same again. It's like walking away from a plane crash; the world changes for you forever.'

The protagonist of his autobiographical 1984 novel, *Empire of the Sun*, is Jim, a British boy also interned by the Japanese near Shanghai. Jim has led a privileged existence in a luxurious house with nine household servants, whom he knows not by name but by function or position, such as Amah, Number One Boy and Number Two Boy. For Jim, the servants are not full human beings but animated objects whose purpose is to do his bidding. Neither especially good nor especially bad, rather a normal, thoughtless boy, he inherits the habit of command and takes his privileged way of life for granted. Not that he fails to notice the difference between his situation and that of most of the population around him; on the contrary, he is curious about life outside the European enclave. It is just that the difference for him is a brute fact about the constitution of the universe.

With the outbreak of war, everything changes. The Japanese sink a British ship and capture an American one, overthrowing the racial hierarchy. An amah slaps Jim in the face on no real provocation. He realises suddenly two things about her that might have been evident earlier, had he stopped to think about them: first, that her life of constant labour has given her considerable strength; and second, that her previous passive obedience flowed neither from consent nor from lack of feeling but from fear, coercion and an absence of alternatives. In that slap is concentrated all the resentment, humiliation and hatred that an adult placed at the orders of a privileged and spoiled child comes to feel; and thus the Japanese victory is also an irreversible moral education for Jim. He will never again be able to conceive of the world as made solely for his convenience.

More than the racial hierarchy is overturned. In the struggle for survival that follows the Japanese occupation of Shanghai, Jim discovers many things: that civilised conduct is a veneer that unaccustomed hardship strips away; that previously prominent people can become insignificant under new conditions; that pride of race, of nation, of position are no protection against demoralisation; that cruelty is common and self-sacrifice rare; in short, that everything he has assumed about the world is wrong.

In *Empire of the Sun*, Ballard describes childhood sights that must affect a person's outlook forever: 'Fifty yards away the corpse of a young Chinese woman floated among the sampans, heels rotating around her head as if unsure in what direction to point that day.' On the way to the camp where he will be interned, illness and death already striking down his fellow prisoners, Jim takes in his surroundings: 'It seemed that the two missionary women on the floor were barely alive, with blanched lips and eyes like those of poisoned mice. Flies swarmed over their faces, darting in and out of their nostrils… Their husbands sat side by side and stared at them in a resigned way, as if a taste for lying on the floor was a minor eccentricity shared by their wives.'

Jim learns that the survival instinct easily trumps most forms of human solidarity. Desperate, his group of prisoners reaches a camp where a British official, evidently left some power and discretion, refuses them entry, fearing they will spread disease. They must seek another camp; more prisoners die on the way.

The internment camp in which Jim eventually finds himself fosters a horrifying loss of moral compunction, but it has its compensations. He forms an alliance of convenience with a young American, Basie, a small-time crook and wheeler-dealer of the kind that tends to do well in such situations. Ballard contrasts Basie with Jim's father, a stern and upright, if distant, figure. 'At home, if he did anything wrong, the consequences seemed to overlay everything for days,' Ballard writes. 'With Basie they vanished instantly. For the first time in his life Jim felt free to do what he wanted.'

In other words, the breakdown of the formalised social order, and its replacement with one based on more ruthless, informal, spontaneously-generated rules, can liberate in a certain sense, in that it permits what was previously impermissible. In Freudian terms, the id escapes the power of the superego; what results both repels and attracts. This lesson Ballard never forgot.

Ballard arrived in England during the austere post-war years, the austerity lengthened by government policy that saw in it an opportunity for ideologically inspired social engineering. (Even now, one occasionally senses nostalgia in medical journals for the era of rationing, which imposed a scientifically-approved diet on the population.) Ballard began medical school but dropped out after two years to become a writer. He never entirely lost his interest in medicine, however, and it is worth noting that doctors are important figures in his novels, the first of which came out in 1962.

All of Ballard's novels have a Robinson Crusoe theme: What happens to man when the props of civilisation are removed from him, as they so easily are, by external circumstances or by the operation of his secret desires, or by both in concert? Ballard's past gave him an awareness of the fragility of things, even when they appear most solid; and in the introduction to his collected short stories, he tells us that he is 'interested in the real future that I could see approaching'. His method: extrapolate something – a trend, a feeling of dissatisfaction – that he detected in the present; magnify it; and then examine its consequences. He was a recorder of what he called 'the visionary present,' a sociological Swift who claimed (half-mistakenly, I think) that he did not write with a moral purpose but instead served as 'a scout who is sent on ahead to see if the water is drinkable or not'.

In Ballard's earlier novels, the decomposition of society results largely from natural processes. For example, in his debut novel, *The Drowned World*, the earth has undergone an extremely rapid warming. (Ballard had an uncanny ability to anticipate future anxieties.) This warming, however, is the consequence not of man's activities but rather of huge sunspots. The sea has risen, flooding almost everything. London is under water, with only the upper heights of the taller buildings left above the surface. Most of the population has retreated to the cooler Arctic circle, while tropical vegetation has taken over the remaining landmasses; the fauna has begun swiftly to devolve to the Triassic era.

In these circumstances, it is not only the physical environment that changes, notes Dr Bodkin, one of the book's characters. 'How often most of us have had the feeling of *déjà vu*, of having seen all this before, in fact of remembering these swamps and lagoons all too well,' he points out. 'However selective the conscious mind may be, most biological memories are unpleasant ones, echoes of danger and terror. Nothing endures for so long as fear.' He adds: 'Just as psychoanalysis reconstructs the original traumatic situation in order to release the repressed material, so we are now being plunged back into the archaeopsychic past, uncovering the ancient taboos and drives that have been dormant for epochs.'

Later in Ballard's work, as in his 1973 novel *Concrete Island*, the cause of the regression to the primitive becomes man-made. 'Soon after three o'clock on the afternoon of April 22nd, 1973, a 35-year-old architect named Robert Maitland was driving down the high-speed exit lane in central London,' the story begins. Maitland's car has a puncture at 70 miles per hour, and it plunges 30 yards down an embankment. Maitland finds himself in a small piece of wasteland, from which the only escape is up the embankment to the highway. He climbs up and tries to attract attention, but 'his jacket and trousers were stained with sweat, mud and engine grease – few drivers, even if they did notice him, would be eager to give him a lift. Besides, it would be almost impossible to slow down here and stop. The pressure of the following traffic... forced them on relentlessly.'

A passing taxi driver sees him and taps his head, signalling that Maitland must be mad. The castaway's situation is a vision of hell: 'Horns blared endlessly as the three lines of vehicles, tail lights flaring, moved towards this junction. As Maitland stood weakly by the roadside, waving a feeble hand, it seemed to him that every vehicle in London had passed and re-passed him a dozen times, the drivers and passengers deliberately ignoring him in a vast spontaneous conspiracy.' Trying to cross the highway, he is injured and thrown back down the embankment. He cannot escape from his desolate patch, isolated amid an agglomeration of millions of people. Now he must live by his wits, wresting from the wasteland whatever living he can.

It is significant that Maitland is an architect, for it is the architects, with their modernist dreams of making the world anew according to implacably abstract principles, who have created the wasteland in the first place. Ballard captures the socially isolating nature of modern architecture – and the modern way of life associated with it – with great symbolic force. The taxi driver, encased in his cage of pressed steel, can see in Maitland only a lunatic with whom he shares no humanity. The other drivers have lost their ability to choose: once on the road, they must inexorably move forward. They do not control the situation; the situation controls them. What should liberate – the car, with its theoretical ability to take you anywhere you want to go, whenever you want to go – becomes dehumanising.

In the same year Ballard published his most controversial book, *Crash*, later made into an equally disturbing film by David Cronenberg. The book is a kind of visionary *reductio ad absurdum* of what Ballard sees as the lack of meaning in modern material abundance, in which erotic and violent sensationalism replace transcendent purpose: the book's characters speed to the sites of auto accidents to seek sexual congress with the dying bodies and torn metal. Ballard's method is Swift's, though with a less general target. To object that Ballard exaggerates the existential predicament of the modern middle classes is to miss the point, just as to object that Swift exaggerates man's absurdity, pretensions and nastiness is to miss the point.

In his next book, *High-Rise*, published in 1975, Ballard sets a small civil war in a luxurious 40-storey apartment building, where 'the regime of trivial disputes and irritations... provided [the] only corporate life' of the 2,000 inhabitants. Robert Laing is a doctor who is divorced, like all of Ballard's protagonists. 'This over-priced cell, slotted almost at random into the cliff face of the apartment building, he had bought after his divorce specifically for its peace, quiet and anonymity,' Ballard writes. It seems to be part of the modern condition that people find difficulty in living together, preferring an isolation in which human contact becomes superficial, fleeting, and primarily instrumental to immediate needs or desires.

Where people have few affective ties but nonetheless live together in close proximity, the potential for conflict is great. Though all the residents are well heeled, a version of class war breaks out in the high-rise, pitting the residents of the upper floors, who have paid the most for their apartments, against those of the lower floors. Boredom and a lack of common purpose provoke aggression, and self-destruction follows. Prosperity is not enough.

If anything, Ballard's vision then darkened. Twenty years after *High-Rise*, prosperity had increased enormously, and Ballard published *Cocaine Nights*, an attack on the very idea of the good life engendered by British consumer society. The novel is set in imaginary rich expatriate enclaves on the Spanish Mediterranean coast, towns 'without either centre or suburbs, that seem to be little more than dispersal ground for golf courses and swimming pools'. As one character says, 'It's Europe's future. Everywhere will be like this soon.'

The utter vacuity of the abundant life that the inhabitants have worked to achieve, enabling them to retire before 50, is reflected in the enclaves' architecture and social atmosphere. 'I looked down on an endless terrain of picture windows, patios and miniature pools,' relates the protagonist, a travel writer.

> Together they had a curiously calming effect, as if these residential compounds were a series of psychological pens that soothed and domesticated... Nothing could ever happen in this affectless realm, where entropic drift calmed the surfaces of a thousand swimming pools.
>
> Everywhere satellite dishes cupped the sky like begging bowls. The residents had retreated to their shady lounges, their bunkers with a view, needing only that part of the external world that was distilled from the sky by their satellite dishes.

The residents are refugees from a disordered world: 'There's excellent security and not a trace of graffiti anywhere – most people's idea of paradise today.' Freed from economic anxiety, they are also 'refugees from time': in fact, they have 'travelled to the far side of boredom' and are now 'desperate for new vices'.

A young tennis coach, Crawford, responsible for arranging the social life of the enclaves, hits on the idea of crime as the solution to the prevailing boredom. Unknowingly, he recapitulates the sociologist Emile Durkheim's view that criminals fulfil an important social function by providing the rest of the population with a cause for solidarity: for one can exercise solidarity only against something and somebody else. 'How do you energise people, give them some sense of community?' Crawford asks. Politics is boring, religion too demanding. 'Only one thing is left which can rouse people, threaten them directly and force them to act together… Crime and transgressive behaviour. [They] provoke us and tap our need for strong emotion, quicken the nervous system and jump the synapses deadened by leisure and inaction.' His conclusion: 'A certain level of crime is part of the necessary roughage of life. Total security is a disease of deprivation.'

By arranging for crimes to be committed at random, including a deliberate fire that kills five, Crawford brings the enclaves back to life, including cultural life. The residents start to play music and participate in theatre productions. Instead of living in solipsistic isolation, they now meet regularly. Ballard is not suggesting that the immolation of people is a worthwhile price if only people take to the violin and footlights as a result. He is suggesting that, absent a transcendent purpose, material affluence is not sufficient – and may lead to boredom, perversity and self-destruction.

In his two most recent novels, *Millennium People* and *Kingdom Come*, Ballard treats England as a country gripped by a consumerist fever, half aware that something more is necessary to lead a bearable human life, and thus vulnerable to an inchoate revolutionism whose inspiration is part fascist, part socialist. The books' characters are, as usual in Ballard, educated and middle class; no member of the underclass ever appears in his pages. This is not accidental. It is the educated class that is essential to running the country and that sets its moral tone; but 'sheltered by benevolent shopping malls', Ballard writes in *Kingdom Come*, it 'waits patiently for the nightmares that will wake [it] into a more passionate world'. Believing in nothing, sated materially, it is capable of anything to escape boredom.

This represents an important insight. When I briefly served as a kind of vulgarity correspondent for a British newspaper – it sent me anywhere the British gathered to behave badly – I discovered to my surprise that the middle classes behaved in crowds with the same menacing disinhibition as their supposed social and educational inferiors. They swore and screamed abuse and made fascistic gestures and urinated in the street with the same abandon that they attributed to the proletarians. It was Ballard who first spotted that the bourgeoisie wanted to proletarianise itself without losing its economic privileges or political power.

In *Millennium People*, the residents of an affluent housing project called Chelsea Marina 'had set about dismantling their middle-class world. They lit bonfires of books and paintings, educational toys and videos… They had quietly discarded their world as if putting out their rubbish for collection. All over England an entire professional caste was rejecting everything it had worked so hard to secure.'

This strikes me as a suggestive metaphor for much that has happened over the last four decades, not only in England (though especially here) but also throughout parts of Western society. We have become bored with what we have inherited, to which, for lack of talent, we have contributed so humiliatingly little. Ballard understood why educated people, haunted by the pointlessness of their lives, feel the need to protest, and he satirised it in *Millennium People*. The book's protagonist, a psychologist, infiltrates the growing middle-class revolutionary movement and attends a protest against a cat show in a London exhibition hall with Angela, a revolutionary:

> Angela stared across the road with narrowed eyes and all a suburbanite's capacity for moral outrage. Walking around the exhibition two hours earlier, I was impressed by her unswerving commitment to the welfare of these luxurious pets. The protest rallies I had recently attended against globalisation, nuclear power and the World Bank were violent but well thought-out. By contrast, this demonstration seemed endearingly Quixotic in its detachment from reality. I tried to point this out to Angela as we strolled along the line of cages.
>
> 'Angela, they look so happy. . . . They're wonderfully cared for. We're trying to rescue them from heaven.'
>
> Angela never varied her step. 'How do you know?'
>
> 'Just watch them.' We stopped in front of a row of Abyssinians so deeply immersed in the luxury of being themselves that they barely noticed the admiring crowds.
>
> 'They're not exactly unhappy. They'd be prowling around, trying to get out of the cages.'
>
> 'They're drugged.' Angela's brows knotted. 'No living creature should be caged. This isn't a cat show, it's a concentration camp.'
>
> 'Still, they are rather gorgeous.'

'They're bred for death, not life. The rest of the litter are drowned at birth. It's a vicious eugenic experiment, the sort of thing Dr Mengele got up to,'

The press not long ago ran obituaries of Peter Cadogan, whom one paper called a 'professional protester'. Another wrote that Cadogan 'spent fifty years on a long quest of resistance to global injustices'. He appeared inseparable from a megaphone, and no man would have been more disappointed to wake one day to a world denuded of injustice. Apparently, someone read the protest poems of William Blake to him on his deathbed, and these roused him temporarily from a coma. Protest was the meaning of his life. His dying words evoked Blake: 'Live differently.' Not better, but differently.

This mind-set can result in the violence from which, as Ballard discovered early in life, we are always but a hairbreadth away, however solidly-founded our comfort may seem. Civilisation's fragility does not make it unreal or valueless – quite the reverse. And while I suspect that Ballard would have disliked seeing conservative implications drawn from his work, they are most certainly there.

A PROPHETIC AND VIOLENT
MASTERPIECE

WHEN, AS A MEDICAL STUDENT, I emerged from the cinema having watched Stanley Kubrick's controversial film of *A Clockwork Orange*, I was astonished and horrified to see a group of young men outside dressed up as droogs, the story's adolescent thugs who delighted in what they called 'ultra-violence'.

The film had been controversial; its detractors, who wanted it banned, charged that it glamorised and thereby promoted violence. The young men dressed as droogs seemed to confirm the charge, though of course it is one thing to imitate a form of dress and quite another to imitate behaviour. Still, even a merely sartorial identification with psychopathic violence shocked me, for it implied an imaginative sympathy with such violence; and seeing those young men outside the theatre was my first intimation that art, literature and ideas might have profound – and not necessarily favourable – social consequences. A year later in Lancashire, a group of young men raped a 17-year-old girl as they sang 'Singin' in the Rain', a real-life replay of one of the film's most notorious scenes.

The author of the book, Anthony Burgess, a polymath who once wrote five novels in a year, came to dislike this particular work intensely, not because of any practical harm to society that the film version of it might have caused but because he did not want to go down in literary history as the author of a book made famous, or notorious, by a film. Irrespective of the value of his other work, however, *A Clockwork Orange* remains a novel of immense power. Linguistically inventive, socially prophetic and philosophically profound, it comes very close to being a work of genius.

The story, set in the England of the near future (the book was published in 1962), is simple. The narrator, Alex, a precocious 15-year-old who has no feeling for others, leads a small gang in many acts of gratuitous, and much enjoyed, violence. Eventually, caught after a murder, he goes to prison, where – after another murder – the authorities offer to release him if he submits to a form of aversive conditioning against violence called the Ludovico Method. On his release, however, he attempts suicide by jumping out of a window, receiving a head injury that undoes his conditioning against violence. Once more he becomes the leader of a gang.

In the final chapter of the book's British version, Alex again rejects violence, this time because he discovers within himself, spontaneously, a source of human tenderness that makes him want to settle down and have a baby. In the American edition – which Stanley Kubrick used – this last chapter is missing: Alex is not redeemed a second time, but returns, apparently once and for all, to the enjoyment of arbitrary and anti-social violence. In this instance it is the British who were the optimists and the Americans the pessimists: Burgess's American publisher, wanting the book to end unhappily, omitted the last chapter.

Burgess had been a teacher (like William Golding, author of *Lord of the Flies*) and evidently sensed a stirring of revolt among the youth of his country and elsewhere in the West, a revolt with which – as a deeply unconventional man who felt himself to be an outsider, however wealthy or famous he became, and who drank deep at the well of resentment as well as of spirituous liquors – he felt some sympathy and might even have helped in a small way to foment. And yet, as a man who was also deeply steeped in literary culture and tradition, he understood the importance of the shift of cultural authority from the old to the young and was very far from sanguine about its effects. He thought that the shift would lead to a hell on earth and the destruction of all that he valued.

He marks the separateness of his novel's young protagonists from their elders by their adoption of a new argot as well as a new form of dress. Vital for groups antagonistic toward the dominant society around them, such argots allow them to identify and communicate with insiders and exclude outsiders. Although I worked in a prison for 14 years, for example, I never came to understand the language that prisoners used as they shouted to one another across landings and between buildings. It was their means of resisting domination. In French *banlieues*, *les jeunes* use an argot derived from words spelled and pronounced backward – and completely incomprehensible to educated speakers of French. A similar form of speech – known as 'backslang' – exists in Liverpool; people of Jamaican descent in Britain use a patois when they want not to be understood by anyone else. The connection between argot and criminal purposes has long been close, of course; and the importance that Burgess ascribes to the new argot in *A Clockwork Orange* suggests that he saw youthful revolt as an expression more of self-indulgence and criminality than of idealism – the latter, shallower view becoming orthodoxy among intellectuals not long after *A Clockwork Orange* appeared.

Burgess's creation of a completely convincing new argot more or less *ex nihilo* is an extraordinary achievement. *Nadsat* (Russian for 'teen'), as its speakers call it, is a mixture of anglicised Russian words – particularly provocative at the height of the Cold War – and Cockney rhyming slang. As a linguistic invention, it is the equal of Orwell's Newspeak. Alex, the narrator, though cold-blooded and self-centred, is intelligent and expresses himself with great force. A vocabulary that is entirely new and incomprehensible at the beginning of the book becomes so thoroughly familiar to the reader at the end that he forgets he has ever had to learn its meaning: it seems completely natural after only a hundred pages. On the very first page, when Alex describes his gang's intention to do a robbery, he says:

[T]here was no real need... of crasting [robbing] any more pretty polly [money] to tolchock [hit] some old veck [man] in an alley and viddy [see] him swim in his blood while we counted the takings and divided by four, nor to do the ultra-violent on some shivering starry [old] grey-haired ptitsa [woman] in a shop and go smecking [laughing] off with the till's guts.

Of course, the lack of real 'need' does not prevent Alex and his gang from robbing in a cruel and violent way, for their cruelty and violence is an end in itself, joyfully engaged in. Not for Burgess was the orthodox liberal view that economic deprivation and lack of opportunity cause crime.

The gang's solipsistic and dehumanising argot reflects this cold-bloodedness. Sexual intercourse, for example, becomes 'the old in-out-in-out', a term without reference to the other participant, who is merely an object. The gang attacks a teacher carrying books home from the library, for no reason other than a free-floating malevolence and joy in cruelty:

Pete held his rookers [hands] and Georgie sort of hooked his rot [mouth] wide open for him and Dim yanked out his false zoobies [teeth], upper and lower. He threw these down on the pavement and then I treated them to the old boot-crush, though they were hard bastards like... The old veck [man] began to make sort of chumbling shooms [sounds] – 'wuf waf wof' – so Georgie let go of holding his goobers [jaws] apart and just let him have one in the toothless rot with his ringy fist, and that made the old veck start moaning a lot then, then out comes the blood, my brothers, real beautiful.

I doubt that a lack of feeling for others has ever been expressed more powerfully.

Burgess intuited with almost prophetic acuity both the nature and characteristics of youth culture when left to its own devices, and the kind of society that might result when that culture became predominant. For example, adults grow afraid of the young and defer to them, something that has certainly come to pass in Britain, where adults now routinely look away as youngsters commit anti-social acts in public, for fear of being knifed if they do otherwise, and mothers anxiously and deferentially ask their petulant five-year-old children what they would like to eat, in the hope of averting tantrums. The result is that adolescents and young men take any refusal of a request as *lèse-majesté*, a challenge to the integrity of their ego. When I refused to prescribe medicine that young men wanted but that I thought they did not need, they would sometimes answer in aggrieved disbelief, 'No? What do you mean, no?' It was not a familiar concept. And in a sense, my refusal was pointless, insofar as any such young man would soon enough find a doctor whom he could intimidate into prescribing what he wanted. Burgess would not have been surprised by this state of affairs: he saw it coming.

When Alex and his gang enter a pub – they are underage, but no one dares challenge them – they spread fear by their mere presence.

Now we were the very good malchicks [boys], smiling good evensong to one and all, though these wrinkled old lighters [people] started to get all shook, their veiny old rookers all trembling round their glasses, and making the suds [drink] spill on the table. 'Leave us be, lads,' said one of them, her face all mappy with being a thousand years old, 'we're only poor old women.'

Intimidation of the aged and contempt for age itself are an essential part of the youth culture: no wonder aging rock stars are eternal adolescents, wrinkled and arthritic but trapped in the poses of youth. Age for them means nothing but indignity.

Alex's parents (one of the things Burgess didn't foresee is the rise of the single-parent family) are afraid of him. He comes home late and plays his music very loud, but 'Pee and em [Father and Mother]... had learnt now not to knock on the wall with complaints of what they called noise. I had taught them. Now they would take sleep-pills.' When Alex's father wants to know what he does at night – recall that Alex is only 15 – he is apologetic and deferential: '"Not that I want to pry, son, but where exactly is it you go to work of evenings?" ...My dad was like humble mumble chumble. "Sorry, son," he said. "But I get worried sometimes."'

When, in a symbolic reversal of the direction of authority, Alex offers his father some money (stolen, of course) so that he can buy himself a drink in the pub, his father says: 'Thanks, son... But we don't go out much now. We daren't go out much, the streets being what they are. Young hooligans and so on. Still, thanks.'

In 1962 the idea that the young would someday impose upon old people in Britain a *de facto* after-dark curfew was still unimaginable, but Burgess, seeing the cloud no bigger than a man's hand on the horizon, imagined that outcome very vividly. With a prophet's imagination, he saw what would happen when the cloud grew until it covered the sky.

With like prescience, Burgess foresaw many other aspects of the youth culture to come: the importance that mind-altering drugs and an industrialised pop music would play in it, for example. (Burgess did not, however, suggest that high culture was necessarily ennobling in itself. Alex, much superior in intelligence to his followers, is a devotee of classical music, listening to which, however, increases his urge to commit violence. No doubt Burgess had in mind those Nazis who could listen with emotion to Schubert *lieder* after a hard day's genocide.)

Burgess foresaw the importance that the youth culture would attach to sexual precocity and a kind of disabused knowingness. In a remarkable rape scene, Alex meets two ten-year-old girls who, like him, are skipping school, in a record shop, where they are listening to pop music with suggestive titles such as 'Night After Day After Night'.

> They saw themselves, you could see, as real grown-up devotchkas [girls] already, what with the old hipswing when they saw your Faithful Narrator, brothers, and padded groodies [breasts] and red all ploshed on their goobers [lips]... [T]hey viddied [saw] themselves as real sophistoes... They had the same ideas or lack of, and the same colour hair – a like dyed strawy. Well, they would grow up real today... No school this afterlunch, but education certain, Alex as teacher.

Their education that afternoon consists of repeated rape by an already experienced 15-year-old.

It would not have surprised Burgess that magazines for 11- or 12-year-old girls are now filled with advice about how to make themselves sexually attractive, that girls of six or seven are dressed by their single mothers in costumes redolent of prostitution, or that there has been a compression of generations, so that friendships are possible between

14- and 26-year-olds. The precocity necessary to avoid humiliation by peers prevents young people from maturing further and leaves them in a state of petrified adolescence. Convinced that they already know all that is necessary, they are disabused about everything, for fear of appearing naive. With no deeper interests, they are prey to gusts of hysterical and childish enthusiasm; only increasingly extreme sensation can arouse them from their mental torpor. Hence the epidemic of self-destructiveness that has followed in the wake of the youth culture.

The world in which youth culture predominates and precocity is the highest achievement is one in which all tenderness is absent. When Alex and his gang attack the teacher, they find a letter in his pocket, which one of them reads out derisively: 'My darling one... I shall be thinking of you while you are away and hope you will remember to wrap up warm when you go out at night.'

Such simple and heartfelt affection and concern for another person are extinct in the world of Alex and his droogs. Alex is incapable of putting himself in the place of anyone else, of 'changing places in fancy with the sufferer', as Adam Smith puts it. Self-absorbed, he is self-pitying but has no pity for others. When he is arrested after the brutal murder of an old woman, he calls the policemen who have arrested him 'bullies' and accuses them when they laugh at him of 'the heighth of... callousness'. Alex is quite incapable of connecting his own savage behaviour with the words that he applies to the police. I was reminded of a case of murder in which I gave testimony recently: the young murderer kicked his girlfriend's head so hard that he broke her jaw in many places and forced her tongue through the back of her throat, and her stomach filled with blood – and a neighbour heard him laugh as he kicked. A policeman, after listening to his lies and evasions for two days, accused him of having no remorse for his deed. 'You have no feelings,' the murderer rejoined. 'I pity your poor wife'

– just like Alex in *A Clockwork Orange*, but without the intelligence and the taste for classical music.

In the world of Alex and his droogs, all relations with other human beings are instrumental means to a selfish, brutal, hedonistic end. And this is the world that so many of my patients now inhabit, a world in which perhaps a third of the British population lives. It is also the world in which having a baby is the fulfilment of a personal human right, and not much else.

But Burgess was not merely a social and cultural prophet. *A Clockwork Orange* grapples as well with the question of the origin and nature of good and evil. The Ludovico Method that Alex undergoes in prison as a means of turning him into a model citizen in exchange for his release is in essence a form of conditioning. Injected with a drug that induces nausea, Alex must then watch films of the kind of violence that he himself committed, his head and eyelids held so that he cannot escape the images by looking away from them – all this to the piped-in accompaniment of the classical music he loves. Before long, such violence, either in imagery or in reality, as well as the sound of classical music, causes him nausea and vomiting even without the injection, as a conditioned response. Alex learns to turn the other cheek, as a Christian should: when he is insulted, threatened, or even struck, he does not retaliate. After the treatment – at least, until he suffers his head injury – he can do no other.

Two scientists, Drs Branom and Brodsky, are in charge of the 'treatment'. The Minister of the Interior, responsible for cutting crime in a society now besieged by the youth culture, says: 'The Government cannot be concerned any longer with outmoded penological theories... Common criminals... can best be dealt with on a purely curative basis. Kill the criminal reflex, that's all.' In other words, a criminal or violent act is, in essence, no different from the act of a rat in a cage, who presses a lever in order to obtain a pellet of food. If you shock the rat with electricity when it presses the lever instead of rewarding it with food, it will soon cease to press the lever. Criminality can be dealt with, or 'cured', in this simple way.

At the time Burgess wrote *A Clockwork Orange*, doctors were trying to 'cure' homosexuals by injecting them with apomorphine, a nausea-inducing drug, while showing them pictures of male nudes. And overwhelmingly, the dominant school of psychology worldwide at the time was the behaviourism of Harvard professor B.F. Skinner. His was what one might call a 'black box' psychology: scientists measured the stimulus and the response but exhibited no interest whatsoever in what happened between the two, as being intrinsically immeasurable and therefore unknowable. While Skinner might have quibbled about the details of the Ludovico Method (for example, that Alex got the injection at the wrong time in relation to the violent films that he had to watch), he would not have rejected its scientific – or rather, scientistic – philosophy.

In 1971, the very year in which the Kubrick film of *A Clockwork Orange* was released, Skinner published a book entitled *Beyond Freedom and Dignity*. He sneered at the possibility that reflection upon our own personal experience and on history might be a valuable source of guidance to us in our attempts to govern our lives. 'What we need,' he wrote, 'is a technology of behaviour.' Fortunately one was at hand. 'A technology of operant behaviour is… already well advanced, and it may prove commensurate with our problems.' As he put it, '[a] scientific analysis shifts the credit as well as the blame [for a man's behaviour] to the environment'. What goes on in a man's mind is quite irrelevant; indeed, 'mind', says Skinner, is 'an explanatory fiction'.

For Skinner, being good is behaving well; and whether a man behaves well or badly depends solely upon the schedule of reinforcement that he has experienced in the past, not upon anything that goes on in his mind. It follows that there is no new situation in a man's life that requires conscious reflection if he is to resolve the dilemma or make the choices that the new situation poses: for everything is merely a replay of the past, generalised to meet the new situation.

The Ludovico Method, then, was not a far-fetched invention of Burgess's but a simplified version – perhaps a *reductio ad absurdum*, or *ad nauseam* – of the technique for solving all human problems that the dominant school of psychology at the time suggested. Burgess was a lapsed Catholic, but he remained deeply influenced by Catholic thought throughout his life. The Skinnerian view of man appalled him. He thought that a human being whose behaviour was simply the expression of conditioned responses was not fully human but an automaton. If he did the right thing merely in the way that Pavlov's dog salivated at the sound of a bell, he could not be a good man: indeed, if all his behaviour was determined in the same way, he was hardly a man at all. A good man, in Burgess's view, had to have the ability to do evil as well as good, an ability that he would voluntarily restrain, at whatever disadvantage to himself.

Being a novelist rather than an essayist, however, and a man of many equivocations, Burgess put these thoughts in *A Clockwork Orange* into the mouth of a ridiculous figure, the prison chaplain, who objects to the Ludovico Method – but not enough to resign his position, for he is eager to advance in what Alex calls 'Prison religion'. Burgess puts the defence of the traditional view of morality as requiring the exercise of free will – the view that there is no good act without the possibility of a bad one – into the mouth of a careerist.

The two endings of *A Clockwork Orange* – the one that Burgess himself wrote and the truncated one that his American publisher wanted and that Kubrick used for his film – have very different meanings.

According to the American-Kubrick version, Alex resumes his life as a violent gang leader after his head injury undoes the influence of the Ludovico Method. He returns to what he was before, once more able to listen to classical music (Beethoven's Ninth) and fantasise violence without any conditioned nausea:

> Oh, it was gorgeosity and yumyumyum. When it came to the Scherzo I could viddy myself very clear running and running on like very light and mysterious nogas [feet], carving the whole litso [face] of the creeching [screaming] world with my cut-throat britva [razor]. And there was the slow movement and the lovely last singing movement still to come. I was cured all right.

Kubrick even suggests that this is a happy outcome: better an authentic psychopath than a conditioned, and therefore inauthentic, goody-goody. Authenticity and self-direction are thus made to be the highest goods, regardless of how they are expressed. And this, at least in Britain, has become a prevailing orthodoxy among the young. If, as I have done, you ask the aggressive young drunks who congregate by the thousand in every British town or city on a Saturday night why they do so, or British football fans why they conduct themselves so menacingly, they will reply that they are expressing themselves, as if there were nothing further to be said on the matter.

The full, British version of *A Clockwork Orange* ends very differently. Alex begins to lose his taste for violence spontaneously, when he sees in a cafe a happy, normal couple, one of whom is a former associate of his. Thereafter, Alex begins to imagine a different life for himself and to fantasise a life that includes tenderness:

> There was Your Humble Narrator Alex coming home
> from work to a good hot plate of dinner, and there
> was this ptitsa [girl] all welcoming and greeting like
> loving… I had this sudden very strong idea that if I
> walked into the room next to this room where the fire
> was burning away and my hot dinner laid on the table,
> there I should find what I really wanted… For in that
> other room in a cot was laying gurgling goo goo goo
> my son… I knew what was happening, O my brothers.
> I was like growing up.

Burgess obviously prefers a reformation that comes spontaneously from within, as it does in the last chapter, to one that comes from without, by application of the Ludovico Method. Here he would agree with Kubrick – an internal reformation is more authentic, and thus better in itself because it is a true expression of the individual. Perhaps Burgess also believes that such an internal reformation is likely to go deeper and be less susceptible to sudden reversal than reformation brought from outside.

Burgess also suggests the somewhat comforting message, at odds with all that has gone before, that Alex's violence is nothing new in the world and that the transformation of immature, violent and solipsistic young men into mature, peaceful and considerate older men will continue forever, as it has done in the past, because deep inside there is a well of goodness, man having been born with original virtue rather than original sin (this is the Pelagian heresy, to which Burgess admitted that he was attracted). There is a never-ending cycle:

> [Y]outh is only being in a way like it might be an animal.
> No, it is not just like being an animal so much as being
> like one of these malenky [small] toys you viddy being

sold in the streets, like little chellovecks [men] made
out of tin and with a spring inside and then a winding
handle on the outside and you wind it up grrr grrr grrr
and off it itties [goes], like walking, O my brothers. But it
itties in a straight line and bangs straight into things bang
bang and it cannot help what it is doing. Being young is
like being like one of these malenky machines.

My son, my son. When I had my son I would
explain all that to him when he was starry enough to like
understand. But then I knew he would not understand
or would not want to understand at all and would do all
the veshches [things] I had done… and I would not be
able to really stop him. And nor would he be able to stop
his own son, brothers. And so it would itty on to like the
end of the world.

And this, surely, is partly right. Four centuries ago Shakespeare
wrote:

> I would there were no age between sixteen and three-
> and-twenty, or that youth would sleep out the rest; for
> there is nothing in the between but getting wenches
> with child, wronging the ancientry, stealing, fighting.

And certainly it is true that criminality, statistically speaking, is an
activity of the young and that there are few prisoners in the prison in
which I worked who had been incarcerated for a crime committed
after the age of 35. There seems to be a biological dimension to
garden-variety wrongdoing.

But a quietistic message – cheerful insofar as it implies that
violence among young men is but a passing phase of their life and

that the current era is no worse in this respect than any past age, and pessimistic in the sense that a reduction of the overall level of violence is impossible – is greatly at odds with the socially prophetic aspect of the book, which repeatedly warns that the coming new youth culture, shallow and worthless, will be unprecedentedly violent and anti-social. And of Britain, at least, Burgess was certainly right. He extrapolated from what he saw in the prime manifestation of the emerging youth culture, pop music, to a future in which self-control had shrunk to vanishing, and he realised that the result could only be a Hobbesian world, in which personal and childish whim was the only authority to guide action. Like all prophets, he extrapolated to the nth degree; but a brief residence in a British slum should persuade anyone that he was not altogether wide of the mark.

A Clockwork Orange is not completely coherent. If youth is violent because the young are like 'malenky machines' who cannot help themselves, what becomes of the free will that Burgess otherwise saw as the precondition of morality? Do people grow into free will from a state of automatism, and, if so, how and when? And if violence is only a passing phase, why should the youth of one age be much more violent than the youth of another? How do we achieve goodness, both on an individual and social level, without resort to the crude behaviourism of the Ludovico Method or any other form of cruelty? Can we bypass consciousness and reflection in our struggle to behave well?

There are no schematic answers in the book. One cannot condemn a novel of 150 pages for failing to answer some of the most difficult and puzzling questions of human existence, but one can praise it for raising them in a peculiarly profound manner and forcing us to think about them. To have combined this with acute social prophecy (to say nothing of entertainment) is near genius.

A DRINKER OF INFINITY

SOMEONE who had known Arthur Koestler told me a little story about him. Koestler was playing Scrabble with his wife, and he put the word 'vince' down on the board.

'Arthur,' said his wife, 'what does "vince" mean?'

Koestler, who never lost his strong Hungarian accent but whose mastery of English was such that he was undoubtedly one of the 20th century's great prose writers in the language, replied (one can just imagine with what light in his eyes): 'To vince is to flinch slightly viz pain.'

How many people could define a word in their first language with such elegant precision, let alone in their fourth, and moreover combine it with such irresistibly wicked humour? One can see in this trifling incident how being with anyone less brilliant than Arthur Koestler must have seemed intolerably dull to any woman who had been in love with him.

As it happens, Koestler's relations with women now have more to do with his reputation than does anything he ever wrote. Since the 1998 publication of David Cesarani's biographical study, Koestler's name has been synonymous with rape, possibly serial in nature, and the abuse of women. I tested this association on several friends with literary interests: though none had read Cesarani's book, in each case the first thought on hearing Koestler's name was of rape. It is doubtful whether any biography has ever affected the reputation of an author more profoundly than did Cesarani's; and its effect is proof, if we needed any, that books have an influence far beyond their actual readership.

Cesarani is a serious scholar, not a man to manufacture sensational claims for nonscholarly purposes; and in fact his widely publicised revelations, which came as a considerable shock, receive a kind of confirmation from a scene in Koestler's novel *Arrival and Departure*, published in 1943.

The book is at least partly autobiographical. Its protagonist (hero would be too positive a word) is Peter Slavek, a young refugee and former Communist militant from an unnamed Balkan country now under Nazi occupation. Slavek arrives in the capital of a neutral country – clearly Portugal – from which he hopes to reach England and enlist in the British forces, the only ones still fighting the Nazis at that time. Koestler himself reached England from Portugal with the same idea in mind, and his description of Lisbon's wartime atmosphere clearly draws on firsthand experience.

While in Lisbon, Slavek falls in love with, or forms an infatuation for, Odette, a young French refugee awaiting a visa for America. Odette has taken no notice of Slavek, but one day she visits a friend's apartment where the Balkan refugee is temporarily staying. The friend is absent, so Slavek and Odette are alone. There follows a scene that suggests that Koestler was as personally acquainted with rape as he was with the fervid atmosphere of wartime Lisbon.

Slavek declares his love for Odette; she rejects him and prepares to leave. 'He jerked himself to his feet, reached the door almost in one jump and got hold of her as she was passing into the hall,' Koestler writes. Then the author says of Slavek that he was doing what several rapists have told me that they sought to do – protect their victims: 'As if the door were a death-trap and she were in danger of falling into it, [he] pressed her against him with a protecting gesture, while with his foot he kicked the door shut.' Odette struggles, but 'her very struggling', Koestler writes, makes Slavek's grip 'close tighter around her, like the noose of a trap' – not the activity of an agent but the operation of a mechanical contrivance.

The situation calms a little, and Slavek realises that he should have let his arms drop with embarrassment, but then 'she began struggling again in renewed fury, and this automatically made him tighten his grip'. Koestler describes Slavek as more terrified than Odette.

Then comes the actual rape:

> She struggled breathlessly, hammering her fists, against his breast... God, how unreasonable she was... All he wanted was to make her understand that he didn't want anything from her... By her furious struggling she caused him to press her back, step by step, from the door. His lips babbled senseless words that were meant to calm; but now it was too late, the flames leapt up, enveloping him... With blind eyes he fell as they stumbled against a couch... [and he] rammed his knee against her legs, felt them give way and a second later her whole body go limp.

After it is all over, Odette cries. Slavek takes her hand, and feels encouraged when she does not withdraw it to explain and justify his actions: 'You know, I am not so sure that you will always regret it, although for the moment you are still angry with me.' Then he contrives to blur the distinction between voluntary and coerced sexual relations: 'Nowadays things often start this way, the end at the beginning I mean. In the old days people had to wait years before they were allowed to go to bed and then found out that they didn't really like each other, it had all been a mirage of their glands. If you start the other way round you won't need to find out whether you really care.'

Odette's reply absolves Slavek of any need to feel remorse: 'The whole point is that if you knock a woman about for long enough and get on her nerves and wear her down, there comes a moment when she suddenly feels how silly all this struggling and kicking is, so much ado about nothing.' Sexual intercourse, then, has no more moral significance than urination or any other physiological function. 'You probably think what an irresistible seducer you are, while in fact all you did was get her to this zero level where she says – after all, why not?' And to confirm the Slavek-Odette-Koestler theory, Slavek and Odette go on to have a short and intense love affair.

Koestler's description of a rape seems to be from the inside; and if Cesarani is right, it gives us the very model of Koestler's conduct and experience. He might even have suffered from (if 'suffered from' is quite the right phrase) what psychiatrists call 'coercive paraphilia': sexual excitement brought on by the act of physical subjugation, a pompous name sometimes being the nearest that medical science can come to an explanation. Slavek's argument, of course, is virtually a rapist's charter. But the uncomfortable fact is that some of the women whom Koestler abused remained friends with him for the rest of their lives. It would take an entire book fully to explore all the evasions in the passage I have quoted, as well as the social and psychological questions it raises.

There is much more to Koestler, of course, than sexual perversity, even if it is difficult nowadays to read anything that he wrote without first donning rape-tinted spectacles. *Arrival and Departure* is not just about Slavek's love life: it passionately engages with the most important political questions of the day.

For example, the book gave the most graphic description until then published of the gassing of the Jews in Eastern Europe, not as isolated massacres but as part of a deliberate genocidal policy; and it drew an explicit comparison – now banal and commonplace, but then brave and arresting – between Hitler and Stalin, pointing out their similarities, despite their enmity. Meeting an intelligent

Nazi agent called Bernard, Slavek asks him why the Nazis, so anti-Communist, nevertheless copied Soviet methods 'to a considerable extent'. Bernard replies:

> There is of course a certain affinity between your ex-fatherland and ours. Both are governed by authoritarian state bureaucracies on a collectivist basis; both are streamlined police states run by economic planning, the one-party system and scientific terror… It is a phase of history as inevitable as was the spreading of the feudal, and later of the capitalist, system. Our two countries are merely the forerunners of the post-individualist, post-liberal era.

To have written this passage at a time when books praising our gallant Soviet allies poured forth from the press – when even conservatives, always very few among the intelligentsia, had replaced their visceral hatred of the Soviet Union with admiration – was an act of considerable courage.

Koestler's reputation as a writer had declined well before Cesarani's revelations. He had become an author of the kind one encounters during late adolescence or early adulthood, whom one catches like the literary equivalent of glandular fever, but to whom, once read, one develops a lifelong immunity. Once one of the world's most famous authors, he became as dated as the youthful fashions of three decades ago.

There were several reasons for this. By 1980, if not before, the burning political issues of his early adulthood – communism, the rise of fascism and the establishment of a Zionist state – were of less concern to new generations of readers. Many regarded Koestler's subsequent obsessions – Indian mysticism, Lamarckian biology, nonreductionist science and parapsychology – as bizarre or even dotty, the symptoms of a mind that had lost its way. In his will he endowed a chair in parapsychology at Edinburgh University. He regarded telepathy and precognition as established facts, largely because of the now-discredited experiments of J.B. Rhine at Duke University. He began to collect examples of startling coincidences, as if they could tell us something about noncausal relations between events. Like Sir Arthur Conan Doyle before him, he seemed to the public to have travelled from serious authorship to spiritualist crankdom.

The penultimate nail in the coffin of his reputation, before Cesarani's revelations, was his double suicide with his wife, who was 20 years younger, in 1983. While he had both severe Parkinson's disease (causing a decline in his mental powers) and leukaemia (from which he was soon to die, in any case), his wife, who swallowed a fatal dose of barbiturates with him, was in perfect health. Many believed – without adequate evidence – that Koestler had bullied his wife into ending her life with him.

This was the second double suicide of a great Central European writer of adopted British citizenship and his wife, the first being that of Stefan and Lotte Zweig. But whereas Zweig killed himself in despair at the state of the world, Koestler killed himself in despair at the state of his health – no doubt a commentary on the direction, not wholly bad, in which the world had moved in the intervening 40 years. But it suggested great egotism and cast doubt on the sincerity, or at least disinterestedness, of all Koestler's previous commitments.

Koestler does not deserve such summary dismissal, for if any figure could claim to have encapsulated in his own life – and recorded – the political, intellectual and emotional tribulations of the 20th century, it is he.

He was born in Budapest in 1905 to assimilated Jewish parents. His father was a businessman who failed most of the time but who occasionally hit the jackpot: immediately before and during the first half of World War I he made a fortune (soon lost) by manufacturing and selling soap that contained radium. Radioactivity was then a recently discovered phenomenon, and many believed the rays to be life-enhancing and disease-curing.

Koestler's father spent the rest of his days dreaming of a new product that would restore his fortune at a stroke; and, in a sense, the young Arthur shared this kind of illusion but transposed it to the intellectual, political, philosophical and spiritual spheres. As a young man, Koestler saw in radical Zionism the answer to his existential problems, though he had no religious belief or cultural or philosophical affinities with Judaism (much later, moreover, he wrote a book still cited by anti-Zionists, *The Thirteenth Tribe*, which claims that most Jews are not of Semitic origin but descendants of the Khazars, a Turkic tribe that converted to Judaism). Then Koestler converted to orthodox Marxist communism, followed by a stage of crusading anti-communism, itself replaced by a prolonged search for a spiritualism founded on evidence and rational inference. Koestler was not a man to do things by philosophical halves: he was a drinker of infinity, to quote the title of one of his books.

Young Arthur, gifted scientifically and mathematically, studied engineering in Vienna but did not graduate. Instead the ardent Zionist went off to Palestine to live on a kibbutz. He did not last long; his personality ultimately would not allow absorption into a collective enterprise. On the verge of starvation, he was saved by a fortuitous appointment as the Palestine correspondent of the Ullstein Trust, the largest German newspaper group, which later assigned him to its Paris office. He then moved to Germany, where he served as the science editor of one newspaper and foreign editor of another, among other exploits flying in a zeppelin to the North Pole via Soviet Russia.

Koestler joined the Communist party, later explaining that it seemed the only viable alternative to Hitler, but this led Ullstein to sack him. Returning to Paris after travelling in the Soviet Union, he wrote political propaganda under Comintern direction until the outbreak of the Spanish Civil War, when a British liberal newspaper assigned him to visit Franco's headquarters.

Denounced as a Communist, he managed to escape, but Franco's forces captured him during a subsequent trip to Spain and sentenced him to death. An international campaign secured his release. Koestler's years as a Comintern agent – in which he, the most egotistical of men, willingly subjected himself to the party's discipline on the grounds that it represented the sole judge of transcendent truth – gave him unparalleled insight into the psychology of party members suddenly accused of counter-revolutionary treason.

He then lived in France, breaking for good with the Communist party over the show trials. When war broke out in 1939, the French government arrested him in Paris for being a potentially hostile alien and imprisoned him in a concentration camp; a second international campaign won his freedom. Fearing re-arrest, he joined the French Foreign Legion and managed, by a very circuitous route, to reach Lisbon. From there he flew – illegally – to London, where he again found himself imprisoned, this time for six weeks. In his prison cell he corrected the proofs of *Darkness at Noon*, which would be his most famous book.

Released from prison, he at once joined the British army, which, he said, had a salutary effect upon his life. 'I found myself transformed from a member of the grey, piteous crowd of refugees – the scum of earth – into a best-selling author,' he wrote. 'This is a dangerous experience for any writer, but before it could turn my head I was also transformed into Private No. 13805661 in 251 Company Pioneer Corps, which was not given to lionising intellectuals.' It says something of Koestler's life until then that he called the three years he spent in blitzed London, where he survived a close bombing, 'among the most uneventful (I almost said peaceful) of my life'.

By the age of 37, Koestler had travelled widely; spoke Hungarian, German, French, Russian and English fluently, as well as some Hebrew (having invented the Hebrew crossword while in Palestine); had been imprisoned several times, including under sentence of death; had been a Zionist, a Communist and an anti-Communist; and had written books in Hungarian, German and English. Shortly after arriving in England, he knew and was friendly with its most prominent writers and intellectuals: George Orwell, Cyril Connolly, Dylan Thomas, Bertrand Russell, Alfred Ayer and many others.

Koestler wrote *Darkness at Noon* in German while living in Paris, expecting at any moment to face arrest. It is the story of Rubashov, a Bolshevik intellectual modelled largely on Nikolai Bukharin, the economist and darling of the party who wound up executed after a 1938 Moscow show trial.

At the time of the book's publication in 1940, and for a long time afterward, the public confession of many old Bolsheviks to self-evidently absurd crimes that carried the death penalty – for example, that from the very beginning of their careers they had served foreign intelligence services – mystified many in the West. How had Communist officials obtained these confessions? Did the Russians have some extremely sophisticated and secret technique of interrogation, unknown in the West?

Of course, some in the West, Communists and ardent fellow travellers, believed that the trials were fair and that the confessions were unforced and entirely veridical. Among the most influential was a prominent British lawyer, D.N. Pritt, who actually wrote a book testifying to the Moscow trials' fairness. As late as 1972, a fellow medical student, at the time a fierce Maoist, tried to convince me that the trials were genuine by lending me transcripts of the proceedings.

So Koestler's imaginary reconstruction of how Rubashov was persuaded to confess, to which he brought his own intimate knowledge of how people thought and acted who had made the party their whole life, was entirely new and original. Koestler's solution to the puzzle was that Rubashov, and those like him, confessed not because of any physical torture (though Rubashov is deprived of sleep, a technique that interrogators did use in obtaining confessions) but because it was logical for them to do so. All their adult lives they had believed that the end justified the means; moreover, and crucially, they had delegated to the party the exclusive right to judge both ends and means. Who were they, then, to object when the party decided that it needed to sacrifice them, irrespective of whether they were guilty of anything?

Koestler is sufficiently sophisticated a novelist not to make Rubashov wholly admirable. Indeed, the Communist has failed to intervene on behalf of his own secretary, Arlova, with whom he has had a love affair, when she is accused of preposterous crimes. He reasons that his life is worth more to the cause than hers.

Koestler has the aristocratic Rubashov interrogated by a proletarian functionary named Gletkin. The climax comes when Gletkin argues that Rubashov's private dissent from the party line must, logically and objectively, lead to civil war and possibly to the destruction of the dictatorship of the proletariat and that therefore his confession 'is the last service the Party will require of you'.

> 'Comrade Rubashov, I hope that you have understood the task which the Party has set you.'
>
> It was the first time that Gletkin called Rubashov 'Comrade'. Rubashov raised his head quickly. He felt a hot wave rising in him, against which he was helpless. His chin shook slightly while he was putting on his pince-nez.
>
> 'I understand.'

Here the pince-nez symbolise the last remnant of a more refined civilisation (Ulu. kluw word them, for example), defeated by a cruder, more ruthless way of life. It is a subtle point that Koestler is making: Rubashov is both beneficiary and destroyer of the old civilisation and is himself destroyed by the offspring of his own destructiveness.

Some on the right have unfairly criticised Koestler, claiming that *Darkness at Noon* implies that subtle argumentation, rather than crude torture, obtained the confessions at the Moscow trials. But nowhere in the book does Koestler suggest that harsher methods to obtain confessions did not play a role – quite the contrary – or that the methods used in Rubashov's case characterised every case. Rather, his novel is philosophical, plausibly pointing to the terrible logical and practical consequences of the belief that the ends justify the means, when those ends have been preordained by authority, whether of history, the great leader or even God.

Darkness at Noon was probably the most influential anti-Communist book ever published, more important (in practice) even than *Animal Farm* or *Nineteen Eighty-Four*. Koestler's standing to write it was undisputed. It is true that it had little resonance in Britain, where it first appeared; and though it sold better in the United States, Communists had even less chance of success there than in Britain, so it again had muted influence. It was in France where the book's impact was decisive: there, after the war, a race took place between the publisher's printing presses and the capacity of the extremely powerful Communist party to buy up and destroy copies as they reached the bookshops. This censorship drive was an important reason why a French referendum on a new constitution, which would have given a preponderant government role to the strongest of the many political parties (then the

Communists), went down to defeat. By trying to silence Koestler's book, the Communists revealed themselves as dictators in the making.

After the publication of *The God That Failed* – containing six essays by prominent intellectuals, including himself, who had been Communists but had become disillusioned to the point of fierce enmity toward their former ideal – and after his participation in the Congress for Cultural Freedom in Berlin in 1950, Koestler shifted his interest. The question of communism seemed settled beyond reasonable doubt, though in practice it needed still to be defeated. Henceforth his attention turned to science and its compatibility (or otherwise) with what one might call mystical or spiritual modes of thought.

He did not leave the practical world behind entirely. He became an ardent campaigner both against the death penalty and in favour of euthanasia (by no means an uncommon combination). His feeling against the death penalty, expressed with characteristic force in his book *Reflections on Hanging*, no doubt arose from his contact with its implementation in Franco's prison. It was also his prison experiences that gave him a life-long interest in the welfare of prisoners and led him to establish the annual Koestler Prizes, awarded to British prisoners who had produced the best literary and artistic work in the previous year. This imaginative and wholly laudable initiative has led to the reverence shown for Koestler's name in British prisons, at least by the better-informed inmates.

Koestler's account of his internment in a Spanish prison, published first as the second half of *Spanish Testament* and then as the whole of *Dialogue with Death* (in my opinion, his greatest book), uncovers a layer of being far deeper than the political. His depiction of the way those condemned to death were taken away to execution is unforgettable:

I had gone to sleep, and I woke up shortly before midnight. In the black silence of the prison, charged with the nightmares of thirteen hundred sleeping men, I heard the murmured prayer of a priest and the ringing of the sanctus bell.

Then a cell door... was opened, and a name was softly called out. 'Que?' – What is the matter – asked a sleepy voice, and the priest's voice grew clearer and the bell rang louder.

And now the drowsy man understood. At first he only groaned; then in a dull voice he called for help: 'Socorro, socorro.'

The same scene is enacted at another cell:

Again, 'Que?' And again the prayer and the bell. This one sobbed and whimpered like a child. Then he cried out for his mother: 'Madre, madre!'

And in his description of the last man removed for execution that night, Koestler subtly indicates the complete inadequacy of political ideology in the face of the mysteries of life and death:

They went to the next cell... He asked no questions. While the priest prayed, he began in a low voice to sing the 'Marseillaise'. But after a few bars his voice broke, and he too sobbed. They marched him off.

And then there was silence again.

No revolutionary triumphalism here, with heroes gladly going to their deaths in the knowledge that the cause will ultimately triumph.

Throughout *Dialogue with Death*, Koestler raises profound existential questions. He becomes almost mystical, foreshadowing his later interests; after his release, he dreams of the Seville prison. 'Often when I wake at night I am homesick for my cell in the death-house… and I feel I have never been so free as I was then.' He continues:

> This is a very curious feeling indeed. We lived an unusual life… The constant nearness of death weighed us down and at the same time gave us a feeling of weightless floating. We were without responsibility. Most of us were not afraid of death, only of the act of dying; and there were times when we overcame even this fear. At such moments we were free — men without shadows, dismissed from the ranks of the mortal; it was the most complete experience of freedom that can be granted a man.

The man who wrote those words was not likely to remain a Communist (as he was when he wrote them). Indeed, it is clear that his initial attraction to communism must have been religious – not that he saw it as the best doctrine with which to oppose Hitler, as he claimed in his subsequent self-justification, or that it represented for him a supposedly pure, rational philosophy. When Koestler saw what communism wrought, both materially and in men's souls, he realised that it could never answer his religious needs.

While he had those needs, he was sufficiently a man of the Enlightenment not to be able to subscribe to any traditional religion. In the 1960s, after all, he produced massive histories of science that commanded the respect of prominent scientists; yet he could not believe that science, at least as then practised, contained all the answers he sought. In his novel *The Age of Longing*, Koestler describes the plight of Hydie, a lapsed Catholic:

Oh, if only she could go back to the infinite comfort of father confessors and mother superiors, of a well-ordered hierarchy which promised punishment and reward, and furnished the world with justice and meaning. If only she could go back! But she was under the curse of reason, which rejected whatever might quench her thirst, without abolishing the urge; which rejected the answer without abolishing the question. For the place of God had become vacant, and there was a draught blowing through the world as in an empty flat before the new tenants have arrived.

Precisely Koestler's own predicament, and that of modern man. It is no wonder that, a few years later, he went to India and Japan to seek the mystical wisdom of Hinduism and Zen Buddhism, or that he sought evidence of man's non-materiality in experiments to prove the reality of extrasensory perception, only a short step from full-blown spiritualism.

Koestler was fully aware, from an early age, of the contradictions in his own character, which helps make him one of the great autobiographers of the last century. In *Arrow in the Blue*, the first volume of his autobiography, he sums himself up as an adolescent: 'The youth of sixteen that I was, with the plastered-down hair, and the fatuous smirk, at once arrogant and sheepish, was emotionally seasick: greedy for pleasure, haunted by guilt, torn between feelings of inferiority and superiority, between the need for contemplative solitude and the frustrated urge for gregariousness.'

And at the end of *The Invisible Writing*, the second volume, Koestler says: 'The contradictions between sensitivity and callousness, integrity and shadiness, egomania and self-sacrifice which appear in every chapter [of the autobiography] would never add up to a credible character in a novel; but this is not a novel… The seemingly paradoxical can be resolved only by holding the figure against the background of his time, by taking into account both the historian's and the psychologist's approach.'

It is precisely because Koestler's life and work so deeply instantiate the existential dilemmas of our age that he is a fascinating figure, unjustly neglected and too often dismissed as a sexual psychopath. He was not a naturally good man (far from it), but he was struggling toward the good by the light and authority of his own intellect; unfortunately, as Hume tells us, reason is the slave of the passions, and Koestler was an exceptionally passionate man.

Once I happened to find two first editions, very cheap, of Koestler's books in a second-hand bookshop that I haunt. 'Ah,' said the bookshop owner, '*The Age of Longing* and *Dialogue with Death*: a complete summary of human life, when you come to think of it.'

IBSEN AND HIS DISCONTENTS

A FAMILY, DR JOHNSON once wrote, is a little kingdom, torn with factions and exposed to revolutions. This is a less than ringing endorsement of family life, of course; and the great Norwegian playwright Henrik Ibsen, whose childhood had been as unhappy as Johnson's, would have agreed with this assessment. But Johnson, unlike Ibsen, went on to remark that all judgment is comparative: that to judge an institution or a convention rightly, one must compare it with its alternatives. Marriage has many pains, says Johnson in *Rasselas*, but celibacy has no pleasures.

Johnson saw human existence as inseparable from dissatisfaction. It is man's nature to suffer from incompatible desires simultaneously – for example, wanting both security and excitement. When he has one, he longs for the other, so that contentment is rarely unalloyed and never lasting.

But most people find it more comforting to believe in perfectibility than in imperfectibility – an example of what Dr Johnson called the triumph of hope over experience. The notion of imperfectibility not only fans existential anxieties but also – by precluding simple solutions to all human problems – places much tougher intellectual demands upon us than utopianism does. Not every question can be answered by reference to a few simple abstract principles that, if followed with sufficient rigor, will supposedly lead to perfection – which is why conservatism is so much more difficult to reduce to slogans than its much more abstract competitors.

The yearning for principles that will abolish human dissatisfactions helps account for the continuing popularity of Ibsen's three most frequently performed plays: *A Doll's House*, *Ghosts* and *Hedda Gabler*.

Each is a ferocious attack on marriage as a powerful source of much human unhappiness and frustration. It is this indictment that gives Ibsen his extraordinary modernity, a modernity that has only seemed to increase over the century and a quarter since he wrote these plays.

The scale of Ibsen's achievement is astonishing. Almost single-handedly he gave birth to the modern theatre. Before him the 19th century, so rich in other literary forms, produced hardly a handful of plays that can still be performed, and the literary power of his work has never since been equalled. It was he who first realised that mundane daily life, relayed in completely naturalistic language, contained within it all the ingredients of tragedy. That he should have transformed the whole of Western drama while writing in an obscure language that was considered primitive   and that he should have produced in 20 years more performable plays than all the British and French playwrights of his era put together, despite their incomparably longer and richer theatrical traditions – is almost miraculous.

Though Ibsen often claimed to be a poet rather than a social critic, lacking any didactic purpose, the evidence of his letters and speeches (quite apart from the internal evidence of the plays themselves) proves quite the opposite – that he was almost incandescent with moral purpose. Contemporaries had no doubt of it; and the first book about him in English, Bernard Shaw's *Quintessence of Ibsenism*, published in 1891 while Ibsen still had many years to live and plays to write, stated forthrightly that his works stood or fell by the moral precepts they advocated. Shaw thought that Ibsen was a Joshua come to blow down the walls of moral convention. I think this judgment is wrong: Ibsen was far too great a writer to be only a moralist, and it is possible still to read or watch his plays with pleasure and instruction without swallowing what he has to say hook, line and sinker.

Still, Ibsen's influence extended far beyond the theatre. He wrote as much to be read as to be performed; and his plays were published, often in relatively large editions, to catch the Christmas market. And Shaw was hardly alone in perceiving their unconventionality. *Ghosts*, for instance, was initially considered so controversial, not to say filthy, that its printed version was handed round semi-clandestinely, few people daring to be seen reading it. By the end of his life, however, a quarter of a century later, most European intellectuals had come to take its moral outlook virtually for granted, and anyone who continued to resist its teachings seemed mired in an unenlightened past.

The comparatively easy acceptance of what Shaw called Ibsenism – 20 or 30 years is a long time in the life of a man, but not of mankind – means that Ibsen must have expressed what many people had thought and wanted to hear but had not dared to say. He was thus both a cause and a symptom of social change; and like many such figures, he was partly right and largely wrong.

What are his moral teachings, at least in the three plays that have forged his enduring image? He was as rabidly hostile to conventional family life as Marx or Engels, but he was a much more effective and powerful critic, because his criticism did not remain on the level of philosophical abstraction. On the contrary, he laid bare the factions and revolutions of family life, its lies and miseries, in compelling and believable dramas; and while it has always been open to the reader or viewer to ascribe the moral pathology exhibited in these plays to the particular characters or neuroses of their *dramatis personae* alone, clearly this was not Ibsen's intention. He was not a forerunner of Jerry Springer; his aim was not titillation or a mere display of the grotesque. He intends us to regard the morbidity his plays anatomise as typical and quintessential (to use Shaw's word), the inevitable consequence of certain social conventions and institutions. He invites us implicitly, and explicitly in *A Doll's House* and *Ghosts*, to consider alternative ways of living in order to eliminate what he considers the avoidable misery of the pathology he brings to light.

It is hardly surprising that feminists celebrate Ibsen. For one thing, his three oft-performed plays repeatedly suggest that marriage is but formalised and legalised prostitution. In *A Doll's House*, Mrs Linde, a childhood friend whom Nora has just encountered after an absence of many years, tells Nora that her marriage has been an unhappy one (I use throughout Michael Meyer's excellent translations):

> NORA: Tell me, is it really true that you didn't love your husband?...
> MRS LINDE: Well, my mother was still alive; and she was helpless and bedridden. And I had my two little brothers to take care of. I didn't feel I could say no.
> NORA: ...He was rich then, was he?

In *Ghosts*, too, marriage for money is a prominent theme. The carpenter Engstrand suggests to Regina, who at this point thinks she is his daughter, that she should marry for that reason. After all, he himself married Regina's mother for money. Like Regina, she had been a servant in the Alving household, until Lieutenant Alving got her pregnant. Mrs Alving discharged her, giving her some money before she left, and then Engstrand married her. Pastor Manders discusses the matter with Lieutenant Alving's widow:

> MANDERS: How much was it you gave the girl?
> MRS ALVING: Fifty pounds.
> MANDERS: Just imagine! To go and marry a fallen woman for a paltry fifty pounds!

The implication is that the transaction would have been reasonable, in the eyes of the respectable pastor, if the sum had been larger – as large as the sum that had 'bought' Mrs Alving. At the play's outset, when she is making arrangements for the opening of an orphanage named in memory of her husband, she explains something to Pastor Manders.

> MRS ALVING: The annual donations that I have made to this Orphanage add up to the sum... which made Lieutenant Alving, in his day, 'a good match'.
> MANDERS: I understand -
> MRS ALVING: It was the sum with which he bought me.

Hedda Gabler alludes only slightly less directly to the mercenary motive of marriage. Mrs Elvsted is another old acquaintance of the main female character, who turns up after an absence of many years and has had an unhappy marriage. She went to Mr Elvsted as a housekeeper and, after the death of his first wife, married him:

> HEDDA: But he loves you, surely? In his own way?
> MRS ELVSTED: Oh, I don't know. I think he finds me useful. And then I don't cost much to keep. I'm cheap.

Marriage, then, is a financial bargain, and a pretty poor one – at least for women. But, of course, there are other reasons for marital unhappiness, especially the irreducible incompatibility of husband and wife. In fact, any apparent happiness is a façade or a lie, maintained by social pressure.

In *A Doll's House*, for example, Nora appears at first to be happily married to Torvald Helmer, a young lawyer on his way up. Helmer treats her like a little girl, sometimes chiding and sometimes indulging her, but never taking her seriously as an adult; and she plays along, acting the featherbrained young woman to almost nauseating perfection. Unbeknownst to Helmer, however, Nora has previously saved his life by obtaining a loan, secured, by a forged signature, that allowed them to spend a year in Italy, whose warmer climate cured the disease that would have killed him.

When Helmer discovers what she has done, he is not grateful and does not see her forgery as a manifestation of her love for him; on the contrary, he condemns her unmercifully and tells her that she is not fit to be mother to their three children. Helmer interprets the episode as if he were the lawyer prosecuting her rather than her husband.

The scales fall from Nora's eyes. Their life together, she sees, has been not only an outward but an inward sham: he is not the man that she, blinded by her acceptance of the social role assigned to her, took him for. She tells him that she is leaving him; and although Helmer offers a more adult, equal relationship between them, it is too late.

Undoubtedly, Ibsen was pointing to a genuine and serious problem of the time – the assumed inability of women to lead any but a domestic existence, without intellectual content (and, in fact, the play was based upon a real case). But if this were its principal moral focus, the play would have lost its impact by now, since the point has long been conceded. Ibsen was not, in fact, a devotee of women's rights: addressing a conference on the subject in Oslo, he said, 'I have never written any play to further a social purpose... I am not even very sure what Women's Rights really are.' With no faith in legislative or institutional solutions to problems, Ibsen had a much larger target: the change of people from within, so that they might finally express their true nature unmediated by the distortions of society.

In *Ghosts*, Mrs Alving's marriage is unhappy not just because she was 'bought'. Her husband was a philandering alcoholic, and she fled from him after a year of marriage, taking refuge in Pastor Manders's house. Although Manders and Mrs Alving felt a mutual attraction – indeed, fell in love – the pastor persuaded her that she had a religious duty to return to her husband. Despite Alving's promise to change, which at the beginning of the play Pastor Manders believes that he kept, Alving continued his dissolute ways until his death. Mrs Alving made it her task to conceal his conduct from the world and from her son, Oswald. But when Alving impregnated the servant with Regina (who is thus Oswald's half-sister), she sent Oswald away and would not allow him to return home while Alving was still alive. While Alving drank himself to death, Mrs Alving made a success of his estate – a success that she allowed to be attributed to Alving, permitting him to die in the odour not only of sanctity but of success.

The lies of Mrs Alving's life spring from the false sense of shame – what will others say? – that traps her into returning to Alving and into covering up for him. Similarly, Manders, as Ibsen portrays him, represents a bogus moralism, in whose code appearance is more important than reality or inner meaning, and avoidance of shame is a better guide to conduct than conscience. This code leads Manders to make wrong decisions even in banal practical matters – for example, whether the orphanage should be insured or not. He discusses this question with Mrs Alving, noting that there had nearly been a fire there the day before. Mrs Alving concludes that the orphanage should be insured. But then Manders indulges in a little oily and dishonest sanctimony:

> MANDERS: Ah, but wait a minute, Mrs Alving. Let us consider this question a little more closely... The Orphanage is, so to speak, to be consecrated to a higher purpose... As far as I personally am concerned, I see nothing offensive in securing ourselves against all eventualities... But what is the feeling among the local people out here?... Are there many people with the right to an opinion... who might take offence?... I am thinking chiefly of people sufficiently independent and

influential to make it impossible for one to ignore their opinions altogether... You see! In town we have a great many such people. Followers of other denominations. People might very easily come to the conclusion that neither you nor I have sufficient trust in the ordinance of a Higher Power... I know – my conscience is clear, that is true. But all the same, we couldn't prevent a false and unfavourable interpretation being placed on our action... And I can't altogether close my eyes to the difficult – I might even say deeply embarrassing – position in which I might find myself.

Of course the opinions of the people whom Manders is propitiating are just as bogus as his own; and when, the next day, the orphanage does in fact burn down, because of Manders's carelessness with a candle, he not only deems it God's judgment on the Alving family but is clearly worried more about his own reputation than about anything else. In fact he finds someone else – Engstrand, the carpenter – willing to take the blame for what he has done. Manders has no conscience, only a fear of what others will say.

His explanation of why he persuaded Mrs Alving to return to her husband displays the same pharisaical fear of public opinion:

> MANDERS: ...a wife is not appointed to be her husband's judge. It was your duty humbly to bear that cross which a higher will had seen fit to assign to you. But instead you... hazard your good name, and very nearly ruin the reputation of others.
> MRS ALVING: Others? Another's, you mean?
> MANDERS: It was extremely inconsiderate of you to seek refuge with me.

Once again there can be no doubt that Ibsen has most accurately put his finger on a pseudo morality in which shame or social disapproval takes the place of personal conscience or true moral principle, and in whose name people – especially women – are made to suffer misery, degradation, and even violence. This is no mere figment of Ibsen's imagination. Indeed, I have observed the consequences of the operation of this pseudo-morality among my young Muslim patients, who are made to suffer the torments of a living hell and are sometimes even killed by their male relatives, solely to preserve the 'good name' of the family in the opinion of others.

By no means, then, was Ibsen exaggerating. When he said that his fellow countrymen were a nation of serfs living in a free country, he meant that their fear of shame and notions of respectability enslaved and oppressed them, even in a land without political oppression.

The third of these portraits of unhappy marriages, *Hedda Gabler*, is the least interesting because it is implausible. Hedda Gabler, the daughter of a general, marries beneath herself, choosing an intellectual who hopes for a chair at the university, though he is actually a petty pedant, without originality or flair. In fact, he is such a milksop, such a pathetic ninny, that it is hard to believe that Hedda, with her very high conception of her own abilities and entitlements, would have married him in the first place. It is therefore difficult to take her consequent travails very seriously. But she ends up killing herself because life, with the bourgeois options it currently offers her, is not worth living.

It is in *A Doll's House* and *Ghosts* that Ibsen offers us not just criticisms but positive prescriptions. And it is because his prescriptions are those of the 1960s, though written 80 years earlier, that we find him still so astonishingly modern and prescient.

When, in *A Doll's House*, Nora tells her husband that she is leaving him, he asks her (just as Pastor Manders would have done) whether she has thought of what other people will say. He then goes on to ask her about her duty:

> HELMER: Can you neglect your most sacred duties?
> NORA: What do you call my most sacred duties?
> HELMER: Do I have to tell you? Your duties to your husband, and your children.

This crucial passage continues with a little psychobabble followed by the justification of radical egotism:

> NORA: I have another duty which is equally sacred.
> HELMER: ...What on earth could that be?
> NORA: My duty to myself.

Nora goes on to explain that she is first and foremost a human being – or that, anyway, she must try to become one. (This sentiment reminds one of Marx's view that men will become truly human only after the revolution has brought about the end of class society. All who had gone before, apparently – and all of Marx's contemporaries – were less than truly human. Little wonder that untold millions were done to death by those who shared this philosophy.) So if Nora is not yet a human being, what will make her one? Philosophical autonomy is the answer:

> NORA: ...I'm no longer prepared to accept what people say and what's written in books. I must think things out for myself and try to find my own answer.

And the criterion she is to use, to judge whether her own answer is correct, is whether it is right – 'or anyway, whether it is right for me'. Postmodernism is not so very modern after all, it seems: Ibsen got there first.

Moments later, Nora makes clear what the consequences of her new freedom are:

> NORA: I don't want to see the children... As I am now
> I can be nothing to them.

And with these chilling words she severs all connection with her three children, forever. Her duty to herself leaves no room for a moment's thought for them. They are as dust in the balance.

When, as I have, you have met hundreds, perhaps thousands, of people abandoned in their childhood by one or both of their parents, on essentially the same grounds ('I need my own space'), and you have seen the lasting despair and damage that such abandonment causes, it is difficult to read or see *A Doll's House* without anger and revulsion. Now we see what Ibsen meant when he said that women's rights were of no fundamental interest to him. He was out to promote something much more important: universal egotism.

It is clear from *Ghosts* as well that Ibsen conceived of a society in which everyone was his own Descartes, working out everything from first principles – or, at least, what he or she believed to be first principles. For example, when Pastor Manders arrives for the first time in Mrs Alving's house, he finds some books that he considers dangerously liberal:

> MRS ALVING: But what do you object to in these books?
> MANDERS: Object to? You surely don't imagine I spend my time studying such publications?
> MRS ALVING: In other words, you've no idea what you're condemning?

> MANDERS: I've read quite enough about these writings to disapprove of them.
>
> MRS ALVING: Don't you think you ought to form your own opinion?
>
> MANDERS: My dear Mrs Alving, there are many occasions in life when one must rely on the judgment of others.

Coming from a character whom Ibsen scorns as ridiculous and bigoted, these words, which contain an obvious truth, are meant to be rejected out of hand. In Ibsen's philosophy, everyone – at least Nature's aristocrats, for in fact Ibsen was no egalitarian or democrat – must examine every question for himself and arrive at his own answer: for example, whether the *Protocols of the Elders of Zion* is historically true – or at least historically true for him.

The object, or at least the obvious consequence, of such independence of judgment is the breakdown of the artificial, socially-constructed barriers that constrain behaviour and (in theory) prevent people from reaching a state of complete happiness, which is to say absence of frustration. Unhappiness in all the plays results from not having followed the heart's inclinations, either by not doing what one wants, or by doing what one does not want, all to comply with some social obligation enforced by the Pastor Manderses of the world:

> MANDERS: ...your marriage was celebrated in an orderly fashion and in full accordance with the law.
>
> MRS ALVING: All this talk about law and order. I often think that is what causes all the unhappiness in the world.

Mrs Alving's son, Oswald, has returned home from Paris not only to attend the opening of the orphanage named for his father but also because he is ill, with tertiary syphilis. He is destined to die soon in a state of either madness or dementia, according to the Parisian specialist (French syphilologists knew more about the disease than any other doctors in the world, and Ibsen was always well informed about medical matters).

At first Oswald – still believing that his father was a fine, upstanding man – concludes that he contracted the disease by his own conduct. In fact, he has congenital syphilis, passed on by his father. (It was formerly objected that Oswald could not have caught syphilis from his father alone, but in fact Oswald's father could have passed on the germs to Oswald through his mother, infecting her only with a subclinical case.) For her part, Mrs Alving is in no doubt that society is responsible for her husband's (and thus her son's) disease:

> MRS ALVING: And this happy, carefree child – for he [Alving] was like a child, then – had to live here in a little town that had no joy to offer him... And in the end the inevitable happened... Your poor father never found any outlet for the joy of life that was in him. And I didn't bring any sunshine into his home... They had taught me about duty and things like that and I sat here for too long believing in them. In the end everything became a matter of duty – my duty, and his duty, and – I'm afraid I made his home intolerable for your poor father.

The way of avoiding such tragedies is for everyone to follow his own inclinations, more or less as they arise. Only associations free of institutional constraint will set men free. Earlier in the play Oswald has described to the scandalised Manders the informal families among whom he mixed in bohemian Paris, after Manders tells Mrs Alving that Oswald has never had the opportunity to know a real home.

> OSWALD: I beg your pardon, sir, but there you're quite mistaken.
> MANDERS: Oh? I thought you had spent practically all your time in artistic circles.
> OSWALD: I have.
> MANDERS: Mostly among young artists.
> OSWALD. Yes.
> MANDERS: But I thought most of those people lacked the means to support a family and make a home for themselves.
> OSWALD: Some of them can't afford to get married, sir.
> MANDERS: Yes, that's what I'm saying.
> OSWALD: But that doesn't mean they can't have a home...
> MANDERS: But I'm not speaking about bachelor establishments. By a home I mean a family establishment, where a man lives with his wife and children.
> OSWALD: Quite. Or with his children and their mother.

We go on to learn that these informal families, precisely because they are based not upon convention, duty or social pressure but upon unconstrained love, are not only equal to conventional families but much superior. Oswald talks of the peace and harmony that he found among them: 'I have never heard an offensive word there, far less ever witnessed anything that could be called immoral.'

And he adds.

> OSWALD: No; do you know when and where I have
> encountered immorality in artistic circles?
> MANDERS: No, I don't, thank heaven.
> OSWALD: Well, I shall tell you. I have encountered
> it when one or another of our model husbands and
> fathers came down to look around a little on their
> own... Then we learned a few things. Those gentlemen
> were able to tell us about places and things of which we
> had never dreamed.

Not only are informal arrangements happier, therefore, than formal ones, but they prevent the spread of the very syphilis from which Oswald suffers. Suffice it to say that this has not been my experience of the last 15 to 20 years of my medical practice.

The right – indeed, the duty – of everyone to decide his own moral principles and to decide what is right for him, without the ghosts of the past to misguide him, leads Mrs Alving to approve of incest, if incest is what makes people happy. While Oswald is still unaware that Regina is his half-sister, he falls in love with her (very quickly, it must be said), and she with him. He wants to marry her.

Mrs Alving discusses the matter with Manders, who by now is aware of the consanguinity of Oswald and Regina:

> MANDERS: ...That would be dreadful.
> MRS ALVING: If I knew... that it would make him
> happy –
> MANDERS: Yes? What then?

> MRS ALVING: If only I weren't such an abject coward,
> I'd say to him: 'Marry her, or make what arrangements
> you please. As long as you're honest and open about
> it – '
> MANDERS:... You mean a legal marriage! ...It's
> absolutely unheard of!
> MRS ALVING: Unheard of, did you say? Put your
> hand on your heart, Pastor Manders, and tell me – do
> you really believe there aren't married couples like that
> to be found in this country?

This is an argument typical of people who wish to abolish boundaries: if these boundaries are not – because they cannot be – adhered to with perfect consistency, then they should be obliterated, as they can only give rise to hypocrisy. Mrs Alving adds the kind of smart-aleck comment that has ever been the stock-in-trade of those to whom boundaries are so irksome: 'Well, we all stem from a relationship of that kind, so we are told.'

It is not that Mrs Alving fails to believe in right and wrong. But what is wrong is betrayal of one's inclinations. When Manders describes his painful self-control in sending her back to her husband when he was in love with her himself, he asks whether that was a crime. Mrs Alving replies, 'Yes, I think so.'

By the end of the play Oswald has asked his mother to kill him with a morphine injection if he has another attack of madness or dementia. In the last scene Oswald does have such an attack, and Mrs Alving's last words in the play, concerning this act of euthanasia, are, 'No; no; no! Yes! No; no!' We never find out whether she goes ahead, and Ibsen refused to say. But he clearly saw it as a matter for everyone to make up his own mind about, to work out for himself, free of legal – which is to say, conventional and institutional – guidance.

The modernity of Ibsen's thought hardly needs further emphasis. The elevation of emotion over principle, of inclination over duty, of rights over responsibilities, of ego over the claims of others, the impatience with boundaries and the promotion of the self as the measure of all things: what could be more modern or gratifying to our current sensibility? Not surprisingly, Ibsen regarded youth rather than age as the fount of wisdom.

'Youth,' he assures us, 'has an instinctive genius which unconsciously hits upon the right answer.'

And Ibsen was profoundly modern in another respect, too. In his own existence he was very conventional. Although attracted to women other than his wife, he always resisted temptation; he dressed correctly; he ostentatiously wore the decorations awarded him by the crowned heads of Europe – which, notoriously, he solicited. He was extremely cautious and careful with money. His habits and tastes were profoundly bourgeois, and he was regular in his habits to the point of rigidity. He could be extremely prickly when he felt his own dignity affronted, and he was a great lover of formality. His wife called him Ibsen, and he signed his letters to her Henrik Ibsen, not Henrik.

His character was formed in an atmosphere of Protestant Pietism. He was inhibited to a degree unusual even among his compatriots. As a child he experienced the trauma of his father's bankruptcy and the descent from prosperity and social respect to poverty and humiliation. He both hated the society in which he grew up and craved high status within it.

Ibsen's character was fixed, but he longed to be different. He was Calvin wanting to be Dionysius. If he couldn't change himself, at least he could change others, and society itself. Like many modern intellectuals, he had difficulty distinguishing his personal problems and neuroses from social problems. Shortly before he wrote *Ghosts*, his son, Sigurd, who had lived almost all his life abroad, had been refused admission to Christiania (Oslo) University by the governing ecclesiastical authorities until he had met such entry requirements as a test of proficiency in Norwegian. Ibsen was furious. He wrote, 'I shall raise a memorial to that black band of theologians.' And he did – Pastor Manders.

There is no evidence that Ibsen ever thought, much less cared, about the effect of his principles on society as a whole. This indifference is hardly surprising, given that he thought that nothing good could come of the great herd of mankind, which he termed the majority, the masses, the mob. He believed that he himself belonged to an aristocracy of intellect, and it is of course in the nature of aristocrats that they should have privileges not accorded to others. But whether we like it or not, we live in a democratic age, when the privileges claimed by some will soon be claimed by all. The charmingly insouciant free love of bohemians is soon enough transmuted into the violent chaos of the slums.

'[*Ghosts*] contains the future,' said Ibsen. He also said that he is most right who is most in tune with the future. But he did not display any interest or foresight into what that future might contain: for him, not whatever is, is right, but whatever will be, is right. Whether the scores of millions who suffered and died in the 20th century because of the destruction of moral boundaries would have agreed with him is another matter.

WHAT MAKES DR JOHNSON GREAT?

A FRIEND OF MINE, Russian by birth but English by adoption, who speaks English more elegantly and eloquently than most native speakers, once asked me of what, precisely, the greatness of Dr Johnson consisted. He was asking only for information, in a spirit of inquiry; but the question took me aback, because the greatness of Dr Johnson was something that I took for granted. If my friend had asked me to name a man whose greatness was his most salient characteristic, I think I would have named Dr Johnson without a second thought.

'But,' my friend continued, 'Dr Johnson was a writer, and the greatness of writers is in their writing. Who reads him now, or feels the need to do so?' He added that he had never read him but still considered himself well-read in English literature.

Johnson's quality of unreadness is not new and is equalled only by that of Walter Scott, whose once-famous historical romances are now read, I suspect, only rarely, and with a sinking heart and a sense of duty – even though *Ivanhoe* was allegedly Mr Blair's favourite reading. Carlyle, in his essay on Boswell's *Life of Johnson*, says that the *Life* far exceeds in value anything Johnson wrote: '[A]lready, indeed,' says Carlyle, '[Johnson's works] are becoming obsolete in this generation; and for some future generations may be valuable chiefly as Prolegomena and expository Scholia to this Johnsoniad of Boswell.' This was written in 1832, less than half a century after Johnson's death, and as literary prophecy was not far from the mark. Boswell has many more readers than Johnson, and probably has had ever since Carlyle passed judgment.

Can a man be really great whose greatest claim to fame is to have been the subject of a great biography, perhaps the greatest ever written?

Of the biographer himself, Macaulay wrote (one year before Carlyle): 'Homer is not more decidedly the first of heroic poets, Shakespeare is not more decidedly the first of dramatists, Demosthenes is not more decidedly the first of orators, than Boswell is the first of biographers. He has no second. He has distanced all his competitors so decidedly that it is not worth while to place them.' This despite the fact that the biography opens with the words, 'To write the life of him who ex-celled all mankind in writing the lives of others… is an arduous and may be reckoned in me a presumptuous task.'

A great biography could be written, at least in theory, about a man who was not of the first importance. Johnson himself wrote a small biographical masterpiece about the reprobate poet Richard Savage, who would by now have been entirely forgotten had Johnson not done so. But great as Boswell's book is, it could not have been written about any man taken at random: Johnson found his Boswell, as the saying goes, but it would be truer to say that Boswell found his Johnson. By the end of the *Life*, most of us are convinced that the final encomium of the writer to his subject was fully justified: 'Such was SAMUEL JOHNSON, a man whose talents, acquirements and virtues were so extraordinary, that the more his character is considered, the more he will be regarded by the present age, and by posterity, with admiration and reverence.'

My friend, who had read his Boswell and knew Johnson's witticisms well enough, persisted in denying that they were grounds for the unanimous conviction he found among educated speakers of English that Johnson deserves an honoured place in the literary pantheon. We might love him for his peculiarities, esteem him for his character, admire him for his learning, wish we had been present to hear his repartee, yet none of this sufficiently accounts for our reverence for him. His Dictionary was no doubt a stupendous achievement, a colossal monument to individual industry and learning, but so was

Alexander Cruden's concordance to the Bible, which provides cross-references for every single word in the King James version. Though Cruden's achievement was of the physical and mental magnitude of Johnson's Dictionary, we do not reverence him in the slightest. Cruden, in fact a very interesting man, is now almost forgotten.

I tried to convey to my friend my personal reaction to Johnson. When I look at Johnson's death mask, I think I see something of his tremendous character and intellect in the huge and craggy features, a rough nobility and a profundity of being, a face that bears the same proportion to the average human visage as the Himalayas do to the Cotswolds: but of course I recognise the objection that I find reflected there only what I was predisposed to find. Likewise, when I look at Joshua Reynolds's portraits of Johnson: those extraordinary pictures by a painter who so loved and reverenced his subject and friend that he painted him precisely as he was – not graceful, not handsome, not elegant – convinced that his appearance would speak for itself, that of a man possessed of unmistakable force of character, an unceasing wrestler with the deepest problems of man's existence, a great soul. We may not always agree with Dr Johnson's answers, but when we look at Reynolds's portraits of him, we can hardly doubt the sincerity, depth and intelligence of his efforts. All the same, I had to admit (under the cross-examination of my friend) that great portraits are no guarantee of the greatness of their sitters.

Macaulay's summary of Boswell's biographical account gives us a clue as to why we are so moved by Johnson and tend to make him a touchstone of what we consider the most admirable, the highest type of man. Thanks to Boswell, says Macaulay, 'Johnson grown old, Johnson in the fullness of his fame and in the enjoyment of a competent fortune, is better known to us than any other man in history.' He continues:

Every thing about him, his coat, his wig, his figure, his
face, his scrofula, his St. Vitus's dance, his rolling walk,
his blinking eye, the outward signs which too clearly
marked his approbation of his dinner, his insatiable
appetite for fish-sauce and veal-pie with plums, his
inexhaustible thirst for tea, his trick of touching the posts
as he walked, his mysterious practice of treasuring up
scraps of orange-peel, his morning slumbers, his midnight disputations, his contortions, his mutterings, his
gruntings, his puffings, his vigorous, acute and ready eloquence, his sarcastic wit, his vehemence, his insolence,
his fits of tempestuous rage, his queer inmates, old Mr
Levett and blind Mrs Williams [who lived for years in his
household at his expense], the cat Hodge and the negro
Frank are all as familiar to us as the objects by which we
have been surrounded from childhood.

What Johnson said of the London of his time, that it contained all
that human life can afford, seems also true of his own life. Johnson is
a good but flawed man, always trying to be, but not always succeeding
in being, a better one: he is proud, he is humble; he is weak, he is
strong; he is prejudiced, he is generous-minded; he is tender-hearted,
he is bad-tempered; he is foolish, he is wise; he is sure of himself,
he is modest; he is idle, he is hardworking; he is opinionated, he is
consumed by doubt; he is spiritual, he is carnal; he is hopeful, he
is despairing; he is sceptical, he is credulous; he is melancholy, he is
light-hearted; he is deferential, he is aware that he has no superior in
the world; he is clumsy of body, he is elegant of mind and diction; he
is a failure, he is triumphant. We never expect to meet anyone who, to
such a degree, encompasses in his being all human vulnerability and
human resilience.

Humility and pride contend in Johnson's heart and mind. He does not object in the slightest to social hierarchy – quite the contrary, and consistent with his profound conservatism, he repeatedly supports it as a necessary precondition of civilisation – and he has no objection to inherited wealth, eminence or influence. Yet when he feels slighted by a nobleman, he objects to the insult to his own worth in the most manly, uncompromising, eloquent and fearless fashion. Writing to Lord Chesterfield, who encouraged him at first to compile his great *Dictionary*, then ignored him entirely during his years of almost superhuman toil, and finally tried to pose as his great patron once he had brought his *Dictionary* to completion, Johnson says in prose whose nobility rings down the centuries: 'Is not a Patron, my Lord, one who looks with unconcern on a man struggling for life in the water, and, when he has reached ground, encumbers him with help? …I hope it is no very cynical asperity, not to confess obligations where no benefit has been received, or to be unwilling that the Publick should consider me as owing that to a Patron, which Providence has enabled me to do for myself.'

His integrity (a virtue no more common in his time than now) shines out from a letter that he wrote to a lady who had asked him to recommend her son to the Archbishop of Canterbury for admission to a university (either Oxford or Cambridge):

MADAM,

I hope you will believe that my delay in answering your letter could proceed only from my unwillingness to destroy any hope that you had formed. Hope is itself a species of happiness, and, perhaps, the chief happiness which this world affords; but, like all other pleasures immoderately enjoyed, the excesses of hope must be expiated by pain… When you made your request to

> me, you should have considered, Madam, what you
> were asking. You ask me to solicit a great man, to whom
> I never spoke, for a young person whom I had never
> seen, upon a supposition which I had no means of
> knowing to be true.

I don't think you could read this letter without perceiving in its writer great intellect, eloquence, wit, knowledge of life derived from deep reflection upon experience and – what perhaps most compels respect – moral seriousness.

Some people might (and did) find Johnson sententious. His precepts roll through our minds like thunder through hills and valleys – but do they have more meaning than thunder has? They often appear obvious, but they are obvious not because they are clichés or truisms or things that everyone knows and has always known, nor are they like the sermons of a jobbing clergyman who goes through the motions of extolling virtue and condemning sin because it is his job to do so. Johnson's precepts are obvious because they are distillations of the lessons of common human experience, and, once expressed, they are impossible to deny.

At every moment, Johnson reflects on the moral meaning and consequences of human life. In his biography of the dissolute poet and his sometime friend Richard Savage, written at an early stage of his career and originally published anonymously, Johnson exhibits both compassion for, and clear-sighted acknowledgment of the faults of, his subject, whose life he treats as an object for moral and psychological reflection. Who could fail to recognise a common human pattern in his delineation of Savage's greatest failing?

> By imputing none of his miseries to himself he
> continued to act upon the same principles and to follow

the same path; was never made wiser by his sufferings, nor preserved by one misfortune from falling into another. He proceeded throughout his life to tread the same steps on the same circle; always applauding his past conduct, or at least forgetting it, to amuse himself with phantoms of happiness which were dancing before him, and willingly turned his eye from the light of reason, when it would have discovered the illusion and shewn him, what he never wanted to see, his real state.

The necessity for honest self-examination, if avoidable misery is to be avoided, could hardly be more eloquently expressed; and it is one of the most serious defects of modern culture and the welfare state that they discourage such self-examination by encouraging the imputation of all miseries to others, and thus have a disastrous effect upon human character.

Johnson was a man of the Enlightenment. He had a great interest in the experimental sciences, for example, and placed a high value on reason. But he was also acutely aware of the limits of the Enlightenment. He could hold irreconcilable dilemmas in his mind without giving way to nihilism or irrationalism. He was profoundly anti-Romantic: his *Life of Savage* ends with an implicit denunciation of the Romantic notion that the possession of talent excuses a man from the demands of the moral life or social existence:

> This relation [the biography] will not be wholly without its use if... those who, in confidence of superior capacities or attainments, disregard the common maxims of life, shall be reminded that nothing will supply the want of prudence, and that negligence and irregularity long

continued will make knowledge useless, wit ridiculous
and genius contemptible.

No one could accuse Johnson of being a mindless conformist; it
is doubtful whether a more individual individual has ever existed; but
he was always prepared to place that limit on his own appetites that,
in the opinion of his acquaintance, Edmund Burke, qualified a man
for freedom.

In his censure of disregard for the common maxims of
life, Johnson displays his deep though flexible conservatism, a
conservatism not of the mulish kind opposed to all possible change
(Johnson invariably praises advances in knowledge and industry,
for example) but of the kind that believes that most men, instead
of reasoning from first principles on all occasions, need the aid of
the accumulated wisdom of custom, precept and prejudice most
of the time if they are to live a moral life in reasonable harmony
and happiness with one another. Johnson criticises Dean Swift,
in his brief biography of him, for his wilful and self-conscious
eccentricity. 'Singularity,' he says, 'as it implies a contempt of the
general practice, is a kind of defiance which justly provokes the
hostility of ridicule; he, therefore, who indulges in peculiar traits, is
worse than others, if he be not better.' Note that Johnson does not
deny the possibility of betterment, nor does he believe that the best
path has always been found already. But he denies that deviation
from the common path, for reasons of vanity, is a virtue; on the
contrary, it is a vice. We might have had fewer social problems
today if this view had had more currency.

A comparison of Johnson's *Rasselas* with Voltaire's *Candide* – by
common consent the two greatest philosophical tales ever written
– makes Johnson's greatness stand forth in sharp relief. Published
in the same year, 1759, both works attacked facile optimism about

human existence. By strange coincidence, both authors had written long poems that addressed the question of optimism before they wrote these two tales exploring the same subject. Johnson's 'The Vanity of Human Wishes' suggests that lasting happiness is not of this world, whether sought in power, wealth or knowledge. Bitterness and disappointment are ever the scholar's lot:

> There mark what Ills the Scholar's Life assail,
> Toil, Envy, Want, the Garret, and the Jail.
> See Nations slowly wise and meanly just,
> To buried Merit raise the tardy Bust.

For Johnson, no form of life is free of care; each has pains at least equal to its joys.

After the Lisbon earthquake of 1755, which killed 30,000 and left the city in ruins, Voltaire wrote a poem that questioned the Leibnizian notion, expressed most pithily in Pope's famous words, 'Whatever is, is right.' Divine Providence being benign, this notion holds, all must be for the best in this, the best of all possible worlds, despite appearances to the contrary, and nothing could be other than it is. Voltaire sharply challenged this view in his 'Poem on the Lisbon Disaster; Or an Examination of the Axiom that All Is Well.'

> Will you say, on seeing this pile of dead:
> 'God is revenged, their death is the price of their crimes'?
> What crime, what fault, have these infants committed
> Who are crushed and bloody on their mother's breast?
> Did Lisbon, which is no more, have more vices
> Than Paris, than London, which are sunk in pleasures?

Voltaire's *Candide*, which has always had more renown than Johnson's *Rasselas*, is nevertheless far the more superficial work, its irony crude and shallow compared with that of *Rasselas*. The surface similarities of the stories only underline their difference in depth. The one, *Candide*, attacks a philosophical doctrine; the other, *Rasselas*, addresses a human condition that is with us still. Portraits of the two authors reveal the difference in their character: Voltaire looks like an unregenerate cynic who wants to shock the world by sneering at it, while Johnson looks like a man determined to penetrate to the heart of human existence. The more serious man is also far the funnier.

Candide, a naive, good-natured young man, lives happily in a Westphalian *schloss*, the home of Baron Thunder-ten-tronckh. He falls under the philosophical spell of the household tutor, Dr Pangloss, who believes that 'all is for the best in this, the best of all possible worlds'. The book traces Candide's subsequent wanderings round the globe, in the course of which he suffers horrible injustices and ill-treatment, as do all his acquaintances.

He witnesses arbitrary misfortunes, including the Lisbon earthquake. In the end, he and Dr Pangloss are reunited on the banks of the Bosphorus, where they find some kind of tranquillity and happiness. Pangloss, absurdly, still maintains his optimism: since 'all events are linked together in the best of all possible worlds', for him their current happiness is the happy consequence of all that they had hitherto suffered and witnessed. Pangloss having been hanged and nearly burned alive by the Inquisition (among many other horrors), the absurdity of his doctrine is evident.

Rasselas is a prince of Abyssinia who, like all royal Abyssinian princes, lives in 'the happy valley' until the time comes for him to ascend the throne. (Interestingly, while Voltaire, the rationalist and universalist, displays considerable contempt for German culture, the patriotic and more locally rooted Johnson shows no contempt whatever for Abyssinian or Egyptian culture, suggesting that rootedness and imaginative sympathy for others are not incompatible.) In the happy valley, Rasselas has all his wants supplied; he lives in luxury among ample and continual amusements, and yet he feels discontent despite the perfection of the place and the ease of his existence.

He and his sister, Nekayah, and a philosophical tutor, Imlac, leave the happy valley and search the world for the right way to live. Imlac acts as a kind of ironical chorus to the ideas of the prince and princess. On their journey they meet the powerful and the powerless, the hermit, the socialite, the sage, the ignoramus, the sophisticate, the peasant: all modes of life, even the most outwardly attractive, have drawbacks, and none answers to all human desires or is free of anxieties and miseries. In the end, the royal pair realise that of the 'wishes that they had formed... none could be obtained'.

The difference in depth of the two books is readily apparent from the difference in the irony that each author employs. Voltaire is heavy and obvious; Johnson, despite his stylistic orotundity, is light and subtle. Candide is expelled from his happy home, Rasselas wants to escape his: already a great difference in depth, for Candide's misfortunes eventuate from outside himself, while Rasselas experiences Man's existential, internally-generated dissatisfaction and restlessness. Since no one could possibly imagine a place better than the happy valley, Johnson confronts us from the first with man's inability ever to be satisfied with what he has, which, he suggests, is his glory but also his misery.

Here is Voltaire on Baron Thunder-ten-tronckh: 'Monsieur the Baron was one of the most powerful lords in Westphalia, for his chateau had a door and some windows.' Yes, Germany was backward at the time, but the satire is heavy-handed. And the objects of Voltaire's satire are similarly unsubtle. Here is the account of the aftermath of the battle between the Bulgars and the Abars in their war about nothing (Candide was written during the Seven Years' War):

At last, while the two kings had Te Deums sung, each in his own camp, Candide took the opportunity to reason on causes and effects. He passed over piles of dead and dying, and first reached a nearby village; it was in ashes; it was an Abar village that the Bulgars had burnt, according to public law. Here badly wounded old men watched their wives die of slit throats, who held their children to their bloody breasts; there, young girls, slit open after having assuaged the natural needs of several heroes, sighed their last; others, half-burnt, begged that they should be killed off. Brains were spread on the ground, beside cut-off arms and legs.

And here is Voltaire's description of the Portuguese reaction to the earthquake of 1755, which Candide and Pangloss witnessed immediately upon their arrival in Lisbon:

After the earthquake that had destroyed three-quarters of Lisbon, the learned men of the country had not found a more effective means of preventing total ruin than that of giving the people a good *auto-da-fé*; it was decided by the University of Coimbra that the spectacle of several people being burnt slowly was an infallible preventative of earthquakes.

This is quite funny, and of course the horrors of war and the excesses of superstition are suitable, if easy, targets of criticism. But there is something irredeemably adolescent in Voltaire's satire, which also lacks real, nonabstract feeling for humanity. Baron Grimm noticed this when the book first came out: a judicious critic writing

247

2,000 years from now, he said, will probably say that the author was only 25 when he wrote it. In fact, Voltaire was 65, 15 years older than Johnson

When we turn to Johnson, we find a mind of a completely different quality. Repeatedly, we marvel at Johnson's wisdom and maturity. Rasselas falls for a time under the spell of a rhetorician in Cairo who extols the control of the passions and emotions. In a chapter titled 'The Prince Finds a Wise and Happy Man', he listens to the rhetorician give a lecture:

> His look was venerable, his action graceful, his pronunciation clear and his diction elegant. He shewed... that human nature is degraded and debased, when the lower faculties predominate over the higher; that when fancy, the parent of passion, usurps the dominion of the mind, nothing ensues but the natural effect of unlawful government, perturbation and confusion.

Rasselas 'listened to him with the veneration due to the instructions of a superior being' and visited him the following day to learn more wisdom from him. But 'he found the philosopher in a room half darkened, and his eyes misty, and his face pale'.

The philosopher's only daughter has died in the night of a fever. 'What I suffer cannot be remedied, what I have lost cannot be supplied.' Rasselas then confronts him with his own fine words about the primacy of reason over sentiments, to which the philosopher replies that Rasselas speaks like one who has never lost anyone. 'What comfort,' asks the philosopher, 'can truth and reason afford me? Of what effect are they now, but to tell me that my daughter will not be restored?'

Rasselas, 'whose humanity would not suffer him to insult misery with reproof, went away convinced of the emptiness of rhetorical sound, and the inefficacy of polished periods and studied sentences'.

Here is real education of both the heart and mind – and confirmation of Imlac's warning to Rasselas to 'be not too hasty... to trust or to admire the teachers of morality: they discourse like angels, but they live like men'. The prince is a callow, young, inexperienced man, yet he is good enough of heart to understand at once that sometimes fellow-feeling must trump logic and argument. And Johnson's profundity is to know that reason's evident limitations do not make it – or even rhetoric's 'polished periods and studied sentences' – valueless, but only limited. Our capacity of reason is magnificent, to be sure, but there are mysteries in human experience that transcend even reason's explanatory powers.

In a later episode, Rasselas and his sister discuss the advantages and disadvantages of early and late marriage, and come to the conclusion that there is no means by which the advantages of both can be reconciled and the disadvantages be avoided. All the things that men desire are not compatible, and therefore discontent is the lot of Man; as Rasselas's sister, Nekayah, puts it: 'No man can, at the same time, fill his cup from the source and from the mouth of the Nile.' A man who understands this will not as a result cease to experience incompatible desires – for example, those for security and excitement – but he will be less embittered that he cannot have everything he wants. An understanding of the imperfectibility of life is necessary for both happiness and virtue.

Throughout his writings, Johnson says things that strike us as obvious – but with the force of revelation. What he says of Richard Savage is, in fact, far truer of himself: '[W]hat no other man would have thought on, it now appears scarcely possible for any man to miss.' His writings appeal to 'whoever will attend to the motions of his own mind', attention that for him is a fundamental duty. Few men have ever paid more serious attention to introspection than Dr Johnson, not as a means of self-indulgence but as necessary to moral improvement and to an understanding of human nature. 'We all know our own state,' he says elsewhere, 'if we could be induced to consider it.' It is Dr Johnson's purpose to recall us to ourselves: perhaps that explains why people now find him so disturbing to read.

He says things that are obvious, but only obvious once he has pointed them out. In *The Rambler*, number 159, for example, he tells us that bashfulness is often a disguised self-importance. The bashful person 'considers that what he shall say or do will never be forgotten; that renown or infamy are suspended upon every syllable.' But, says Johnson, 'He that considers how little he dwells upon the condition of others, will learn how little the attention of others is attracted by himself.'

Every chapter of *Rasselas* contains thoughts so penetrating that they could only be those of a man of the character portrayed by Boswell. Johnson is brandy to Voltaire's thin beer (a strange reversal of national comestibles). Take the visit of Rasselas and Imlac to the Pyramids. When Imlac proposes the trip, Rasselas objects that it is men, not their past works, that interest him. Imlac replies: 'To judge rightly of the present we must oppose it to the past; for all judgment is comparative, and of the future nothing can be known.' Having established that 'to see men we must see their works', Imlac continues: 'If we act only for ourselves, to neglect the study of history is not prudent; if we are entrusted with the care of others, it is not just.'

When they finally arrive at the Pyramids, Imlac's reflections are profound:

> [F]or the pyramids, no reason has ever been given
> adequate to the cost and labour of the work. The

narrowness of the chambers proves that it could afford no retreat from enemies, and treasures might have been reposited at far less expense with equal security. It seems to have been erected only in compliance with that hunger of imagination which preys incessantly upon life, and must be always appeased by some employment. Those who have already all that they can enjoy must enlarge their desires. He that has built for use till use is supplied must begin to build for vanity.

And finally:

I consider this mighty structure as a monument of the insufficiency of human enjoyments.

The last chapter of the book is titled 'The Conclusion, in which Nothing Is Concluded.' This is not a facile irony, as it might have been if a postmodernist had written it; it is a statement of the difficulties with which Johnson wrestled all his life – as we all must, if we pause for thought.

When one considers that Voltaire was no inconsiderable person and yet was shallow by comparison with Johnson, and that Johnson wrote *Rasselas* in a week to pay for his mother's medical treatment and funeral, one begins to grasp the intellectual and moral dimension of the man. What a mighty mind, so furnished that it could write such a book in a week, to pay such comparatively trifling bills! Of course the speed of his work also explains why Johnson was always aware, and felt deeply guilty, that he had not achieved as much as he might had he applied himself more diligently, and that 'I have neither attempted nor formed any scheme of Life by which I may do good and please God' (this on his 62nd birthday). Johnson was never satisfied with himself and did not blame the world for his dissatisfaction; 50 years after he was cheekily disobliging to his impoverished father, the GREAT SAMUEL JOHNSON, in Boswell's phrase, stood bareheaded for an hour in the rain in Uttoxeter marketplace in atonement for his sin.

Johnson is an unusual writer, in that he is far greater than the sum of his parts. For all the excellence of *Rasselas*, Johnson is not among the greatest imaginative writers of English literature; only a few lines of his poetry are now remembered; his essays, though vastly more self-analytically honest and morally useful than anything Freud wrote, do not appeal to an age that prefers psychobabble to true reflection, and in which self-exculpation is *de rigueur*.

But his Dictionary – 43,000 definitions and 110,000 citations from literature, a work of near-unimaginable proportions when one considers the labour of devising for oneself the definition of even one word – provides a key to his abiding greatness. His definition of the word 'conscience' is 'the knowledge or faculty by which we judge the goodness or wickedness of ourselves'. Above all, Johnson saw the exercise of judgment as the supreme human duty; however inviting it is for human beings to avoid judgment, because it is impossible to judge correctly of everything, it is inescapably necessary to make judgments. Truly, he was as Boswell described him, a man whose extraordinary 'character' compels 'admiration and reverence' – and illuminates every line he wrote. 'His mind resembled the vast amphitheatre, the Coliseum of Rome,' Boswell wrote. 'In the centre stood his judgment, which like a mighty gladiator, combated those apprehensions that, like the wild beasts of the arena, were all around in cells, ready to be let out upon him.'

And, of course, upon us. I think I can return an answer to my once-Russian friend.

WHAT THE NEW ATHEISTS DON'T SEE

PARLIAMENT'S FIRST AVOWEDLY atheist member, Charles Bradlaugh, would stride into public meetings in the 1880s, take out his pocket watch and challenge God to strike him dead in 60 seconds. God bided his time but got Bradlaugh in the end. A slightly later atheist, Bertrand Russell, was once asked what he would do if it proved that he was mistaken and if he met his maker in the hereafter. He would demand to know, Russell replied with all the high-pitched fervour of his pedantry, why God had not made the evidence of his existence plainer and more irrefutable. And Samuel Beckett came up with a memorable line: 'God doesn't exist – the bastard!'

Beckett's wonderful outburst of disappointed rage suggests that it is not as easy as one might suppose to rid oneself of the notion of God. (Perhaps this is the time to declare that I am not myself a believer.) At the very least, Beckett's line implies that God's existence would solve some kind of problem – actually, a profound one: the transcendent purpose of human existence. Few of us, especially as we grow older, are entirely comfortable with the idea that life is full of sound and fury but signifies nothing. However much philosophers tell us that it is illogical to fear death, and that at worst it is only the process of dying that we should fear, people still fear death as much as ever. In like fashion, however many times philosophers say that it is up to us ourselves, and to no one else, to find the meaning of life, we continue to long for a transcendent purpose immanent in existence itself, independent of our own wills. To tell us that we should not feel this longing is a bit like telling someone in the first flush of love that the object of his affections is not worthy of them. The heart hath its reasons that reason knows not of.

Of course, men – that is to say, some men – have denied this truth ever since the Enlightenment, and have sought to find a way of life based entirely on reason. Far as I am from decrying reason, the attempt leads at best to Gradgrind and at worst to Stalin. Reason can never be the absolute dictator of man's mental or moral economy.

The search for the pure guiding light of reason, uncontaminated by human passion or metaphysical principles that go beyond all possible evidence, continues, however; and recently a small epidemic of books has declared success, at least if success consists of having slain the inveterate enemy of reason, namely religion. The philosophers Daniel Dennett, A.C. Grayling, Michel Onfray and Sam Harris, the biologist Richard Dawkins and the journalist and critic Christopher Hitchens have all written books roundly condemning religion and its works. Evidently there is a tide in the affairs, if not of men, at least of authors.

The curious thing about these books is that the authors often appear to think they are saying something new and brave. They imagine themselves to be like the intrepid explorer Sir Richard Burton, who in 1853 disguised himself as a Muslim merchant, went to Mecca and then wrote a book about his unprecedented feat. The public appears to agree, for the neo-atheist books have sold by the hundred thousand. Yet with the possible exception of Dennett's, they advance no argument that I, the village atheist, could not have made by the age of 14 (Saint Anselm's ontological argument for God's existence gave me the greatest difficulty, but I had taken Hume to heart on the weakness of the argument from design).

I first doubted God's existence at about the age of nine. It was at the school assembly that I lost my faith. We had been given to understand that if we opened our eyes during prayers God would depart the assembly hall. I wanted to test this hypothesis. Surely, if I opened my eyes suddenly, I would glimpse the fleeing God? What I saw instead, it turned out, was the headmaster, Mr Clinton, intoning the prayer with one eye closed and the other open, with which he beadily surveyed the children below for transgressions. I quickly concluded that Mr Clinton did not believe what he said about the need to keep our eyes shut. And if he did not believe that, why should I believe in his God? In such illogical leaps do our beliefs often originate, to be disciplined later in life (if we receive enough education) by elaborate rationalisation.

Dennett's *Breaking the Spell* is the least bad-tempered of the new atheist books, but it is deeply condescending to all religious people. He argues that religion is explicable in evolutionary terms – for example, by our inborn human propensity, at one time valuable for our survival on the African savannahs, to attribute animate agency to threatening events.

For Dennett, to prove the biological origin of belief in God is to show its irrationality, to break its spell. But of course it is a necessary part of the argument that all possible human beliefs, including belief in evolution, must be explicable in precisely the same way; or else why single out religion for this treatment? Either we test ideas according to arguments in their favour, independent of their origins, thus making the argument from evolution irrelevant, or all possible beliefs come under the same suspicion of being only evolutionary adaptations – and thus biologically contingent rather than true or false. We find ourselves facing a version of the paradox of the Cretan liar: all beliefs, including this one, are the products of evolution, and all beliefs that are products of evolution cannot be known to be true.

One striking aspect of Dennett's book is his failure to avoid the language of purpose, intention and ontological moral evaluation, despite his fierce opposition to teleological views of existence: the coyote's 'methods of locomotion have been ruthlessly optimised for efficiency'. Or: 'The stinginess of Nature can be seen everywhere we look.' Or again: 'This is a good example of Mother Nature's stinginess in the final accounting combined with absurd profligacy in the incidentals.' I would go on but I fear the point is clear. (And Dennett is not alone in this difficulty: Michel Onfray's *Atheist Manifesto*, so rich in errors and inexactitudes that it would take a book as long as his to correct them, says on its second page that religion prevents mankind from facing up to 'reality in all its naked cruelty'. But how can reality have any moral quality without having an immanent or transcendent purpose?)

No doubt Dennett would reply that he is writing in metaphors for the layman, and that he could translate all his statements into a language without either moral evaluation or purpose included in it. Perhaps he would argue that his language is evidence that the spell still has a hold over even him, the breaker of the spell for the rest of humanity. But I am not sure that this response would be psychologically accurate. I think Dennett's use of the language of evaluation and purpose is evidence of a deep-seated metaphysical belief (however caused) that Providence exists in the universe, a belief that few people, confronted by the mystery of beauty and of existence itself, escape entirely. At any rate, it ill-behoves Dennett to condescend to those poor primitives who still have a religious or providential view of the world: a view that, at base, is no more refutable than Dennett's metaphysical faith in evolution.

Dennett is not the only new atheist to employ religious language. In *The God Delusion*, Richard Dawkins quotes with approval a new set of Ten Commandments for atheists, which he obtained from an atheist website, without considering odd the idea that atheists require commandments at all, let alone precisely ten of them; nor does their metaphysical status seem to worry him. The last of the atheist's Ten Commandments ends with the following: 'Question everything.' Everything? Including the need to question everything, and so on *ad infinitum*?

Not to belabour the point, but if I questioned whether George Washington died in 1799, I could spend a lifetime trying to prove it and find myself still, at the end of my efforts, having to make a leap, or perhaps several leaps, of faith in order to believe the rather banal fact that I had set out to prove. Metaphysics is like nature: though you throw it out with a pitchfork, it always returns. What is confounded here is surely the abstract right to question everything with the actual exercise of that right on all possible occasions. Anyone who did exercise his right on all possible occasions would wind up a short-lived fool.

This sloppiness and lack of intellectual scruple, with the assumption of certainty where there is none, combined with adolescent shrillness and intolerance, reach an apogee in Sam Harris's book *The End Of Faith*. It is not easy to do justice to the book's nastiness; it makes Dawkins's claim that religious education constitutes child abuse look sane and moderate.

Harris tells us, for example, that 'we must find our way to a time when faith, without evidence, disgraces anyone who would claim it. Given the present state of the world, there appears to be no other future worth wanting.' I am glad that I am old enough that I shall not see the future of reason as laid down by Harris; but I am puzzled by the status of the compulsion in the first sentence that I have quoted. Is Harris writing of a historical inevitability? Of a categorical imperative? Or is he merely making a legislative proposal? This is who-will-rid-me-of-this-troublesome-priest language, ambiguous no doubt, but not open to a generous interpretation.

It becomes even more sinister when considered in conjunction with the following sentences, quite possibly the most disgraceful that I have read in a book by a man posing as a rationalist: 'The link between belief and behaviour raises the stakes considerably. Some propositions are so dangerous that it may be ethical to kill people for believing them. This may seem an extraordinary claim, but it merely enunciates an ordinary fact about the world in which we live.'

Let us leave aside the metaphysical problems that these three sentences raise. For Harris, the most important question about genocide would seem to be: 'Who is genociding whom?' To adapt Dostoevsky slightly, starting from universal reason I arrive at universal madness.

Lying not far beneath the surface of all the neo-atheist books is the kind of historiography that many of us adopted in our hormone-disturbed adolescence, furious at the discovery that our parents sometimes told lies and violated their own precepts and rules. It can be summed up in Christopher Hitchens's drumbeat in *God Is Not Great*: 'Religion spoils everything.'

What? The Saint Matthew Passion? The Cathedral of Chartres? The emblematic religious person in these books seems to be a Glasgow Airport bomber – a type unrepresentative of Muslims, let alone communicants of the poor old Church of England. It is surely not news, except to someone so ignorant that he probably wouldn't be interested in these books in the first place, that religious conflict has often been murderous and that religious people have committed hideous atrocities. But so have secularists and atheists, and though they have had less time to prove their mettle in this area, they have proved it amply. If religious belief is not synonymous with good behaviour, neither is absence of belief, to put it mildly.

In fact, one can write the history of anything as a chronicle of crime and folly. Science and technology spoil everything: without trains and IG Farben, no Auschwitz; without transistor radios and mass-produced machetes, no Rwandan genocide. First you decide what you hate, and then you gather evidence for its hatefulness. Since man is a fallen creature (I use the term metaphorically, rather than in its religious sense), there is always much to find.

The thinness of the new atheism is evident in its approach to our civilisation, which until recently was religious to its core. To regret religion is, in fact, to regret our civilisation and its monuments, its achievements and its legacy. And, in my own view, the absence of religious faith, provided that such faith is not murderously intolerant, can have a deleterious effect upon human character and personality. If you empty the world of purpose, make it one of brute fact alone, you empty it (for many people, at any rate) of reasons for gratitude, and a sense of gratitude is necessary for both happiness and decency. For what can soon, and all too easily, replace gratitude is a sense of entitlement. Without gratitude, it is hard to appreciate, or be satisfied with, what you have: and life will become an existential shopping spree that no product satisfies.

A few years back, the National Gallery held an exhibition of Spanish still-life paintings. One of these paintings had a physical effect on the people who sauntered in, stopping them in their tracks; some even gasped. I have never seen an image have such an impact on people. The painting, by Juan Sanchez Cotán, now hangs in the San Diego Museum of Art. It shows four fruits and vegetables, two suspended by string, forming a parabola in a grey stone window.

Even if you did not know that Sanchez Cotán was a 17th century Spanish priest, you could know that the painter was religious: for this picture is a visual testimony of gratitude for the beauty of those things that sustain us. Once you have seen it, and concentrated your attention on it, you will never take the existence of the humble cabbage – or of anything else – quite so much for granted, but will see its beauty and be thankful for it.

The painting is a permanent call to contemplation of the meaning of human life, and as such it arrested people who ordinarily were not, I suspect, much given to quiet contemplation.

The same holds true with the work of the great Dutch still-life painters. On the neo-atheist view, the religious connection between Catholic Spain and Protestant Holland is one of conflict, war and massacre only: and certainly one cannot deny this history. And yet something more exists. As with Sanchez Cotán, only a deep reverence, an ability not to take existence for granted, could turn a representation of a herring on a pewter plate into an object of transcendent beauty, worthy of serious reflection.

I recently had occasion to compare the writings of the neo-atheists with those of Anglican divines of the 17th and 18th centuries. I was visiting some friends at their country house in England, which had a library of old volumes; since the family of the previous owners had a churchman in every generation, many of the books were religious. In my own neo-atheist days, I would have scorned these works as pertaining to a non-existent entity and containing nothing of value. I would have considered the authors deluded men, who probably sought to delude others for reasons that Marx might have enumerated.

But looking, say, into the works of Joseph Hall, DD, I found myself moved: much more moved, it goes without saying, than by any of the books of the new atheists. Hall was bishop of Exeter and then of Norwich; though a moderate Puritan, he took the Royalist side in the English civil war and lost his see, dying in 1656 while Cromwell was still Lord Protector.

Except by specialists, Hall remains almost entirely forgotten today. I opened one of the volumes at random, his *Contemplations Upon the Principal Passages of the Holy Story*. Here was the contemplation on the sickness of Hezekiah:

> Hezekiah was freed from the siege of the Assyrians, but
> he is surprised with a disease. He, that delivered him
> from the hand of his enemies, smites him with sickness.

God doth not let us loose from all afflictions, when he redeems us from one.

To think that Hezekiah was either not thankful enough for his deliverance, or too much lifted up with the glory of so miraculous a favour, were an injurious misconstruction of the hand of God, and an uncharitable censure of a holy prince; for, though no flesh and blood can avoid the just desert of bodily punishment, yet God doth not always strike with an intuition of sin: sometimes he regards the benefit of our trial; sometimes, the glory of his mercy in our cure.

Hall surely means us to infer that whatever happens to us, however unpleasant, has a meaning and purpose; and this enables us to bear our sorrows with greater dignity and less suffering. And it is part of the existential reality of human life that we shall always need consolation, no matter what progress we make. Hall continues:

When, as yet, he had not so much as the comfort of a child to succeed him, thy prophet is sent to him, with the heavy message of his death: 'Set thine house in order; for thou shalt die, and not live.' It is no small mercy of God, that he gives us warning of our end... No soul can want important affairs, to be ordered for a final dissolution.

This is the language not of rights and entitlements but of something much deeper – a universal respect for the condition of being human.

For Hall, life is instinct with meaning: a meaning capable of controlling man's pride at his good fortune and consoling him for his ill fortune. Here is an extract from Hall's *Characters of Virtues and Vices*:

He is an happy man, that hath learned to read himself, more than all books; and hath so taken out this lesson, that he can never forget it: that knows the world, and cares not for it; that, after many traverses of thoughts, is grown to know what he may trust to; and stands now equally armed for all events: that hath got the mastery at home; so as he can cross his will without a mutiny, and so please it that he makes it not a wanton: that, in earthly things, wishes no more than nature; in spiritual, is ever graciously ambitious: that, for his condition, stands on his own feet, not needing to lean upon the great; and can so frame his thoughts to his estate, that when he hath least, he cannot want, because he is as free from desire, as superfluity: that hath seasonably broken the headstrong restiness of prosperity; and can now manage it, at pleasure: upon whom, all smaller crosses light as hailstones upon a roof; and, for the greater calamities, he can take them as tributes of life and tokens of love; and, if his ship be tossed, yet he is sure his anchor is fast. If all the world were his, he could be no other than he is; no whit gladder of himself, no whit higher in his carriage; because he knows, that contentment lies not in the things he hath, but in the mind that values them.

Though eloquent, this appeal to moderation as the key to happiness is not original; but such moderation comes more naturally to the man who believes in something not merely higher than himself but higher than mankind. After all, the greatest enjoyment of the usages of this world, even to excess, might seem rational when the usages of this world are all that there is.

In his *Occasional Meditations*, Hall takes perfectly ordinary scenes – ordinary, of course, for his times – and derives meaning from them. Here is his meditation 'Upon the Flies Gathering to a Galled Horse':

> How these flies swarm to the galled part of this poor beast; and there sit, feeding upon that worst piece of his flesh, not meddling with the other sound parts of his skin! Even thus do malicious tongues of detractors: if a man have any infirmity in his person or actions, that they will be sure to gather unto, and dwell upon; whereas, his commendable parts and well-deservings are passed by, without mention, without regard. It is an envious self-love and base cruelty, that causeth this ill disposition in men: in the mean time, this only they have gained; it must needs be a filthy creature, that feeds upon nothing but corruption.

Surely Hall is not suggesting (unlike Dennett in his unguarded moments) that the biological purpose of flies is to feed off injured horses, but rather that a sight in nature can be the occasion for us to reflect imaginatively on our morality. He is not raising a biological theory about flies, in contradistinction to the theory of evolution, but thinking morally about human existence. It is true that he would say that everything is part of God's Providence, but, again, this is no more (and no less) a metaphysical belief than the belief in natural selection as an all-explanatory principle.

Let us compare Hall's meditation 'Upon the Sight of a Harlot Carted' with Harris's statement that some people ought perhaps to be killed for their beliefs:

With what noise, and tumult, and zeal of solemn justice, is this sin punished! The streets are not more full of beholders, than clamours. Every one strives to express his detestation of the fact, by some token of revenge: one casts mire, another water, another rotten eggs, upon the miserable offender. Neither, indeed, is she worthy of less: but, in the mean time, no man looks home to himself. It is no uncharity to say, that too many insult in this just punishment, who have deserved more... Public sins have more shame; private may have more guilt. If the world cannot charge me of those, it is enough, that I can charge my soul of worse. Let others rejoice, in these public executions: let me pity the sins of others, and be humbled under the sense of my own.

Who sounds more charitable, more generous, more just, more profound, more honest, more humane: Sam Harris or Joseph Hall, DD, late lord bishop of Exeter and of Norwich?

No doubt it helps that Hall lived at a time of sonorous prose, prose that merely because of its sonority resonates in our souls; prose of the kind that none of us, because of the time in which we live, could ever equal. But the style applies to the thought as well as to the prose; and I prefer Hall's charity to Harris's intolerance.

THE SPECTRES HAUNTING DRESDEN

THE FOUNDATIONS OF HITLER'S bunker were uncovered during the building frenzy in Berlin that followed the reunification of Germany. An anguished debate ensued about what to do with the site, for in Germany both memory and amnesia are dangerous, each with its moral hazards. To mark the bunker's site might turn it into a place of pilgrimage for neo-Nazis, resurgent in the East; not to mark it might be regarded as an attempt to deny the past. In the end, anonymous burial was deemed the better, which is to say the safer, option.

Nowhere in the world (except, perhaps, in Israel or Russia) does history weigh as heavily, as palpably, upon ordinary people as in Germany. More than 60 years after the end of World War II, the disaster of Nazism is still unmistakably and inescapably inscribed upon almost every town and cityscape, in whichever direction you look. The urban environment of Germany, whose towns and cities were once among the most beautiful in the world, second only to Italy's, is now a wasteland of functional yet discordant modern architecture, soulless and incapable of inspiring anything but a vague existential unease, with a sense of impermanence and unreality that mere prosperity can do nothing to dispel. Well-stocked shops do not supply meaning or purpose. Beauty, at least in its man-made form, has left the land for good, and such remnants of past glories as remain serve only as a constant, nagging reminder of what has been lost, destroyed, utterly and irretrievably smashed up.

Nor are the comforts of victimhood available to the Germans as they survey the devastation of their homeland. Walking with the widow of a banker through the one small square in Frankfurt that has been restored to its medieval splendour, I remarked how beautiful a city Frankfurt must once have been, and how terrible it was that such beauty should have been lost forever.

'We started it,' she said. 'We got what we deserved.'

But who was this 'we' of whom she spoke? She was not of an age to have helped or even to have supported the Nazis, and therefore (if justice requires that each should get his desert) it was unjust that she should bear the guilty burden of the past. And Germans far younger than she still bear it. I went to dinner with a young businessman, born 20 years after the end of the war, who told me that the forestry company for which he worked, and which had interests in Britain, had decided that it needed a mission statement. A meeting ensued, and someone suggested *Holz mit Stolz* ('Wood with Pride'), whereupon a two-hour discussion erupted among the employees of the company as to whether pride in anything was permitted to the Germans, or whether it was the beginning of the slippery slope that led to… well, everyone knew where. The businessman found this all perfectly normal, part of being a contemporary German.

Collective pride is denied the Germans because, if pride is taken in the achievements of one's national ancestors, it follows that shame for what they have done must also be accepted. And the shame of German history is greater than any cultural achievement, not because that achievement fails to balance the shame but because it is more recent than any achievement, and furthermore was committed by a generation either still living or still existent well within living memory.

The moral impossibility of patriotism worries Germans of conservative instinct or temperament. Upon what in their historical tradition can they safely look back as a guide or a help? One young German conservative historian I met took refuge in Anglophilia – his England, of course, being an England of the past. He needed a refuge, because Hitler and Nazism had besmirched everything in his own land. The historiography that sees in German history nothing but a prelude to Hitler and Nazism may be intellectually unjustified, the product of the historian's bogus authorial omniscience, but it has emotional and psychological force nonetheless, precisely because the willingness to take pride in the past implies a preparedness to accept the shame of it. Thus, Bach and Beethoven can be celebrated but not as Germans; otherwise they would be tainted. The young German historian worked for a publishing house with a history lasting almost four centuries, but its failure to go out of business during the 12 years of the Third Reich cast a shadow both forward and backward, like a spectral presence that haunts a great mansion.

The impossibility of patriotism does not extinguish the need to belong, however. No man is, or can be, an island; everyone, no matter how egotistical, needs to belong to a collectivity larger than himself. A young German once said to me, 'I don't feel German, I feel European.' This sounded false to my ears: it had the same effect upon me as the squeak of chalk on a blackboard, and sent a shiver down my spine. One might as well say, 'I don't feel human, I feel mammalian.' We do not, and cannot, feel all that we are: so that while we who live in Europe are European, we don't feel European.

In any case, can a German feel European unilaterally, without the Portuguese (for example) similarly and reciprocally feeling European rather than Portuguese? From my observations of the French, they still feel French, indeed quite strongly so. Nearly half a century after the Treaty of Rome, they can't be said to like the Germans; to think otherwise is to mistake a marriage of convenience for the passion of Romeo and Juliet.

A common European identity therefore has to be forged deliberately and artificially; and one of the imperatives for attempting to do so is the need of Germans for an identity that is not German (the other, which dovetails neatly, is the French drive to recover world influence). And since the Germans are very powerful in Europe, by weight of their economy, their need to escape from themselves by absorbing everyone into a new collective identity will sooner or later be perceived in the rest of Europe as the need to impose themselves – as a return to their bad old habits. New identities can indeed be forged, but usually in the crucible of war or at least of social upheaval: not, in the context, an inviting prospect.

On no city does history weigh heavier than on Dresden. It is 64 years since the bombing that forever changed the basis of the city's renown. Overnight, the Florence of the Elbe became a perpetual monument to destruction from the air, famed for its rubble and its corpses rather than its baroque architecture and its devotion to art. And then came communism.

You meet people in Dresden who, until a few years ago, knew nothing but life under Hitler, Ulbricht and Honecker. Truly the sins of their fathers were visited upon them, for they brought neither the Nazis nor the Communists to power and there was nothing they could do to escape them. For such people, the sudden change in 1990 was both liberation and burden. Avid to see a world that had been previously forbidden them, they took immediate advantage of their new freedom to visit the farthest areas of the globe, the more exotic the better. But the liberation brought with it a heightened awareness of the man-made desert of their own pasts, seven-eighths of their lives, truly an expense of spirit in a waste of shame. Never was Joy's grape burst more decisively against veil'd Melancholy's palate fine.

When I last visited Dresden in 2004, nearly a decade and a half after reunification and after the expenditure of untold billions of deutsche marks and euros, the city was still incompletely Westernised. Its unemployment rate was three times that of Germany as a whole, so high in fact that all the city dwellers I met believed the official figures to be manipulated downward, for propaganda purposes: it being inconceivable to them, as the result of long and incontrovertible experience, that any government would tell the truth about anything. And while some parts of the city have taken on the feverish vulgarity that for so many people in the modern world is the manifestation, prerequisite, and only meaning and value of freedom, others still have that disintegrating deadness peculiar to communism, where paint flakes and stucco crumbles, where stale smells always linger in stairwells and electric light casts a yellowing gloom the colour of cheap paper that has aged.

Not all Dresden was bombed, of course; on the banks of the Elbe there are still the magnificent villas of the haute bourgeoisie. Some of them have been bought and restored by rich 'Wessis,' as the inhabitants of the former West Germany are still, not altogether affectionately, known; but others remain unrestored, uninhabited and deteriorating, at night appearing, unlit, like the set of a Gothic horror movie. One expects bats or vampires to emerge. For more than 40 years they were the homes of Dresden 'workers of the brain' (to use Communist terminology), but such was their dilapidation that, immediately after reunification, they were declared unfit for habitation according to the standards of the West, and their residents moved elsewhere.

To the moral complications of a Nazi past were added those of a Communist past, the greatest of which was an awareness of just how widespread the practice of denunciation had been. On some estimates, a sixth of the population of the former German Democratic Republic were *Mitarbeiter* – collaborators with the secret police, the Stasi – and had spied upon and denounced their neighbours, friends, relatives and even spouses. Once the archives opened and people could read their security dossiers for themselves, they discovered in many cases that those to whom they had relayed their private thoughts had relayed them in turn to the Stasi, in return, practically, for nothing except the informer's satisfaction of being on the right side of the powerful. Those whom people had thought were their best friends turned out to be the very informers whose denunciation had resulted in their otherwise inexplicable failure to gain promotion in their work, sometimes for decades. Such discoveries were not conducive to a favourable or an optimistic view of human nature or the trust upon which a secure social life is built. The GDR, founded on a political theory that made a fetish of human solidarity, turned everyone into an atom in the asocial ether.

The destruction of Dresden on the night of February 13, 1945, by the Royal Air Force, and on the following two days by the US Army Air Corps, necessitated the rebuilding of the city, with only a small area around the famous Zwinger restored to its former glory. Dresden had been all but destroyed once before, by the armies of Frederick the Great (if Frederick was enlightened, give me obscurantism); but at least he replaced the Renaissance city recorded in the canvases of Bellotto with a baroque one, not with a wilderness of totalitarian functionalism whose purpose was to stamp out all sense of individuality and to emphasise the omnipresent might of the state. The bombing of Dresden was a convenient pretext to do what Communists (and some others) like to do in any case: the systematisation of Bucharest during Ceauşescu's rule, or the replacement of the medieval city of Alès, 25 miles from my house in France, by mass housing of hideous inhumanity on the orders of the Communist city council, being but two cases in point.

Despite this, the Communists used the destruction of Dresden for propaganda purposes throughout the four decades of their rule. The church bells of the city tolled on every anniversary of the bombing, for the 20 minutes it took the RAF to unload the explosives that created the firestorm that turned the Florence of the Elbe into a smoking ruin as archaeological as Pompeii. 'See what the capitalist barbarians did,' was the message, 'and what they would do again if they had the chance and if we did not arm ourselves to the teeth.' Needless to say, the rapine of the Red Army went strictly unmentioned.

But the bombing caused some unease in Britain even at the time. Was it justified? The issue of the war, after all, was by then hardly in doubt; and, in any case, both the ethics and efficacy of bombing civilian areas had been questioned, not only by left-wing politicians and George Bell, bishop of Chichester, but by the air force commanders themselves. A debate has simmered ever since, occasionally coming to a boil as when a statue commemorating the head of the RAF's Bomber Command, Arthur Harris, was unveiled in London in 1992 or, more recently, when the Queen paid a state visit to Germany and failed to utter an apology for the bombing.

I don't think any decent, civilised person can look at pictures of Dresden after the bombing without being overcome by a sense of shock. The jagged ruins of walls emerging from fields of rubble, as far as the eye can see or the camera record, are a testament, of a kind, to human ingenuity. Only the long development of science and knowledge could have achieved this. As for the funeral pyres of bodies, piled up with their legs and arms emerging from the mass, or the corpses of the people boiled alive in the fountains in which they had taken refuge… one averts not only one's eyes but one's thoughts.

Yet the idea sometimes propounded by those who seek to condemn the bombing as an atrocity equal to, and counterbalancing, Nazi atrocities – that Dresden was some kind of city of the innocents, concerned only with the arts and having nothing to do with the war effort, cut off from and morally superior to the rest of Nazi Germany – is clearly absurd. It is in the nature of totalitarian regimes that no such innocence should persist anywhere; and it certainly didn't in Dresden in 1945. For example, the Zeiss-Ikon optical group alone employed 10,000 workers (and some forced labour), all engaged – of course – in war work. Nor had Dresden's record been very different from the rest of Germany's. Its synagogue was burned down during the reichspogromnacht [illegible] in November 1938, the Gauleiter of Saxony, who had his seat in Dresden, was the notoriously brutal and corrupt Martin Mutschmann. The bombing saved the life of at least one man, the famous diarist Victor Klemperer, one of the 197 Jews still alive in the city (out of a former population of several thousand). He and the handful of remaining Jews had been marked down for deportation and death two days after the bombing; in the chaos which ensued, he was able to escape and tear the yellow star from his coat.

Eighteen years after the end of the war, in 1963, the pro-Nazi historian David Irving published his first book, *The Destruction of Dresden*. In those days he was either less pro-Nazi than he later became or more circumspect – the memory of the war still being fresh – but it was probably not entirely a coincidence that he devoted his first attention to an event that Churchill suspected might be a blot on the British escutcheon. But Irving – later a leading Holocaust denier, who lost a famous libel suit against a historian who exposed him as such and went on to serve a prison sentence in Austria, in my view imposed because of a wrongful law, for the offence – clearly accepted in 1963 that there had been a Nazi genocide against the Jews, and he ended his book with an admission that the bombing (which he called 'the biggest single massacre in European history') was 'carried out in the cause of bringing to their knees a people who, corrupted by Nazism, had committed the greatest crimes against humanity in recorded time'.

There were faint signs of Irving's later acceptance of the Nazi worldview in this book, though they probably went unnoticed at the time. Describing the state of medical services in Dresden after the bombing, he mentioned that 'a vast euthanasia-hospital for mentally incurables' was transformed into a hospital for the wounded, without any remark upon the very concept of a 'euthanasia-hospital for mentally incurables': an institution that, by itself, would be sufficient to negate one meaning of his ambiguous description of Dresden in a chapter heading as 'The Virgin Target'. (Did he mean that it had never yet been attacked, or that the city was an innocent virgin?)

Of course, it would be absurd to pretend that the bombing of Dresden was conducted in order to put an end to the evil of its 'euthanasia-hospital', however vast, or to rescue Victor Klemperer from certain death. Among other motives for bombing, no doubt, was the need to demonstrate to the advancing Russians the tremendous firepower of the West, despite its relative weakness in land armies.

Irving's book was influential, however, precisely because he hid, or had not yet fully developed, his Nazi sympathies. It achieved its greatest influence through *Slaughterhouse-Five*, Kurt Vonnegut's famous counter-cultural anti-war novel, published six years later, which makes grateful acknowledgement of Irving's book, whose inflated estimate of the death toll of the bombing it unquestioningly accepts. Vonnegut, an American soldier who was a prisoner of war in Dresden at the time of the bombing, having been captured during the land offensive in the west, writes of the war and the bombing itself as if it took place in no context, as if it were just an arbitrary and absurd quarrel between rivals, between Tweedledum and Tweedledee, with no internal content or moral meaning – a quarrel that nevertheless resulted in one of the rivals cruelly and thoughtlessly destroying a beautiful city of the other.

But Vonnegut, to whom it did not occur that his subject matter was uniquely unsuited to facetious, adolescent literary experimentation, was writing an anti-war tract in the form of a post-modern novel, not a historical re-examination of the bombing of Dresden or of Germany as a whole. The problem that has bedevilled any such re-examination is fear that sympathy for the victims, or regret that so much of aesthetic and cultural value was destroyed, might be taken as sympathy for Nazism itself. The difficulty of disentangling individual from collective responsibility for the evils perpetrated by the Nazi regime is unresolved even now, and perhaps is inherently unresolvable.

True, Hitler was immensely popular; on the other hand, he never won a majority of the votes in anything that resembled a free election, and public enthusiasm in dictatorships cannot be taken entirely at face value (in his diaries, Klemperer himself veers between thinking that most Germans were Nazis and that the enthusiasm was bogus and more or less forced). The Germans entered into the spirit of violence and denunciation with a will, but on the other hand intimidation was everywhere. A witness to the burning of the Dresden synagogue on Kristallnacht who was overheard publicly to liken it to the worst times of the Middle Ages was seized by the Gestapo and taken away: an object lesson to all those who saw or learned about his fate. And those who say that Nazism was the inevitable consummation of German history, inherent in all that had gone before, must explain why so many German Jews (my grandfather among them, a major in the imperial German army during the Great War) were deeply and patriotically attached to both the country and its culture, and why so many of them were so blind for so long. Their lack of foresight is surely as eloquent as the historian's hindsight.

By the end of the war, 600,000 Germans had been killed by the bombing campaign, and a third of the population rendered homeless. Yet when the war was over, none among the many millions affected could express his grief and despair openly, for to have done so would have rendered him open to the charge of Nazi sympathies. The East Germans could toll the bells for Dresden each anniversary of the bombing only because the government enforced the myth that all the Nazis originated from, and were now located in, West Germany. But normal, personal, un-ideological grief was not permitted.

W.G. Sebald, an expatriate German author who lived in England, where he died in a car crash in 2001, pointed out a curious lacuna in German literature of memoirs or fictional accounts of the bombing and its after-effects. Millions suffered terribly, yet there is hardly a memoir or a novel to record it. Anything other than silence about what they experienced would have seemed, and still would seem, indecent and highly suspect, an attempt to establish a moral equivalence between the victims and perpetrators of Nazism.

Foreigners, such as the Swedish writer Stig Dagerman, could write about the sufferings of the Germans immediately after the war, but not the Germans themselves. Victor Gollancz, a British publisher of Polish-Jewish origin who could not be suspected in the slightest of Nazi sympathies and who had spent the entire 1930s publishing books warning the world of the Nazi peril, wrote and published a book in the immediate aftermath of the war called *In Darkest Germany*, in which he drew attention to the plight of the Germans living (and starving) among the ruins, which he observed on a visit there. To the charge that the Germans had brought it all on themselves and deserved no less, he replied with a three-word question: 'And the children?' His book was furnished with many affecting pictures, perhaps the most poignant among them that of the comfortably-attired Gollancz lifting the foot of a little German boy to demonstrate his pitiful footwear to the camera.

But for several decades it was impermissible for Germans to allude publicly to their own sufferings of the period, much of which must have been innocent, unless it be considered that all Germans were equally guilty *ex officio*, as it were. No doubt the impermissibility of publicly-expressed complaint, and therefore of resentment, was a powerful stimulus of the *Wirtschaftswunder*, the economic miracle, into which the Germans in the West threw their potentially resentful energies after the war, for lack of anywhere else to direct them. But this left a legacy of deep emptiness that all the reflective Germans I have met seem to feel. Perhaps it explains also the German longing to travel greater than that of any other nation I know.

In the last few years, best-selling books have begun to appear in Germany to record the suffering of the Germans during and after the war. Is this dangerous self-pity an implicit national self-exculpation? Or is it a sign of health, that at last Germans can approach their own past unencumbered by the psychological complexes bequeathed to them by their parents and grandparents?

As I walked through Dresden, I lamented the loss of an incomparable city, while thinking how difficult it must be to be a German, for whom neither memory nor amnesia can provide consolation.

AFTER EMPIRE

AS SOON AS I qualified as a doctor, I went to Rhodesia, which was to transform itself into Zimbabwe five years or so later.

In the next decade I worked and travelled a great deal in Africa and couldn't help but reflect upon such matters as the clash of cultures, the legacy of colonialism and the practical effects of good intentions unadulterated by any grasp of reality. I gradually came to the conclusion that the rich and powerful can indeed have an effect upon the poor and powerless – perhaps can even remake them – but not necessarily (in fact, necessarily not) in the way they wanted or anticipated. The law of unintended consequences is stronger than the most absolute power.

I went to Rhodesia because I wanted to see the last true outpost of colonialism in Africa, the final gasp of the British Empire that had done so much to shape the modern world. True, it had now rebelled against the mother country and was a pariah state: but it was still recognisably British in all but name. As Sir Roy Welensky, the Prime Minister of the short-lived and ill-fated Federation of Rhodesia and Nyasaland, once described himself, he was 'half-Polish, half-Jewish, one hundred percent British'.

Until my arrival at Bulawayo Airport, the British Empire had been for me principally a philatelic phenomenon. When I was young, Britain's still-astonishing assortment of far-flung territories – from British Honduras and British Guiana to British North Borneo, Basutoland, Bechuanaland and Swaziland – each issued beautiful engraved stamps, with the Queen's profile in the right upper corner, looking serenely down upon exotic creatures such as orang-utans or frigate birds, or upon natives (as we still called and thought of them) going about their natively tasks, tapping rubber or climbing coconut palms. To my childish mind, any political entity that issued such desirable stamps must have been a power for good. And my father – a Communist by conviction – also encouraged me to read the works of G.A. Henty, late-19th century adventure stories extolling the exploits of empire builders, who by bravery, sterling character, superior intelligence and *force majeure* overcame the resistance of such spirited but doomed peoples as the Zulu and the Fuzzy-Wuzzies. Henty might seem an odd choice for a Communist to give his son, but Marx himself was an imperialist of a kind, believing that European colonialism was an instrument of progress toward History's happy denouement; only at a later stage, after it had performed its progressive work, was empire to be condemned.

And condemned Rhodesia most certainly was, loudly and insistently, as if it were the greatest threat to world peace and the security of the planet. By the time I arrived, it had no friends, only enemies. Even South Africa, the regional colossus with which Rhodesia shared a long border and which might have been expected to be sympathetic, was highly ambivalent toward it: for South Africa sought to ingratiate itself with other nations by being less than wholehearted in its economic cooperation with the government of Ian Smith.

I expected to find on my arrival, therefore, a country in crisis and decay. Instead, I found a country that was, to all appearances, thriving: its roads were well maintained, its transport system functioning, its towns and cities clean and manifesting a municipal pride long gone from England. There were no electricity cuts or shortages of basic food commodities. The large hospital in which I was to work, while stark and somewhat lacking in comforts, was extremely clean and ran with exemplary efficiency. The staff, mostly black except for its most senior members, had a vibrant *esprit de corps*, and the hospital, as I discovered, had a reputation for miles around for the best of medical care. The rural poor would make immense and touching efforts to reach it: they arrived covered in the dust of their long journeys. The African nationalist leader and foe of the government, Joshua Nkomo, was a patient there and trusted the care implicitly, for medical ethics transcended all political antagonisms.

The surgeon for whom I worked, who came from England, was the best I have ever known and a man of exemplary character. Devoting his enormous technical accomplishment to the humblest of patients, he seemed not only capable of every surgical procedure, but he was a brilliant diagnostician, his clinical intuition honed by a relative lack of high-tech aids: so much so that others in the hospital regarded him as the final court of appeal. I never knew him to be mistaken, though like every other doctor he must have made errors in his time. He saved the lives of hundreds every year and inspired the most absolute trust and confidence in his patients. He never panicked, even in the direst emergency; and he knew what to do when a man had been half eaten by a crocodile or mauled by a leopard, when a child had been bitten in the leg by a puff adder, or when a man appeared with a spear driven through his skull. When called in the early hours of the morning, as he frequently was, he was as even-tempered as if attending a social event. Greater love hath no man…

He was not a missionary, however; he was infused by nothing resembling a religious spirit, only by a profound medical ethic and an enthusiasm for his art and science. He wanted a varied and interesting surgical practice, and he wanted to save human life; and the Rhodesia of the time offered him ideal conditions for using his skills to maximum benefit (even the best of surgeons relies on a well-organised hospital to achieve results). Within a short time of the political hand over in 1980, however, he returned to England – not because of any racial feeling or political antagonism but simply because the swift degeneration of standards in the hospital made the high-level practice of surgery impossible. The institution that had seemed to me on my arrival to be so solid and well founded fell apart in the historical twinkling of an eye.

In leaving Zimbabwe and returning to England, he accepted a much reduced standard of living, whatever the nominal value of his income. Talleyrand said that he who had not experienced the *ancien régime* (as an aristocrat, of course) knew nothing of the sweetness of life. The same might be said of him who had not experienced life as a colonial in Africa. I, whose salary was by other standards small, lived at a level that I have scarcely equalled since. It is true that Rhodesia lacked many consumer goods at that time, due to the economic sanctions imposed upon it: but what I learned from this lack is how little consumer goods add to the quality of life, at least in an equable climate such as Rhodesia's. Life was no poorer for being lived without them.

The real luxuries were space and beauty – and the time to enjoy them. With three other junior doctors, I rented a large and elegant colonial house, old by the standards of a country settled by whites only 80 years previously, set in beautiful grounds tended by a garden 'boy' called Moses (the 'boy' in garden boy or houseboy implied no youth: once, in East Africa, I was served by a houseboy who was 94, who had lived in the same family for 70 years, and who would have seen the suggestion of retirement as insulting). Surrounding the house was a red flagstone veranda where breakfast was served on linen in the cool of the morning, the soft light of the sunrise spreading through the foliage of the flame and jacaranda trees; even the harsh cry of the go-away bird seemed grateful on the ear. It was the only time in my life when I have arisen from bed without a tinge of regret.

We worked hard: I have never worked harder, and I can still conjure up the heavy feeling in my head, as if it were full of lead shot and could snap off my neck under its own weight, brought about by weekends on duty, when from Friday morning to Monday evening I would get not more than three hours' sleep. The luxury of our life was this: that, our work once done, we never had to perform a single chore for ourselves. The rest of our time, in our most beautiful surroundings, was given over to friendship, sport, study, hunting – whatever we wished.

Of course, our leisure rested upon a pyramid of startling inequality and social difference. The staff who freed us of life's little inconveniences lived an existence that was opaque to us, though they had quarters only a few yards from where we lived. Their hopes, wishes, fears and aspirations were not ours; their beliefs, tastes and customs were alien to us.

Our very distance, socially and psychologically, made our relations with them unproblematical and easy. We studiously avoided that tone of spoiled and bored querulousness for which colonials were infamous. We never resorted to that supposed staple of colonial conversation, the servant problem, but were properly grateful. Like most of the people I met in Rhodesia, we tried to treat our staff well, providing extra help for them for the frequent emergencies of African life – for example, illness among relatives. In return, they treated us with genuine solicitude. We assuaged our conscience by telling ourselves – what was no doubt true – that they would be worse off without our employ, but we couldn't help feeling uneasy about the vast gulf between us and our fellow human beings.

By contrast, our relations with our African medical colleagues were harder-edged, because the social, intellectual and cultural distance between us was far reduced. Rhodesia was still a white-dominated society, but for reasons of practical necessity, and in a vain attempt to convince the world that it was not as monstrous as made out, it had produced a growing cadre of educated Africans, doctors prominent among them. Unsurprisingly, they were not content to remain subalterns under the permanent tutelage of whites, so that our relations with them were superficially polite and collegial, but human warmth was difficult or impossible. Many belonged secretly to the African nationalist movement that was soon to take power; and two were to serve (if that is the word to describe their depredations) as ministers of health.

Unlike in South Africa, where salaries were paid according to a racial hierarchy (whites first, Indians and coloured second, Africans last), salaries in Rhodesia were equal for blacks and whites doing the same job, so that a black junior doctor received the same salary as mine. But there remained a vast gulf in our standards of living, the significance of which at first escaped me; but it was crucial in explaining the disasters that befell the newly independent countries that enjoyed what Byron called, and eagerly anticipated as, the first dance of freedom.

The young black doctors who earned the same salary as we whites could not achieve the same standard of living for a very simple reason: they had an immense number of social obligations to fulfil. They were expected to provide for an ever-expanding circle of family members (some of whom may have invested in their education) and people from their village, tribe and province. An income that allowed a white to live like a lord because of a lack of such obligations scarcely raised a black above the level of his family. Mere equality of salary, therefore, was quite insufficient to procure for them the standard of living that they saw the whites had and that it was only human nature for them to desire – and believe themselves entitled to, on account of the superior talent that had allowed them to raise themselves above their fellows. In fact, a salary a thousand times as great would hardly have been sufficient to procure it: for their social obligations increased *pari passu* with their incomes.

These obligations also explain the fact, often disdainfully remarked upon by former colonials, that when Africans moved into the beautiful and well-appointed villas of their former colonial masters, the houses swiftly degenerated into a species of superior, more spacious slum. Just as African doctors were perfectly equal to their medical tasks, technically speaking, so the degeneration of colonial villas had nothing to do with the intellectual inability of Africans to maintain them. Rather, the fortunate inheritor of such a villa was soon overwhelmed by relatives and others who had a social claim upon him. They brought even their goats with them, and one goat can undo in an afternoon what it has taken decades to establish.

It is easy to see why a civil service, controlled and manned in its upper reaches by whites, could remain efficient and uncorrupt but could not long do so when manned by Africans who were supposed to follow the same rules and procedures. The same is true, of course, for every other administrative activity, public or private. The thick network of social obligations explains why, while it would have been out of the question to bribe most Rhodesian bureaucrats, yet in only a few years it would have been out of the question not to try to bribe most Zimbabwean ones, whose relatives would have condemned them for failing to obtain on their behalf all the advantages their official opportunities might provide. Thus do the very same tasks in the very same offices carried out by people of different cultural and social backgrounds result in very different outcomes.

Viewed in this light, African nationalism was a struggle as much for power and privilege as it was for freedom, though it co-opted the language of freedom for obvious political advantage. In the matter of freedom, even Rhodesia – certainly no haven of free speech – was superior to its successor state, Zimbabwe. I still have in my library the oppositionist pamphlets and Marxist analyses of the vexed land question in Rhodesia that I bought there when Ian Smith was premier. Such thoroughgoing criticism of the rule of Mr Mugabe would be inconceivable – or else fraught with much greater dangers than opposition authors experienced under Ian Smith. And indeed, in all but one or two African states, the accession to independence brought no advance in intellectual freedom but rather, in many cases, a tyranny considerably worse than the preceding colonial regimes.

Of course, the solidarity and inescapable social obligations that corrupted public and private administration in Africa also gave a unique charm and humanity to life there and served to protect people from the worst consequences of the misfortunes that buffeted them. There were always relatives whose unquestioned duty it was to help and protect them if they could, so that no one had to face the world entirely alone. Africans tend to find our lack of such obligations puzzling and unfeeling – and, in this, they are not entirely wrong.

These considerations help explain the paradox that strikes so many visitors to Africa: the evident decency, kindness and dignity of the ordinary people, and the fathomless iniquity, dishonesty and ruthlessness of the politicians and administrators. This contrast recently struck me anew when a lawyer asked me to prepare a report on a Zimbabwean woman who had stayed illegally in England.

She was in her 40s and clearly in a disturbed state of mind. Mostly she looked down at the floor, avoiding all eye contact. When she looked up, her eyes seemed focused on infinity, or at least upon another world. She spoke hardly a word: her story was told me by her niece, a nurse who had come (or fled) to England some years before, and with whom she now stayed.

During the war of 'liberation', her brother had enlisted in the Rhodesian army. One day, the nationalist guerrillas came to her village and commanded her parents to tell them where he was, that they might kill him as a traitor to the African cause. But not knowing his whereabouts, her parents could not answer: and so, in front of her eyes, and making her watch (she was 17 years old at the time), they tied her parents to trees, doused them in gasoline, and burned them to death. (At this point in the story, I could not help but recall the argument, common among radicals at the time, that those African countries that liberated themselves by force of arms faced a better, brighter future than those that had been handed independence on a plate, because the war of liberation would forge genuine leadership and national unity. Algeria? Mozambique? Angola? Guinea-Bissau?)

Whether or not it was witnessing this terrible scene that turned her mind, she was never able thereafter to lead a normal life. She did not marry, a social catastrophe for a woman in Zimbabwe. She was taken in and looked after by a cousin who worked for a white farmer, and she spent her life staring into space. Then the 'war veterans' arrived, those who had allegedly fought for Zimbabwe's freedom – in reality, groups of party thugs intent upon dispossessing white farmers of their land in fulfilment of Mr Mugabe's demagogic and economically disastrous instructions. The white farmer and his black manager were killed and all the workers whom the farm had supported driven off the land. Hearing of her aunt's plight, her niece in England sent her a ticket.

This story illustrates both the ruthless appetite for power and control unleashed in Africa by the colonial experience – an appetite made all the nastier by some of the technological appurtenances of the colonialists' civilisation – and the generosity of the great majority of Africans. The niece would look after her aunt uncomplainingly for the rest of her life, demanding nothing in return and regarding it as her plain duty to do so, also asking nothing from the British state. Her kindness toward her aunt, who could contribute nothing, was moving to behold.

My Zimbabwean experiences sensitised me to the chaos I later witnessed throughout Africa. The contrast between kindness on the one hand and rapacity on the other was everywhere evident, and I learned that there is no more heartless saying than that the people get the government that it is fit for. Who, in all honesty, could deserve an Idi Amin or a Julius Nyerere? Certainly not the African peasants I encountered. The fact that such monsters could quite explicably emerge from the people by no means meant that the people deserved them.

The explanations usually given for Africa's post-colonial travails seemed to me facile. It was often said, for example, that African states were artificial, created by a stroke of a European's pen that took no notice of social realities; that boundaries were either drawn with a ruler in straight lines or at a natural feature such as a river, despite the fact that people of the same ethnic group lived on both sides.

This notion overlooks two salient facts: that the countries in Africa that do actually correspond to social, historical and ethnic realities – for example Burundi, Rwanda and Somalia – have not fared noticeably better than those that do not. Moreover in Africa, social realities are so complex that no system of boundaries could correspond to them. For example, there are said to be up to 300 ethnic groups in Nigeria alone, often deeply intermixed geographically: only extreme balkanisation followed by profound ethnic cleansing could have resulted in the kind of boundaries that would have avoided this particular criticism of the European map-makers. On the other hand, pan-Africanism was not feasible: for the kind of integration that could not be achieved on a small national scale could hardly be achieved on a vastly bigger international one.

In fact, it was the imposition of the European model of the nation-state upon Africa, for which it was peculiarly unsuited, that caused so many disasters. With no loyalty to the nation but only to the tribe or family, those who control the state can see it only as an object and instrument of exploitation. Gaining political power is the only way ambitious people see to achieving the immeasurably higher standard of living that the colonialists dangled in front of their faces for so long. Given the natural wickedness of human beings, the lengths to which they are prepared to go to achieve power – along with their followers, who expect to share in the spoils – are limitless. The winner-take-all aspect of Africa's political life is what makes it more than usually vicious.

But it is important to understand why another explanation commonly touted for Africa's post-colonial turmoil is mistaken – the view that the dearth of trained people in Africa at the time of independence is to blame. No history of the modern Congo catastrophe is complete without reference to the paucity of college graduates at the time of the Belgian withdrawal, as if things would have been better had there been more of them. And therefore the solution was obvious: train more people. Education in Africa became a secular shibboleth that it was impious to question.

The expansion of education in Tanzania, where I lived for three years, was indeed impressive. The literacy rate had improved dramatically, so that it was better than that of the former colonising power, and it was inspiring to see the sacrifices villagers were willing to make to enable at least one of their children to continue his schooling. School fees took precedence over every other expenditure. If anyone doubted the capacity of the poor to make investments in their own future, the conduct of the Tanzanians should have been sufficient to persuade him otherwise. (I used to lend money to villagers to pay the fees, and – poor as they were – they never failed to repay me.)

Unfortunately there was a less laudable, indeed positively harmful, side to this effort. The aim of education was, in almost every case, that at least one family member should escape what Marx contemptuously called the idiocy of rural life and get into government service, from which he would be in a position to extort from the only productive people in the country – namely, the peasants from whom he had sprung. The son in government service was secure income, social security and old-age pension rolled into one. Farming, the country's indispensable economic base, was viewed as the occupation of dullards and failures, and so it was hardly surprising that the education of an ever-larger number of government servants went hand in hand with an ever-contracting economy. It also explains why there is no correlation between a country's number of college graduates at independence and its subsequent economic success.

The naive supposition on which the argument for education rests is that training counteracts and overpowers a cultural worldview. A trained man is but a clone of his trainer, on this theory, sharing his every attitude and worldview. But in fact what results is a curious hybrid, whose fundamental beliefs may be impervious to the education he has received.

I had a striking example of this phenomenon recently, when I had a Congolese patient who had taken refuge in this country from the terrible war in Central Africa that has so far claimed up to three million lives. He was an intelligent man and had that easy charm that I remember well from the days when I traversed – not without difficulty or discomfort – the Zaire of Marshal Mobutu Sese Seko. He had two degrees in agronomy and had trained in Toulouse in the interpretation of satellite pictures for agronomic purposes. He recognised the power of modern science, therefore, and had worked for the UN Food and Agricultural Organisation, and was used to dealing with Western aid donors and investors as well as academics.

The examination over, we chatted about the Congo: he was delighted to meet someone who knew his country, by no means easily found in England. I asked him about Mobutu, whom he had known personally.

'He was very powerful,' he said. 'He collected the best witch doctors from every part of Zaire. Of course, he could make himself invisible; that was how he knew everything about us. And he could turn himself into a leopard when he wanted.'

This was said with perfect seriousness. For him the magical powers of Mobutu were more impressive and important than the photographic power of satellites. Magic trumped science. In this he was not at all abnormal, it being as difficult or impossible for a sub-Saharan African to deny the power of magic as for an inhabitant of the Arabian peninsula to deny the power of Allah. My Congolese patient was perfectly relaxed: usually Africans feel constrained to disguise from Europeans their most visceral beliefs, for which they know the Europeans usually feel contempt as primitive and superstitious. And so, in dealing with outsiders, Africans feel obliged to play an elaborate charade, denying their deepest beliefs in an attempt to obtain the outsider's minimal respect. In deceiving others about their innermost beliefs, often very easily, and in keeping their inner selves hidden from them, they are equalising the disparity of power. The weak are not powerless: they have the power, for instance, to gull the outsider.

Perhaps the most baleful legacy of British and other colonials in Africa was the idea of the philosopher-king, to whose role colonial officials aspired, and which they often actually played, bequeathing it to their African successors. Many colonial officials made great sacrifices for the sake of their territories, to whose welfare they were devoted, and they attempted to govern them wisely, dispensing justice even-handedly. But they left for the nationalists the instruments needed to erect the tyrannies and kleptocracies that marked post-independence Africa. They bequeathed a legacy of treating ordinary uneducated Africans as children, incapable of making decisions for themselves. No attitude is more grateful to the aspiring despot.

To take one example: the marketing boards of West Africa. Throughout West Africa, millions of African peasants under British rule set up small plantations for crops such as palm oil and cocoa. (Since cocoa trees mature only after five years, this is another instance of the African peasant's ability both to think ahead and delay gratification by investment, despite great poverty.) Then the British colonial governments had the idea, benignly intended, of protecting the peasant growers from the fluctuations of the marketplace. They set up a stabilisation fund, under the direction of a marketing board. In good years the marketing board would withhold from the peasants some of the money their crops produced; in bad years it would use the money earned in the good years to increase their incomes. With stable incomes, they could plan ahead.

Of course, for the system to work, the marketing boards would have to have monopoly purchasing powers. And it takes little imagination to see how such marketing boards would tempt an aspiring despot, such as Dr Nkrumah, with grandiose ideas: he could use them in effect to tax Ghana's producers in order to fund his insane projects and to subsidise the urban population that was the source of his power, as well as to amass a personal fortune. A continent away, in Tanzania, Nyerere used precisely the same means to expropriate the peasant coffee growers, in the end causing them to pull up their coffee bushes and plant a little corn instead, which at least they could eat, to the great and further impoverishment of the country.

The idea behind the marketing boards was a paternalist colonial one: that peasant farmers were too simple to cope with fluctuating prices and that the colonial philosopher-kings had therefore to protect them from such fluctuations – this despite the fact that it was the simple peasants who grew the commodities in the first place.

After several years in Africa, I concluded that the colonial enterprise had been fundamentally wrong and mistaken, even when, as was often the case in its final stages, it was benevolently intended. The good it did was ephemeral; the harm, lasting. The powerful can change the powerless, it is true; but not in any way they choose. The unpredictability of humans is the revenge of the powerless. What emerges politically from the colonial enterprise is often something worse, or at least more vicious because better equipped, than what existed before. Good intentions are certainly no guarantee of good results.

A Note On The Author

Theodore Dalrymple is a British doctor and writer, born in 1949, who has worked on four continents and, for many years, in a hospital and a prison in a British inner city. His work has appeared in *The Spectator*, *The Daily Telegraph*, *The Guardian*, *The Sunday Telegraph*, *The Daily Mail*, *New Statesman* and many other newspapers and magazines.

He now shares his time between England and France.

Later this year, Monday Books will publish *Second Opinion*, a further collection of Dalrymple pieces.

Also from
Monday Books

Wasting Police Time / **PC David Copperfield** (ppbk, £7.99)

The best-selling inside story of the
lunacy of modern British policing,
written by a serving police officer
who dared to question the stifling
bureaucracy and politically-correct
orthodoxy that has left Britain's
criminal justice system a laughing
stock.

'Very revealing' – *The Daily Telegraph*
'Passionate, important, interesting and genuinely
revealing' – *The Sunday Times*
'Graphic, entertaining and sobering' – *The Observer*
'A huge hit... will make you laugh out loud'
– *The Daily Mail*
'Hilarious... should be compulsory reading for our
political masters' – *The Mail on Sunday*
'More of a fiction than Dickens'
– **Tony McNulty MP, former Police Minister**
(On a BBC *Panorama* programme about PC Copperfield, McNulty
was later forced to admit that this statement, made in the House of
Commons, was itself untrue)

**From all good bookshops, online from
www.mondaybooks.com or via 01455 221752.**

Just published:

Perverting The Course Of Justice / **Inspector Gadget**
(ppbk, £7.99)

A senior serving policeman picks up where PC Copperfield left off and reveals how far the insanity extends – children arrested for stealing sweets from each other while serious criminals go about their business unmolested.

In Foreign Fields / **Dan Collins**
(ppbk, £7.99)

A staggering collection of 25 tales of
astonishing, medal winning bravery
by British soldiers, Marines and
RAF men in Iraq and Afghanistan.

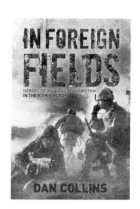

'**Enthralling and awe-inspiring untold stories**'
– *The Daily Mail*

'**Astonishing feats of bravery illustrated in laconic,
first-person prose**' – *Independent on Sunday*

'**The book everyone's talking about... a gripping account
of life on the frontlines of Iraq and Afghanistan**'
– *News of the World*

'**An outstanding read**' – *Soldier Magazine*

**From all good bookshops, online from
www.mondaybooks.com or via 01455 221752.**

When Science Goes Wrong / Simon LeVay
(ppbk, £7.99)

We live in times of astonishing scientific progress. But for every stunning triumph there are hundreds of cock-ups, damp squibs and disasters. Escaped anthrax spores and nuclear explosions, tiny data errors which send a spacecraft hurtling to oblivion, innocent men jailed on 'infallible' DNA evidence…just some of the fascinating and disturbing tales from the dark side of discovery.

'Spine-tingling, occasionally gruesome accounts of well-meant but disastrous scientific bungling'
– *The Los Angeles Times*

'Entertaining and thought-provoking'
– *Publisher's Weekly*

'The dark – but fascinating – side of science… an absorbing read' – *GeoTimes*

From all good bookshops, online from www.mondaybooks.com or via 01455 221752.